Inside
Private Equity

Inside
Private Equity

The Professional
Investor's Handbook

JAMES M. KOCIS

JAMES C. BACHMAN IV

AUSTIN M. LONG III

CRAIG J. NICKELS

John Wiley & Sons, Inc.

Published by John Wiley & Sons, Inc., Hoboken, New Jersey.
Published simultaneously in Canada.

Quote from *The Silicon Boys and Their Valley of Dreams*, David A. Kaplan, Perenniel, 1999. Used with permission of the author.

Two articles by Tom Judge copyright.

Microsoft Excel is a trademark of Microsoft Corporation. PowerPoint is a trademark of Microsoft Corporation.

For more information about the patented methodologies referenced this book visit http://www.alignmentcapital.com.

For general information on our other products and services or for technical support, please contact our Customer Care Department within the United States at (800) 762-2974, outside the United States at (317) 572-3993 or fax (317) 572-4002.

Wiley publishes in a variety of print and electronic formats and by print-on-demand. Some material included with standard print versions of this book may not be included in e-books or in print-on-demand. If this book refers to media such as a CD or DVD that is not included in the version you purchased, you may download this material at http://booksupport.wiley.com. For more information about Wiley products, visit www.wiley.com.

Library of Congress Cataloging-in-Publication Data:

Inside private equity : the professional investor's handbook / James M. Kocis [et al.].
    p. cm. – (Wiley finance series)
Includes bibliographical references and index.
ISBN 978-0-470-42189-5 (cloth)
1. Private equity.   2. Venture capital.   3. Portfolio management.   4. Investments.
I. Kocis, James M.
    HG4751.I57 2009
    332.63'22–dc22
                                                              2008045556

10 9 8 7 6 5 4 3 2 1

*To Nick Vallario
and in memory of Shao Xin Kai*

Contents

PART TWO

Measurements and Comparisons

PART THREE

Topics on Risk

Foreword

started to invest in venture capital partnerships on behalf of the AT&T pension fund in 1980. Please note that I referred to venture capital and not private equity. It was not until the late 1980s that Stan Pratt and Steven Galante, then of Venture Economics, and Ned Regan, former Controller of the State of New York, coined the phrase "private equity." Three unrelated events urged me to venture into venture investing in 1980. In 1979 the Department of Labor issued final regulations applying "the prudent man rule" to the investment of corporate pension fund monies in alternative investments. On Labor Day 1974, President Gerald Ford signed into law the "Employee Retirement Income Security Act" (ERISA), which governed the administration of corporate pension plans and assets. However, it was not until "final regulations" were issued in 1979 that corporate pension funds felt comfortable making investments in venture capital. The second event related to the consolidation of all pension funds held by the 23 telephone operating companies owned by AT&T. All of the assets of those funds were transferred to the Bell System Trust. One of my responsibilities was to examine the individual holdings in every publicly traded stock portfolio transferred into the Bell System Trust. Much to my amazement I found about six investments listed at the very end of one of those portfolios with an "L.P." following the name of the investment. Meeting Ray Held, then of the Manufacturers Hanover Trust Company, was the third event. Ray taught me a great deal about investing in venture capital including the knowledge that "L.P." meant "Limited Partner." I like to think that I taught Ray a little about what makes institutional investors tick. Those three events led me to start investing in venture capital partnerships.

During 1979 about $160 million in total was committed to venture capital partnerships. To the best of my knowledge only five institutions were making such investments in January of 1980. Morgan Stanley and J. P. Morgan had made commitments to venture capital using "Partners" money and three endowments, from east to west, Harvard, Yale, and Stanford had invested in venture capital in the late 1970s. I am aware of a few other "venture" events during the late 1970s. Ned Heizer, one of the founders of the National Venture Capital Association (NVCA), had raised an $80 million fund from insurance companies and banks to invest in start-ups, and some wealthy families like the Bessemer, Rockefeller, and Whitney families had supported venture-like investments for many years. I believe that "Jock" Whitney gave Eddie Rickenbacker, the most decorated American combat pilot of World War I, the funds to create Eastern Airlines back in 1938.

During 1980 I discovered that there was very little information available about venture capital that I could get my hands on. There were no performance numbers available. In fact, it was almost impossible to get my hands on any information. I did have the opportunity to chat with a handful of venture capitalists, and two names kept coming up in those telephone calls: Stan Pratt and Dick Testa. Stan was the owner of Venture Economics and the publisher and editor of the *Venture Capital Journal*. Dick Testa was a founder of the Boston law firm of Testa, Hurwitz & Thiebault. Dick was instrumental in working with the Securities and Exchange Commission to create one of the country's first high-tech initial public offerings, Digital Equipment Corporation. I knew that I needed to talk with both Stan and Dick. I called each of them, and both men graciously agreed to meet with me. I flew to Boston early one morning, met with both, and flew back in the evening. Both of these gentlemen were a wealth of information. Not only did they know every venture capitalist in this country, they knew all of the entrepreneurs and chief executive officers of every start-up that had been created by venture capitalists. The next day back in my office the telephone started ringing off the wall. The word was out. The AT&T pension fund was making investments in venture capital partnerships.

A general partner would call me and say that they were raising a venture capital fund. If they said they were raising "a fund," I learned to conclude that they were raising their first "institutional money" fund. If they were raising a second fund they would proudly say, "We are raising our second fund." The general partner asked if he and his partners could visit me in my office. I, of course, said "yes." After all, I was trying to invest, and the more general partners I could meet the better. At the appointed time and place all of the general partners arrived. This usually meant two or three people. They would present a "hard copy slide show." Keep in mind that this was before PowerPoint. They would begin by discussing their individual backgrounds and experiences. This would be followed by their deal flow and investment strategy. Then a discussion of their investment decision-making process and, finally, the size and scope of the fund they were hoping to raise. At that point they asked for a commitment. I probably should not admit this, but my strategy and due diligence process were as simple as simple can get. My strategy was to invest in venture capital. Since all of the funds being raised during the early 1980s were seed, start-up, and early-stage partnerships, that turned out to be my strategy. Here is the part I probably should not reveal, but I have nothing to lose now. If I could understand their strategy and investment decision-making process and if both made sense, I mean common sense, then I was halfway home. During that meeting I also looked into the eyes of each of the general partners and asked myself, "Do I trust this person?" If the answer to all of the above was "yes," then I made a commitment to their partnership. There was none of this nonsense that they would get back to me with my allocation. The general partners and I had a golden handshake, and they were on their way to the next fundraising meeting.

In 1981 IBM introduced the personal computer, and for quite a few years venture capitalists invested in computer hardware. In fact they put so much money into hardware that they created over 70 Winchester drive companies. This might be referred to as the first bubble in venture capital. As the personal computer became a commodity, venture capitalists began investing in software. The mid to late 1980s was not a good time for venture capital. And the stock market crash of 1987 created very chilly conditions, and a good venture firm was lucky to have one IPO a year.

Asset allocation is a crucial aspect of managing institutional money. It probably accounts for 90 or 95 percent of the total performance of an institutional portfolio. As soon as we started investing pension fund money in venture capital I was under pressure to come up with an expected return for venture capital that could be used in the algorithm that was used in asset allocation. I finally decided to look at the historic long-term return of large capitalized public stocks and discovered that the average annual return of that asset class since the Great Depression was 10 percent. I decided that if venture capital could provide a 50 percent premium, or 15 percent, that would be attractive enough to attract investors. To check my theory I looked at the return on small capitalized stocks, the closest public investment to venture capital. That average annual return was 12 percent, and I decided that a 25 percent premium would be adequate. Amazingly that number is also 15 percent. I felt pretty good about my discovery and mentioned my new expected return of 15 percent at a Venture Economics conference a few months later. Since most of the conference attendees were general partners, I was taken to task for trying to ruin the venture industry. They were talking about returns of 25 to 35 percent. If you look back at the average annual return on private equity since 1980, I think you will find it is very close to my expected return.

In 1983 we made our first venture capital investment in Europe. It was a commitment to Alta-Berkeley in London. In those days many venture firms in England created an investment vehicle in the form of a "unit trust" and registered that trust on the Isle of Jersey in the Channel Islands to avoid the taxation of partnerships in England. The Isle of Jersey has its own parliament and is not subject to English law. My friend, Sir Ronald Cohen, fought successfully to change the tax law in England so that today partnerships are widely used not only in England, but on the continent as well. Two years later we made our first investment in Japan. It was called Japan America and was managed by Japan Associated Finance Companies (Jafco). Their first investment was in a 150-year-old, family-owned, high school textbook publisher. I wondered what I had gotten myself into until they took the company public about three years later at a multiple of around 20.

By 1987 I knew that I needed a method to evaluate each of our partnership investments against some sort of benchmark. I decided to calculate the return for all of the partnerships that we had committed to in one single year, using all of the cash flows and values as if they were one partnership. I could then compare the returns on each of the individual partnerships with the return for all of the partnerships for that year on the assumption that all of those partnerships were investing in the same economic and venture capital environment. Hence, the "vintage year" concept was born.

When 1989 rolled around, we were receiving quite a few distributions of newly issued common stock in venture-backed companies. Distributions did not become meaningful until the late 1980s. Remember, this was a primarily venture capital portfolio consisting of seed, start-up, and early-stage investments. I did not know whether to hold or sell these stocks. Beth Dater of Warburg Pincus Counselors had a terrific track record of managing small stock mutual funds. I asked her if she would manage all of the venture capital distributed stocks for the AT&T venture portfolio. When she and I met with Lionel Pincus, he agreed to take the assignment because he was friendly with my boss. However, I think that he said that managing distributed stocks would never be "a business." About five years later Warburg Pincus was managing around $8 billion worth of "distributed" stocks.

Bart Holaday was managing the venture capital portfolio at First Chicago. He and I were concerned that venture capital firms were placing a very different valuation on exactly the same venture investment where there were a number of different partnerships invested in the same company. We came up with a one-page valuation policy for the industry. We were getting nowhere until Stan Golder, a highly respected venture capitalist, and a founder of Golder, Thoma, Cressy, publicly supported our effort. In fact, that gave us an entrée to the NVCA, which promptly said they were not interested in our proposed valuation policy. It is interesting that within six months both the European and British Venture Capital Associations adopted our one-page policy. It also started to appear in offering memorandums and even in textbooks. I do not think that the NVCA ever adopted our policy. All of this took place in 1990.

That same year Bob Black of Kemper Investments and I decided it would be a good idea if limited partners got together periodically like the venture general partners did as part of the NVCA. We drew up a list of a dozen or so limited partners on a cocktail napkin and invited them to a meeting in November 1990. We met at a Marriott Courtyard just outside O'Hare Airport near Chicago. Everyone we invited showed up, and we got a meeting room for no cost because at least 10 of the attendees spent the night at the motel. We all chipped in for a buffet lunch and agreed to meet again. A few months later I was an attendee at a Venture Economics Forum and several general partners accused me of trying to form a "cartel" to control terms and conditions. Anyone associated with the private equity industry knows that never happened. I understand that now the Institutional Limited Partners Association (ILPA) has a couple of hundred paying members and an executive director with a staff of 8 or 10. I never visualized that happening.

In 1993 I was at my wits' end trying to keep track of well over a hundred partnerships. Then I met Jim Kocis. He had approached Mitchell Hutchins about developing a Windows version of a private equity system to little avail. Then Jim came to see me and I said that AT&T would put up $25,000 a year for a few years to develop such a system. The rest is history. Today the Burgiss Group helps over 200 clients monitor and manage billions of dollars of private equity assets.

By late 1995 the AT&T pension fund had received all of its paid-in cash calls in the form of cash or stock distributions and still held a venture portfolio worth billions of dollars

Why am I telling you all of this? Because I wish I had this book, *Inside Private Equity*, in January of 1980. However, that would have been impossible at that time. Today four knowledgeable, experienced authors, James M. Kocis, James C. Bachman IV, Austin M. Long III, and Craig J. Nickels have created this very helpful and informative handbook on private equity. I urge every current and future investor in private equity to read this book. So, read on.

> Tom Judge
> Former Investor in Venture Capital

Tom Judge was inducted into the Private Equity Hall of Fame in 1995 and was considered the dean of institutional investors during his 15-year private equity tenure at AT&T. During those 15 years, he created and managed the AT&T venture capital portfolio that grew from zero in 1980 to commitments of $1.5 billion in 180 partnerships formed by 90 firms. He retired from AT&T in September 1995. He is an honorary Kauffman Fellow. Tom also co-founded *the Institutional Limited Partners Association, which has grown to a membership of over 200 institutions.*

Prior to managing the venture capital portfolio for the AT&T Investment Management Corporation, he was involved in all aspects of the administration of employee benefit assets at AT&T for 17 years. Tom has been a frequent speaker at private equity and pension fund conferences and seminars worldwide. He holds an undergraduate degree from the Pennsylvania State University and earned his MBA at Seton Hall University.

Preface

MEASURES MATTER

This book focuses on a particular form of investing, the ownership of private assets, which we simply refer to as private equity. This once-sleepy backwater is now a raging river, overflowing its banks and flooding the marketplace. Newspapers now often refer to private equity as if it were something of importance to everyone. And indirectly it may be, but investing in private equity is primarily done by specialized firms and wealthy individuals or institutions with long-term horizons, with tens of millions or even billions to invest. Private equity has nothing to offer the casual or short-term investor.

There are fascinating books that weave tales of venture capitalists building great companies from scratch. There are fast-paced accounts of the buyout of the century. There are guidebooks for entrepreneurs seeking venture capital. There are detailed private equity case books that use proprietary data to explain the more general behavior of the asset class or to defend a particular theory. This book is none of these.

This book was primarily written for those with the most at risk, those that supply the money, a great deal of it, the limited partners. Whether you are the head of a pension group, an administrator at a fund of funds, an investment officer at a foundation or endowment, or an analyst charged with monitoring a portfolio of private equity assets, we expect that you will find something of interest here. But *Inside Private Equity* may have interest for others. If you are a fund manager, doing the work of investing in companies and reporting back to your limited partners, you may benefit from seeing the world from their perspective. We believe that this text also has something to offer those who provide specialized services to the private equity industry, such as accountants, attorneys, and consultants.

The authors have a broad range of experience and exposure to private equity. Two of us, Messrs. Kocis and Bachman, design, develop, and support large-scale, commercial private equity portfolio management systems at the Burgiss Group, whose clients include many of the largest private equity investors in the world. The other two authors, Messrs. Long and Nickels, are practitioners who run, have run, and have advised large private equity programs. Austin runs Alignment Capital, a private equity consultancy. Craig is Director of Private Markets for Washington University in St. Louis.

In our work we put particular emphasis on measurement. *Inside Private Equity* arose from our belief that the general understanding of how to invest in, monitor, and measure the performance and risk of private equity has not kept up with its scale and importance. In this book we focus on what *you* can measure. Our explanations and examples are meant to illustrate concepts and basic principles. Our examples use simple numbers and are broken down into steps. Critically, every analytical technique we write about has been put to the test of managing large portfolios of private assets. Some of them are tried-and-true and may be somewhat obvious, but we hope that much of what we present here is new to you.

Building a portfolio of private equity assets takes years or even decades. Since most private equity funds have a term of 10 years or more, almost all of the analysis that you will do will be on partially realized investments. Measuring private equity will make you get used to thinking in terms of long-term interim results. This requires a very different mind-set from the public markets, where today's investments can be measured tonight.

Despite this long-term horizon, interim results can be used for decisions that matter. Investors can, for example, actively manage their private equity portfolios by selling (or buying) positions in partnerships. Measuring performance midstream is also critical for the ongoing investment process. Often the decisions about new investment opportunities and follow-on investments are made from the performance characteristics of funds that are only part way through their lives. Interim results also serve as a gauge of the health of a private equity fund or portfolio. Without them, your reports to investment boards and other stakeholders would seem bare.

The analytical techniques that we write about are useful at several levels of abstraction and scale. For example, you can calculate the IRR on a company, a fund, a group of funds that originated in the same year, or on a whole portfolio of funds. The result from each tells a different story, but the principles are precisely the same.

As you apply these techniques, you may be drawn to compare your performance results with industry norms. When you do, you should be aware that research in private equity is still in its infancy. Unlike research in the public markets, where practitioners and academics can mine rich veins of transactional data, the literature on private equity is sparse and is mainly based on selected sets of proprietary data.

In our collective work, we get to see a great deal of private data. From our point of view, the current state of commercially available information about private equity is a mess. We know that universe data about private equity is rightly hard to get, assemble, maintain, and audit. We also believe that the industry, with its emphasis on quartile returns, is currently poorly served. We are not alone in our criticism. In this text, we avoid the use of proprietary data.

Unfortunately, there are aspects of the private equity industry that are driven by hype, myth, and folklore. We have heard our share of nonsense, where achieving a high IRR is a goal unto itself. What usually gets lost amidst the hype are the true measures of wealth creation and risk. For example, we often see the average IRRs published in trade publications and journals. We think this kind of analysis is at best misleading and at worst plain silly. Investors should focus instead on the effects that this type of investing has on the investor. The return, as most prominently measured by the IRR, is at best a proxy for the overall wealth generated. As you will see, a high IRR does not necessarily mean that a great deal of wealth was generated.

We start this text with a brief introduction, lay out some perspectives, and describe a structured investment approach. We describe a simple data framework before introducing standard asset-class measures and analytical techniques. We address some of the challenges of quarterly reporting in the face of partial or incomplete data. We beat the IRR into submission, providing an exhaustive review of its calculation, anomalies, and variations. We delve deeply into the topic of peer universes and benchmarks. We introduce aspects of visualizing the performance of investments that we have found to be particularly helpful. We then introduce more advanced measures such as the Index Comparison Method, which allows you to compare your investments to the public markets. We move on to topics on risk, where we present techniques that help you uncover both how and where wealth was gained and lost. Finally, we broadly introduce two methodologies for cash flow modeling before wrapping up.

As practitioners, we know that private equity isn't all that mysterious. But we run a risk here. Secret societies thrive in the dark. Mystique sells. Yet recent events have shown that the world has grown suspicious of private equity, its means, and its motives. There are episodic calls to take legislative actions to control it and to create accounting standards to constrain it. On balance, we think that the private equity industry could benefit from a little more light.

As a close friend of ours who runs a major pension fund reminds us: "Private equity is only 20 percent of my assets but takes 80 percent of my time." We hope that this book helps you better manage these assets and your time. Finally, and pragmatically, we know that every measure needs a context, that experience counts, and that insight comes in ways that cannot be predicted. We hope that this book adds to your knowledge, stimulates thinking, and helps you invest wisely.

We welcome hearing from you.

James M. Kocis
James C. Bachman IV
Austin M. Long III
Craig J. Nickels

Acknowledgments

This book was made possible with the help of Tim Moore, who knocked our heads together, and Tom Judge for providing an enormous opportunity. Special thanks to Andrew Conner, David A. Kaplan, and Chihtsung Lam.

Much of this work would not have been possible without the help of Kendra Alaishuski, Stephen Bruhns, Joseph Fung, Berlin Lai, Romit Mukherjee, Lorna Palmer, Ana Perez, James Rearden, and the rest of the team at the Burgiss Group. Nelson Lacey, thanks for the connections. And of course, for making it possible in hurry, Skyler Balbus, Bill Falloon, Meg Freeborn, Kevin Holm, and Laura Walsh at Wiley. This book would also not have been possible without the continuing support from Laureen Costa, Julian Shles, Larry Unrein, Sandy Zablocki, and the rest of the crew at J.P. Morgan Asset Management.

Then there are the host of others we must thank including Anthony Aronica, Susan Carter, Linda Costa, Paul Finlayson, Tom Gotsch, Leslie Halladay, Pat Haverland, Linda Hoffman, Guy Holappa, Mark McBride, Jesse Reyes, Stephen Roseme, Louis Sciarretta, and Cheng Wang.

For research above and beyond the call of duty, Joan Siminitus and Anita Matt for helping find a critical reference.

Special thanks to Alice Heatherington and Zoe Westhof for their careful editing and diplomatic delivery of constructive criticism. Finally a big thanks to the crew at La Isla, for the best coffee in Hoboken, NJ.

How to Use This Book

This book builds on itself. If you are new to private equity, we think that you should read it from front to back, for the concepts and terms we introduce early on are needed for understanding what we explain later. In lieu of reading it from cover to cover, please refer to our guidance below. If you plan on reading only one chapter, read Chapter 16, The Private Equity Professional.

We have broken this text into four parts.

Part One is largely background and sets the foundation for the technical discussions that follow. There are no equations in Part One.

- For those new to private equity, reading the first two chapters is a good start. These two chapters will give you a sense of private equity, its beginnings, what drove its growth, and where it is today. If all you want is a general understanding of the asset class, you can probably stop here.
- To get a general understanding of a structured approach to private equity portfolio management, and how it fits into a larger program of investment, read Chapter 3, Managing the Investment Process. This chapter draws heavily from the experience of Messrs. Long and Nickels.
- If you are responsible for tracking or monitoring a portfolio of private equity investments, you should read Chapter 4, Capturing a Portfolio. This chapter sets the stage for the discussions on measurements that follow by describing the basic data you will need to capture.
- To understand some of the challenges of tracking the underlying investments that a private equity fund makes, its portfolio holdings, read Chapter 5, Tracking Portfolio Holdings.

Part Two covers the fundamental techniques you can use to measure, compare, and present the performance of this asset class.

- For anyone wanting to understand the performance measurements, Chapters 6 and 7 are required reading. These chapters explore multiples and many variations on the theme of return, as most prominently measured by the IRR.

- For those trying to compare their portfolio with benchmarks or universes, read Chapter 8.
- We present a short critique on private equity research that we have encountered in Chapter 9. Read this chapter as a prelude to more advanced topics.
- If you are responsible for quantitative due diligence or for preparing summary presentations, read Chapter 10. It presents some charting techniques that we have found interesting and useful.
- To understand how to compare the performance of your investments to the public markets, read Chapter 11, which presents Long & Nickels' Index Comparison Method (ICM).

Part Three wades into deeper water, helping you to extract more information from your portfolio.

- To understand what part luck and skill played in picking investments for a private equity portfolio, read Chapter 12, Performance Attribution.
- To better understand how wealth has been created, read Chapter 13, The Concentration of Wealth.
- To understand what effect the size of a portfolio has on performance expectations, read Chapter 14, The Diversification of Portfolios.
- To become acquainted with the general techniques of cash flow modeling, read Chapter 15, Cash Management Models.

Part Four is the wrap-up, outlining our view of the private equity professional and summarizing the contents.

About the Authors

James M. Kocis

jkocis@burgiss.com

Jim is the founder and president of the Burgiss Group, one of the leading providers of software and services to the private equity limited partner community. Jim's involvement with the private equity industry began in the late 1980s with a consulting engagement with Mitchell-Hutchins. He and his team designed Private i, the world's most popular program for private equity portfolio management. Private i is used to manage in excess of $1 trillion of private equity investments. Jim's previous book is *The Paradox Programmer's Guide: PAL By Example*, coauthored with Alan Zenreich, published by Random House. Jim has a BS in Chemical Engineering from the New Jersey Institute of Technology.

James C. Bachman IV, CAIA

jbachman@burgiss.com

James is the Head of Research at the Burgiss Group. In this role, he is principally responsible for research-related initiatives as well as expanding the technology platform's portfolio management capabilities. Prior to the Burgiss Group, James worked at the Bridgeton Companies, an alternative investment boutique. As one of Bridgeton's first employees, James played a significant role in the firm's capital management, derivatives brokerage, and research and development divisions.

James obtained his BA in Economics and Business Administration as an Omicron Delta Epsilon graduate from Muhlenberg College and received his MBA from Texas A&M University at Commerce. Additionally, he holds the Chartered Alternative Investment Analyst designation. James is a member of the CFA Institute's Global Investment Performance Standards (GIPS) Private Equity Working Group.

Austin M. Long III, JD, CPA

along@alignmentcapital.com

Austin is the head of Alignment Capital, a private equity consultancy. Austin has been active in the private markets since 1987, when he cofounded what was to become the University of Texas Investment Management Company's (UTIMCO) private investment group. When he left in 2000, the UTIMCO private equity program had $2.2 billion in commitments. Austin is a former co-chair of the Institutional Limited Partners Association. He is a frequent speaker at industry gatherings. Austin co-founded Alignment Capital Group in 2001 with Craig Nickels.

Austin received his BA degree from Baylor in 1970, his Masters in Professional Accounting from The University of Texas at Austin in 1981 and his JD degree from DePaul University in 1987. He is a Certified Public Accountant and has been admitted to the bars of Illinois and Texas. Austin is a member of the CFA Institute's Global Investment Performance Standards (GIPS) Private Equity Working Group.

Craig J. Nickels, CFA
craig.nickels@wustl.edu
Craig is the Director of Private Markets for Washington University in St. Louis where his responsibilities include the oversight and management of the University's private market investments within the multi-billion dollar endowment. Included asset classes are private equity (venture, buyout, mezzanine, and so on), real estate, and real-assets.

Craig graduated from The University of Texas at Austin with a BBA in Finance in 1981. He was awarded the Chartered Financial Analyst Designation in 1986. Craig is a member of the Chartered Financial Analysts Institute and the CFA Society of St. Louis. Craig is also a member of the CFA Institute's Global Investment Performance Standards (GIPS) Private Equity Working Group.

Austin Long and Craig Nickels are the inventors of U.S. patent #7,058,583, Method for Calculating Portfolio Scaled IRR and U.S. patent #7,421,407, Process and System for Determining Correlation of Public and Private Markets and Risk of Private Markets. For summaries, see Appendix H.

Setting the Foundation

CHAPTER 1

Background

"There is always a critical job to be done," said Doriot. "There is a sales door to be opened, a credit line to be established, a new important employee to be found, or a business technique to be learned. The venture investor must always be on call to advise, to persuade, to dissuade, to encourage, but always to help build. Then venture capital becomes true creative capital—creating growth for the company and financial success for the investing organization."
—Georges Doriot quoted in Ante, *Creative Capital*, p. 173

This chapter introduces private equity by tracing some of the history and evolution of one of its earliest forms, venture capital. We then explain some of the major forms of private equity investing. We present some unsolicited advice about how to start a program of private equity investing and then let you in on a big secret.

OWNING COMPANIES

On December 12, 1980, Apple Computer, owned by its employees and a few venture capital firms, went public (Apple n.d.). From that day forward, Apple was a public company and was required to comply with the regulations of the U.S. Securities and Exchange Commission. With that event, early investments in Apple by venture capitalists paid off. Since then, Apple has been required to have external audits, comply with government filings, and invite public scrutiny. Further, Apple's officers had increased liability and were subject to rules that made public their compensation and personal transactions involving the company.

If you buy a single share of Apple today, you instantly own a piece of the company. As a shareholder, you receive financial reports, have voting and other rights, and are invited to the annual meeting. Most importantly, by owning that share of Apple, you have standing—you have equity. Yet you can leave this all behind with one electronic order—it's as easy as selling that share.

Private companies are an entirely different matter. What do you own when you have put some of your hard-earned cash into a private company? As your transaction was private, it was largely unregulated. Need to cash out your private equity in that company? Good luck. Who will you sell it to? Will anyone buy it? And so, realistically, what is it worth? What rights do you have?

VENTURE CAPITAL'S BEGINNINGS

Investing in private companies, whether through sweat equity or with money, is as old as business. Venture capital is but one form of private equity investing and is generally understood to be the business of investing in new or young enterprises with innovative ideas.

WHAT WE CALL PRIVATE EQUITY

Owning equity in a private company led to the obvious and simple term *private equity*. We like that broad term and will use it throughout this book. It is common to see this term used to describe the world of buyouts. We like two other terms, *venture capital* because it describes itself; and, to describe everything in private equity that is not venture capital, including buyouts and mezzanine, *corporate finance*.

A broader term, *alternative investments*, is used to describe many types of investment, including venture capital, corporate finance, hedge funds, distressed debt, timber, energy, and real estate investments.

Some historians mark the beginning of venture capital to the 1930s and 1940s, when wealthy families, such as the Vanderbilts, Rockefellers, and Bessemers began private investing in private companies. These so-called angel investors have a following still. One of the first venture capital firms, J. H. Whitney & Company, was founded in 1946 (J. H. Whitney n.d.). They are still in business today, having raised their sixth outside fund, for $750 million, in 2005 (Hsu and Kenney 2004).

Many people credit General Georges F. Doriot, an influential teacher and innovator at Harvard, for helping institutionalize venture capital after the Second World War. Doriot is perhaps best known for his role in the formation of American Research & Development Corporation (ARDC). With ARDC, Doriot raised outside capital solely for investment in companies. In its 25-year history, ARDC helped fund more than a hundred companies. Its most notable financial success was Digital Equipment Corporation, which turned a $70,000 investment into $355 million.

In 1958, early venture capital got a boost from the U.S. government when the Small Business Administration was authorized to license businesses as Small Business Investment Companies (SBICs). This license gave these finance companies the ability to leverage federal funds to lend to growing companies. SBIC companies became very popular in the 1960s.

In the United States, the big boosts for venture capital came in the 1970s. The first was the reduction of the capital gains tax. This was of little concern to tax-exempt institutions, but was of profound importance to encourage venture capitalists (Bushner et al. 1994, p. 7). The second was from the U.S. Congress in 1974, when it enacted the Employee Retirement Income Security Act (ERISA), a set of pension reforms designed to help goad U.S. pension managers into more balanced custodianship. Unfortunately, this act was a source of confusion and a damper on venture investing until it was clarified in 1979 to explicitly permit pension funds to invest in assets like venture capital. In effect, the U.S. Congress said: "It is your responsibility to meet the pension obligations to which your organization has committed. Do not be foolhardy, but as well, do not be completely risk-averse. Take risks commensurate with rewards. Balance your portfolio. Diversify. We will be watching."

U.S. pension funds paid heed. In the late 1970s and early 1980s, a few added a small amount of venture capital to their pension portfolios. A few endowments joined in. It is easy today to view this start as timid, but this was uncharted territory. Fund sizes were small. Players were few or had no track record. Pension funds worth hundreds of millions or billions were at that time known to make mere $500,000 commitments to $10,000,000 first-time venture capital funds. You might not blame them. What investment professional wanted to own more than 10 percent of a new and "extremely risky" venture? Better to stand side by side with a few other brave souls. However small these amounts were, they were a start. With confidence gained by experience, pension funds, endowments, and foundations began to commit larger sums to bigger funds. Today, it is not uncommon for these same institutions to commit $50 million or more to a fund.

This start was tentative for a number of other reasons as well. Compared to more traditional investments, such as public equities and government and corporate bonds, an investment in a fund is always more difficult to buy, sell, or even value. These funds are, by design, long-term investments: most have a 10-year initial term. Many are not fully liquidated for 12 or more years. This illiquidity posed further complications to traditional investment managers. And to these managers, venture capital seemed a messy business with a language and practice all its own. To top it off, standards were lacking, there were few participants, and business systems and best practices were nonexistent.

Yet, in a way, the small size of the industry contributed to its early success. This community of investors and fund managers was close-knit. With much of the early activity centered in Boston and Silicon Valley and with money rather scant, general partners (GPs) from different firms collaborated on deals. Practices evolved. Supporting services, particularly in the legal and investment banking areas, grew or expanded alongside. Specialty firms emerged. Periods of retrenchment weeded out the tourists.

So, by fits and starts, the industry grew. Extraordinary monetary returns in the early 1980s attracted new investors and new capital at the wrong time. Industry-wide returns fell, and many first-time investors got cold feet and dropped out. Yet the industry grew, in part because those who stuck with it were rewarded for their persistence. This cycle was repeated in the early 1990s, when returns suffered and another set of investors bailed out. Those with patience hit the jackpot with the sky-high returns of the mid-1990s. Along the way, many of these pioneering investors quietly increased their allocations to this asset class from a modest 2 percent or 3 percent to 5 percent, 10 percent, or more. To some, the rebalancing of their asset allocation targets came through gain and reinvestment in their own portfolio, without having to commit additional capital. For others, gains from pension assets due to private equity were well above pension funding obligations, adding significantly to their bottom line.

Recent history is bubble created, bubble deflated, and beyond. The world went crazy with IT spending in the run-up to the Y2K computer software panic and the advent of the World Wide Web. Venture capitalists became, for a time, masters of the universe. The downturn that followed chastened for a time, but did not fundamentally change the practice of private equity. Despite excesses and carelessness, many investors in private equity made money. Lots of it. But after the boom, the IPO market vanished and the record level of investing in private equity of 2000 was followed by an unexpected and dramatic drop in 2001.

THE VERY RECENT PAST

Despite this cyclicality, venture capital continues to attract new investors. In many ways it has become institutionalized. Taking advantage of this trend, some experienced investment teams have left the larger institutional investors and formed their own funds of funds. Meanwhile, a continuing crop of investors, having started their portfolios with funds of funds, are beginning to make their own investments directly in funds.

Some suggest that alternative assets may come to dominate the portfolios of some very long-term investors. David Swensen (2000) at Yale University has championed aggressive strategies that emphasize alternative investments over more traditional investments. Where timidity and lack of understanding have kept institutional investors from allocating more than 5 percent of a portfolio, we are now in an age where some institutions have over 50 percent of their portfolios in these assets. Many institutions have reaped the benefits of these aggressive strategies, but in light of the events of late 2008, may now be facing challenges associated with the illiquidity of this asset class.

WHAT MAKES A VENTURE CAPITALIST?

Whatever your preference for this narrative, it is at least agreed that something changed in the marketplace when, with relatively modest investments, these investors helped create a process. This process has become known as venture capital investing and the people behind it, venture capitalists or VCs.

What makes a venture capitalist? Money, of course. Sometimes lots of it. But money is often the least of it. A venture capitalist has got to think he has the stuff that can help make an enterprise work: experience, contacts, knowledge, perseverance, and wisdom. A venture capitalist measures success day by day, by building great companies.

Although many pioneering venture capitalists used their own money, not all did. Venture capital funds, in which money from many investors is pooled, helped change the scale of the process. What had been self-limiting suddenly had the potential to do bigger things. Over time, the venture capital process was applied to a broader set of private investments, and so a more general industry term arose: private equity. Over the past 50 years, private equity has fueled the fortunes of thousands, launched worldwide enterprises, and helped shape whole industries.

PRIVATE EQUITY IS OWNERSHIP OF A COMPANY

Apple Computer is a particularly successful example of venture capital investing. But there are hundreds of companies that benefited from venture capital backing. Netscape, Google, eBay, Cisco, Sun Microsystems, Amazon, and Genentech are also notable companies that were backed by venture capital. That venture capital is associated with these firms and their success is a good thing, but these companies are more the exception than the rule. For every company that makes it big, there are dozens of venture-backed companies that never made their investors a cent. In fact, it is the nature of the business that many venture-backed companies lose all of the money investors put into them.

In its broadest context, private equity is simply a stake, large or small, in a private company. Buying into a company is interesting for a variety of reasons, not the least of which is that a small stake can turn into a big stake as the company grows. In 1985, Merrill Lynch bought a stake in a company called Innovative Market Systems (IMS), which had created an electronic information network (Bloomberg 2001). IMS was later renamed Bloomberg. By 1990, Merrill had invested a total of $39 million for a 30 percent stake in Bloomberg (*New York Times* 1996). In 1996 Merrill sold back to Bloomberg a portion, and Merrill booked a $155 million gain. In July 2008, Merrill finally sold their remaining 20 percent interest for $4.5 billion (Clark 2008). Not a bad investment.

To have the interest and attention of institutional investors, a company or an idea has to have large-scale potential. No private equity investor is interested in acquiring partial ownership of the independent dry-cleaner that does your shirts and blouses. Yet they might express interest in a new idea for cleaning everyone's laundry using nanobots, proving the technology, growing a business around it, and taking it public or selling it for a big profit.

Venture capital may help create household names, but private equity isn't all about venture capital. The buyout, a form of corporate finance, can be used to change the ownership or the type of ownership of a company through a variety of means.

In one of its most common forms, the leveraged buyout (LBO) takes a public company private through a combination of debt and equity financing. One of the central ideas behind this form of restructuring is that the addition of substantial amounts of debt to the balance sheet of the company helps create changes that unlock hidden value.

Once the company is private and freed from some of the regulatory and other burdens of being a public company, the central goal of buyout is to discover means to build this value. In many cases, this work has included refocusing the mission of the company, selling off noncore assets, freshening product lines, streamlining processes, and often, replacing existing management. A happy conclusion to this disruptive process is that the company, reinvigorated, is brought public again or sold at a profit to a strategic buyer. This process may take years. For example the buyout of Kinko's by Clayton, Dublier & Rice took seven years and it was sold to Federal Express for $2.4 billion in cash (Clayton, Dublier & Rice 2004).

But such happy endings aren't guaranteed.

There are variations on the theme of buyouts, including Leveraged Buy-out, Management Buyout, Management Buy-In, Employee Buyout, Institutional Buyout, and Buy-In Management Buyout. These have the acronyms LBO, MBO, MBI, EBO, IBO, and, of course, BIMBO.

COMMON FORMS OF PRIVATE INVESTING

There are many ways to acquire interests and develop the value of private companies. In general terms, two of the determining factors are how much work you want to do and how close you want to be to the daily operations of the company.

1. **Hands On, Hands Dirty Ownership**

    So you want to be really close to the action? Buy a company and run it. There is no better way to understand that the application of both hard work and money is only a start, and by no means is it a guarantee of success.

2. **Hands On Ownership**

    If you have the appetite to acquire ownership in a company without intermediaries, you can buy into what is called a direct investment. Your capital is exchanged for securities in the form of debt, equity, or some hybrid instrument in the company. With this cash infusion and some guidance, the company expands, increases its market share, finishes the development of a product, or brings a new product to market.

    Direct investing usually takes substantial resources, only one of which is money. Young or growing companies need all kinds of advice, management, discipline, and simple moral support. Your connections could come into play, bringing in a key hire, getting the legal help when needed, mentoring staff. Building companies is hard work—pursuing this type activity is the very definition of a venture capitalist or buyout professional.

    You get out of a direct investment by selling your position when it makes sense. The upside? A significant return on your money and the satisfaction that comes from creating something of value. The potential downside? You lose all the time, money, and personal commitment you invested.

3. **Hands Off Ownership**

As you get further from the action, you have less responsibility. You can have ownership in companies without any operational responsibility in two ways: a co-investment and as a limited partner in a fund.

A co-investment is as a kind of silent partner alongside a direct investor, who may be a fund manager. In this case you are called a co-investor and your responsibility is usually limited to supplying capital.

The most common investment vehicle, a private equity fund, is a legal entity formed to invest in companies. This is the way that most investors get exposure to private equity. These funds are generally set up in the form of a limited partnership and have a fixed term. As a limited partner, you commit money to the fund, the fund manager calls your capital to make investments in companies, and so you come to indirectly own positions in portfolio companies.

The managers of the fund, the general partners (GPs), charge management fees to run the fund. Their principal role is to find, negotiate with, and dedicate themselves to improving the operations, products, or strategies of the companies they invest in to increase their value. When the time is ripe, the partnership then sells its position in these companies and passes on the majority of the profits to its limited partners.

By investing in private equity partnerships, you get the benefit of ownership without as much involvement, liability, or control. As a limited partner in a fund, you are more of an observer than a participant. The general partners choose the companies in which to invest and monitor their progress. Private equity firms use other resources they deem appropriate to help make these companies succeed, including money, time, and talent. The general partners earn a fee for this work, and this fee includes a portion of the profits.

4. **Arm's Distance Ownership**

You commit to a private equity fund of funds. This is a good alternative for those without the resources to directly invest in individual funds. Investing in a fund of funds has similarities to investing in a fund, in that you are investing in a team that will make decisions for you.

In general, the closer you are to the direct ownership of a company, the more control you have and usually, the more work involved. If you are buying a direct position in a company, you assume a higher degree of responsibility for the success or failure of the venture and may end up committing much more than money to assure this success. The risk of loss is higher but so is the potential reward. With an investment in a fund as a limited partner, you are privy to the details of the company investments that the fund makes. Limited partners with significant positions or expertise are often asked to be on the advisory board of a fund. Finally, when you invest through a fund of funds, your active involvement is even less.

Successful private equity investing depends on personal relationships, trust, carefully crafted agreements, compensation, and a host of other hard and soft factors. Put all of these things together and it is most easily and often described as an alignment of interests between GP and LP.

WHY INVEST IN PRIVATE EQUITY?

> *When you're telling these little stories, here's a good idea: have a point. It makes it so much more interesting for the listener.*
> —Steve Martin to John Candy in *Planes, Trains and Automobiles*

When you bring a private equity opportunity into an institution for the first time, think of yourself as bringing an exotic animal into the boardroom. You will need to explain yourself. "Here is what the private equity animal looks like. It has special needs. It cannot live on its own. It requires special handling and feeding. We don't know everything we need to know about it quite yet. We are going to have to learn how to take care of it." And then you'd better be ready to explain to them why you've brought it into the boardroom. Have a point.

It may not always be about a golden egg. Diversifying a portfolio and seeking returns above the market may be enough, but getting into private equity should be a deliberate act. You may have a host of reasons. Corporate venture groups may invest in private companies for their strategic fit. Governmental institutions may emphasize employment or regional development. Endowments and foundations are perpetual investors, with a natural tolerance for the illiquid nature of private equity investments.

Most importantly, know that the commitment to build a private equity program relies on consistency that must bear up under the weight of uneven monetary rewards. If it is just money that you are after, being in the game at the right time may make all the difference. Get cold feet, skip a year, and you may destroy all of your hard work. We will discuss this more in depth in Chapter 13, The Concentration of Wealth.

FINALLY: THE BIG SECRET

Today, the business of investing in private equity is an industry unto itself, employing tens of thousands of people across the globe, from dedicated sales forces to specialized legal firms. Even though it has its focus on private transactions, private equity is in the public eye and is subject to a great deal of scrutiny, press, and curiosity. With private equity firms' indirect employment of millions of people, the public offering and notoriety of firms like Blackstone, and attempts by the U.S. Congress to regulate and tax private equity in new ways, its shadow looms large. Also within this mass of activity, private companies are being taken public or are being acquired by public companies and public companies are taken private only to be taken public again: eBay buys Skype; Intel buys a manufacturing division split off by a buyout. As a result, the portfolios of most limited partners are likely to contain a significant amount of transitory undistributed public assets.

The big secret is that the business of private equity isn't that private.

CONCLUSIONS

Although investing in a company can be a casual affair, the business of private equity investing requires substantial resources and a long-term horizon. This chapter briefly looked at the history of private equity investing, described its common forms, and presented some general background.

CHAPTER 2

Private Equity Perspectives

This chapter describes and introduces the private equity industry from several different perspectives. Along the way, we introduce companies, funds, funds of funds, and investors.

WORKING IN PRIVATE EQUITY

At the height of the dot-com mania, so   ist was talking to an entrepreneur.

"How are your sales going?" asked the VC.

"Great," said the entrepreneur. "We just closed our second round."

The inside joke is that the venture capitalist was asking about the health of the entrepreneur's company, its products, and their potential for sales. The entrepreneur, a bit full of himself and oblivious to the outside world, was telling the VC that he had gotten more venture capital funding for his enterprise, whatever it was, however it was doing. Products? What products? This disconnect was typical of that time. Same universe, different planets.

To the casual observer, private equity may sound like one thing, with one set of concerns and only one point of view. The business media tends to paint it as such. The truth is that it is more complicated, and it would not be a stretch to say that private equity is largely in the eye of the beholder.

To a company struggling to raise capital, private equity may seem barbaric, a ritualistic dance with the rich, powerful, and capricious. To an employee in that company, private equity may seem a threat. To an entrepreneur with the next hot idea, it may feel like a game. To a venture capitalist, it may be an opportunity to help invent the next new thing. To a potential limited partner (LP) investor, it may have an allure of mystery or simply the burden of a mandate passed down from on high. To a long-time investor, it may seem challenging, exciting, or like a tough way to earn a living.

Two strangers meet on a plane, and both say, "I work in private equity." What does this mean? We introduce the broad strokes of private equity and its various perspectives with a simple metaphor.

THE WORLD OF PRIVATE EQUITY

Think of private equity as a world unto itself. This world can be a bit insular at times, with significant barriers to entry. For most people, private equity is a world apart, requiring large amounts of capital and specialized expertise to enter. In the United States for example, investing in private equity is only open to accredited investors, those who meet high minimum regulatory standards. These barriers mean that private equity investing is done mostly by wealthy individuals and institutional investors, such as endowments, foundations, and pension funds, who generally have money to invest, long-term horizons, and the resources to manage it.

In this world of private equity, there are several distinct points of view. This chapter explains the roles of its players, companies, funds, funds of funds, and investors.

THE COMPANY PERSPECTIVE

The private equity industry exists because companies throughout the world have a continuing need for capital and that need is underserved by the more traditional financial markets.

Start-up companies, often with unproven business models, need seed capital. Early-stage companies, whose products need further work before getting to market, require development capital. Growing companies can consume tremendous amounts of capital just attempting to meet the demand for their products or services. Companies in need of restructuring, developing new product lines, or expanding into new markets all need capital.

The term that is most often used in the private equity industry to characterize the speed at which capital is consumed by a company is its "burn rate." This measure, how fast a company burns through cash, can tell you something important about its stage of development.

So companies are central to private equity, its raison d'être. Throughout this chapter, we will build on a simple diagram, shown in Figure 2.1,

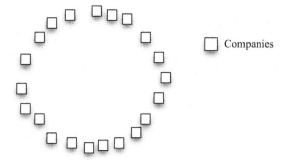

FIGURE 2.1 Companies seeking funding through private equity can be of any size or industry.

to highlight the relationships between the major types of organizations in private equity. This outer ring represents those seeking capital, companies.

Private equity can be attractive to any company, big or small, private or public. But private equity is considered a very expensive form of capital. If the owner of a company sells a piece of the business to a private equity firm, you can assume that they bought into it for good reasons. Should the owner fail to run it properly, the private equity investors may be happy to take it over.

Capital from private equity firms can also be expensive from the standpoint of the loss of control. A bank may not be able to replace the owner and take over the company, but a private equity firm usually can, and probably will, assume control when called upon to protect its investment.

Anyone who sells a portion of a company to a private equity firm and expects only money, with no strings attached, is naive. We can assume that most company owners who seek out private equity financing are not naive. Nothing comes for free. If done with eyes wide open, an entrepreneur looking to grow a business with outside capital understands the benefits that come from working with a team that builds companies for a living.

Company owners also understand the stakes involved and the financial incentives that help drive success when a private equity firm becomes involved. The private equity team works side-by-side with company owners, providing them needed guidance through hands-on management and tapping their network of specialists in operations, law, engineering, and finance. In an ideal relationship between company owners and a private equity fund manager, all interests are aligned.

DEFINITION: FUND MANAGER

A fund is only a legal entity, a pact between general and limited partners. The organization that actually runs a private equity fund is called the *fund manager*.

For example, Accel Partners is the name of a venture capital firm that has raised many funds over its long life. One of the funds that Accel Partners raised is the Accel India Venture Fund (Accel Partners 2008).

Many people tend to use the terms *fund*, *fund manager*, and *GP* interchangeably.

Company owners seeking private equity capital should prepare themselves well for the conversation with a GP. There are a number of books and resources that help describe this process, which is almost an art unto itself. Regional private equity and venture capital associations often sponsor events where budding entrepreneurs and company owners can tell their two-minute story, their elevator pitch, to a group of GPs in one forum. The general rule is to keep it brief, but be prepared to answer hard questions.

THE FUND PERSPECTIVE

Most institutions equate investing in private equity with investing in funds. The purpose of a private equity fund is to leverage both the expertise of a fund manager and the capital of its investors.

Most funds are organized as limited partnerships and have a fixed lifespan, usually 10 years. Although the partners can extend the life of a fund by agreement, at the end of the term the partnership usually dissolves—the fund is said to be self-liquidating. Other legal structures, such as evergreen funds, have no fixed term and may live on indefinitely. Some investors have opt-out rights, that is, the right to decline to invest in particular portfolio companies.

Funds are formed by general partners, with limited partners as members. The general partners manage the fund and assume the bulk of the liability of the partnership. The limited partners supply the bulk of the capital. The 99/1 rule, a rule of thumb, is the ratio of capital ultimately supplied by the LPs to that supplied by the GPs. The 1 percent or more supplied by the general partners is meant to further the alignment of interests between partners. With their own capital at risk, GPs are said "to have skin in the game."

Fundraising is the business of selling the vision of a fund to investors. This is an involved process, and usually involves first describing the strategy of the fund in a private placement memorandum (PPM), a document that attempts to cast their approach as a unique opportunity. The real work of fundraising starts by getting the PPM to dozens or even hundreds of potential investors and meeting with as many as possible. This process is known as a "road show." One of the things a GP might sell to potential investors is the elusive deal flow, that is, their access to potential investments in companies. Many fund managers emphasize the proprietary nature of their deal flow.

The definitive sign that fundraising has been successful is a closing, the signing of partnership documents. Somewhat counterintuitively, a closing does not necessarily mean that participation in the fund is closed; it means that the fund is definitively in operation. It is not uncommon to have several closings for a fund. Funds can be of any size, but the final size of the fund and the total number of investors may not be known until well after the fund has started operation, when the fund has its final closing.

Most funds are independent, and most fund managers are careful to create balance in the group of investors that they sign. In contrast, a "captive fund" has only one principal source of capital, often a parent company. Most captive funds are focused around a core investment strategy that supports the general mission of its parent. A "semicaptive fund" may have a dominant source of funding, while welcoming outside investors.

Intel Capital (2007) is an example of a captive fund. From its Web site (www.intel.com/capital/download/factsheet.pdf),

> *Intel Capital, Intel's global investment organization, makes equity investments in innovative technology start-ups and companies worldwide. Intel Capital invests in a broad range of companies offering hardware, software and services targeting enterprise, home, mobility, health, consumer Internet, semiconductor manufacturing, and cleantech.*

GETTING DOWN TO WORK

In many private equity firms, the real work begins after a fund is closed. At some firms, the work may have already begun.

As we mentioned, during fundraising some GPs boast of "proprietary deal-flow." This usually means that their teams have already been hard at work and may have more than a few candidate companies in which to invest. We can presume that these deals are characterized as proprietary either because no one else knows about them or the GP has already signed an agreement to provide funding to them. The other choice is that the use of the word *proprietary* is pure hyperbole.

We do know that with larger, more established fund operations, whole teams are dedicated to generating deal-flow. Some firms employ junior associates to make thousands of cold calls to companies every year to generate deal-flow.

THE INVESTMENT PERIOD

The first few years of a fund are what is called the investment period. During this critical time, companies are found, capital is called from investors, and investments in companies are made. The process is not as easy as it sounds. After initial screening, most potential investments are rejected. A fund will invest in a company only after extensive due diligence, a process meant to substantiate the strategic, financial, tax, legal, and personnel aspects of a business. (We describe an investment process from a different perspective, that of the LP, in Chapter 3.)

The capital from LPs is only requested as needed by the GP for operations and specific investment opportunities. This creates challenges of cash flow management for LPs. (We discuss this at length in Chapter 15.) Some of this capital is in the form of management fees that help fund the operations of the fund manager, legal fees, and the costs of doing due diligence. The bulk of the capital drawn during this period is for investment purposes, as the GP discovers and makes investments in companies. A draw of capital from an investor is known as a "capital call" or a "takedown."

Once the GP invests in a company, it becomes part of the fund's portfolio and so is often referred to as a "portfolio company." In many parts of the world, a portfolio company is also referred to as an "investee company."

Fund managers are a diverse lot. Some private equity teams are small and focus on young companies not yet making money; others direct their efforts to building up already profitable companies. Some funds focus on a particular industry sector, others on a particular region, and others still on a type of transaction. Some of the biggest fund management companies are public and know few bounds. The mega buyout funds are taking part in some of the largest and most complex financial transactions imaginable.

Figure 2.2 shows that funds invest in companies, and that two or more funds can, and often do, invest in the same company.

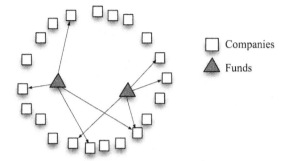

FIGURE 2.2   Funds invest in companies. Some funds specialize in particular types of companies, industries, or a particular region. For a variety of reasons, two or more funds often invest in the same company.

OTHER GPs AND ROUNDS

Quite often, two or more GPs invest in the same company. The GPs may be complementary in their approaches and so bring different things to the table. The company may require more capital than one GP is able or comfortable providing. One GP may provide capital to the company as a start-up and another may add capital during a period of expansion. This funding can happen all at once or at different times, and it is important to distinguish when the financing occurred. Whenever a company receives funding, it is referred to as a "round of financing" (or more simply a "round"). Each round is usually referred to as a "Series." The first round of financing is called Series A, the second Series B, and so on.

Two numbers are associated with the value of the company at each round of financing. The first value, the value of the company before the financing event, is the pre-money valuation. A second value, the post-money valuation, adds on the capital supplied in the round to the value of the company before the financing.

You may also encounter two more terms related to rounds. A round that only involves those currently invested in a company, with no new investors, is known as an "inside round." When a new, unrelated investor adds capital, it is known as an "outside round." A "down round" is a financing event that begins with a lower valuation for the company than the previous round. This is generally not a good thing. The hope of the GP is that with every successive round, the value of the company will increase. However disappointing it may be, a down round is a happier alternative for all involved than letting the company run out of capital. In that case, everybody loses.

Each successive round of financing of a portfolio company has the potential to dilute the ownership established by the prior rounds. This depends on the specific terms that the GP negotiated with the company.

Once an investment in a company is made, the central mission of the GP is to make the company successful. This is usually a lot of work and may take years to accomplish. As the fund manager repeats this process and builds a portfolio of companies, this work gets more complicated and becomes increasingly demanding. This is where the skills of the GP are tested. Fund managers have to be continually critical, some might say ruthless, in their continuous assessment of each portfolio company's chances for success.

Fund managers provide written reports to their limited partners on a regular basis, usually quarterly. These reports should describe in detail significant events, including investments, company descriptions, product developments, and other milestones. These reports also provide a consolidated schedule of investments that reveals the current carrying cost of every company, its current market value, and ideally, any proceeds from the investment in the company.

Companies that repeatedly fail to live up to their expectations should be written down in value or written off altogether as quickly as possible. Portfolio companies that show no promise of an exit and are kept on the books of a fund are known as the "living dead." This type of holding can sap the energy and limited resources of a fund manager.

After all this work on a company, the ideal outcome for a portfolio company is that it is sold to another company at a high multiple of its cost to the fund or possibly better yet, taken public through an IPO. On average, relatively few venture capital investments in portfolio companies make it big, but those that do reward fund managers with both money and reputation. The reputation gained from a string of successful exits for portfolio companies is critical to the continued fortune of the GP.

Success can create success and, in effect, create a brand. Some private equity firms, with long track records of accomplishment, are relieved of many of the chores of marketing by being a brand. Entrepreneurs seek them out. Investors try to throw money at them. These firms are few and far between.

Figure 2.3 depicts the relationships of fund manager, limited partner, funds, and companies. It is important to note that limited partners often invest in more than one fund and successive funds can invest in the same company.

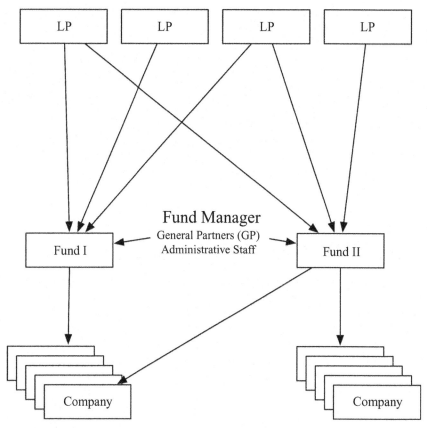

FIGURE 2.3 Each fund is a separate legal entity established by the fund manager. Capital is supplied by limited partners to funds and on through to companies. The fund manager is the firm that raises and manages funds.

Successful fund managers work in overlapping cycles of fundraising, investing in companies, building value, exiting investments, and liquidating funds. These dynamic phases and this cyclicality help align the interests of all concerned.

LIFE AS A GP

The life of a general partner can be frenetic. A start-up phase of a fund is followed by several years of investing in a portfolio of companies. As capital is put to work and the fund is depleted, the GP goes back on the road to raise a new fund. The performance of the first fund, its track record, becomes part of the next road show. Meanwhile, work continues on the first fund, proving out their strategy. If fundraising is successful, the cycle continues. Some believe that a private equity firm is not fully tested until it attempts to raise a third fund, as the second fund can often be raised without a clear picture of how successful the first fund will be.

A private equity firm must keep raising funds, or it dies. A failure to raise a fund is not unusual and is not always fatal, but without fresh infusions of capital, a GP can only complete work on current funds. In some cases, failing to raise a fund is viewed as a temporary setback, and the GPs will continue work on their current portfolio, later recast their message, and try fundraising again at a more favorable time.

HOW FUND MANAGERS MAKE MONEY

> *In the 16th and 17th centuries, when European traders were travelling to the New World and the Far East, voyages were funded by private investors, each of whom took a share of the risk and a share of the profits in proportion to his or her investment. By custom, the captain of the ship took 20 percent of the value of the cargo. That rule still applies: private-equity firms generally take a carried interest of 20 percent of the capital gain made by the funds under their management.*
>
> —Sir Ronald Cohen (2007, p. 22)

Fund managers make money primarily in two ways:

1. The fund manager charges a management fee to cover the cost of running the fund. This is usually from 2 to 2.5 percent of the committed capital to the fund, but many variations of fee structures exist. Usually the management fees scale down in the later years of the fund, when investments are being realized and there is less to do.
2. The fund manager takes a cut of the profits, called the "carried interest" or more simply the "carry." Today the carry is usually 20 percent, but it can be 30 percent or more. This tradition, as explained in the quote above, is a nautical term related to a captain's compensation for a voyage. The carry may not start until a defined percent profit, a "hurdle rate" (also known as "preferred return"), is returned to the LP investors. Once the fund meets that threshold, it enters the catch-up period, during which the GP receives the majority of distributions until

the agreed-upon profit split is met. Carry earned in the early life of a fund may also be subject to being returned to investors if subsequent investments lose money. This is known as "clawback."

THE FUNDS OF FUNDS PERSPECTIVE

A private equity fund of funds straddles the world of general partner and a limited partner investor. Instead of investing in companies, a private equity fund of funds invests in private equity funds.

Although they impose an additional layer of fees on investors, funds of funds can have very clear benefits. Among them, a fund of funds structure creates an easy way to invest in private equity for investors who may lack the knowledge or other resources to do so. Some investors invest in funds of funds as a springboard for a program of their own design. Funds of funds can also provide investors significant diversification, by geography, stage, and industry, with only one commitment. As well, many funds of funds have long-term relationships with some of the best fund managers in the industry.

By investing in funds on a large scale, a fund of funds has all the hallmarks of a traditional limited partner, including long-term horizons and a great deal of capital. As an LP, a fund of funds screens investments, performs due diligence on the track record of managers, invests according to a plan, and has constituents to report to on a regular basis.

Yet a fund of funds is also a general partner. As a GP, its main source of capital is not itself, but instead is raised periodically from third parties. This requires fundraising activity that looks very similar to that of a GP. A fund of funds charges fees for management and is rewarded with incentives for good performance. Like a GP, a fund of funds draws capital to meet its obligations and distributes cash when its investments are realized. The difference is that a fund of funds usually invests in funds, not companies. Figure 2.4 creates the role of a fund of funds on our evolving diagram, pointing out that it can invest directly in companies as an adjunct to their main investing in funds.

On both sides of its operations, the part that is LP and the part that is GP, the differences are largely differences in scale. A fund of funds may have hundreds of investors, some with very small slices of the fund. Because of its scale, a fund of funds is heavily dependent on automation, with systems to allocate capital in a myriad of ways. Funds of funds usually have or outsource sophisticated systems or services that help in administration. Running a fund of funds well requires an experienced investment team backed by a skilled administrative staff and sophisticated infrastructure.

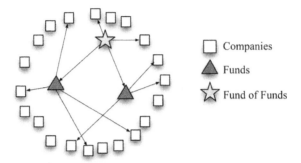

FIGURE 2.4 A fund of funds primarily invests in funds, but can also invest directly in companies.

As with many GPs, some funds of funds specialize. For example, several funds of funds focus on acquiring positions in limited partnerships from willing sellers looking for liquidity—these partnerships positions are known as "secondaries."

THE INVESTOR

Ultimately, most money comes from LPs. An investor in private equity usually has substantial long-term assets or liabilities that can benefit from additional diversification and potential for higher returns while absorbing some added risk.

Typical private equity investors include endowments, foundations, public and private pension funds, financial services companies, and family investment offices. Another important set of service providers, represented by advisors and gatekeepers, may invest on the behalf of others. Investors in private equity have three main opportunities in the private equity world: funds, funds of funds, or companies.

- Investors can invest in a fund, where they join a small circle of investors in a limited partnership. The investment initially takes the form of a commitment to the fund. The size of the commitment determines their pro rata share of the fund; an investor with a commitment of $15 million in a $100 million fund has a 15 percent share. The commitment is a pledge to provide capital over time, usually over the first five years, as the fund invests in companies. Major investors are often asked to sit on an advisory board for the fund and so gain additional insight into its operations and provide valuable input.

■ Investors can leverage their efforts by investing in a fund of funds. A typical fund of funds provides, at the cost of another layer of fees and expenses, ownership in dozens of funds and as a result, exposure to a much more highly diversified portfolio of companies.

■ Investors can also put money to work directly in a company. This is known as a direct investment. Here the investor's money is exchanged for equity, debt, or a combination of both in the company. This type of activity requires more time, attention, and expertise. Another form of this, called a "co-investment," allows the investor to invest directly in a company alongside another more hands-on investor, typically a fund.

Directly and indirectly, an ownership pattern emerges. The investor owns a fund, which owns positions in companies. A fund of funds owns positions in funds, which own positions in companies. The investor adds an occasional co-investment. Within the large but still limited world of companies, overlapping interests are common. Two or more funds often invest in the same company. An investor can also invest in a company without the help of a GP. An investor with hundreds of investments and thousands of indirect interests in companies will often have a large overlap of ownership in companies.

THE INVESTOR'S PERSPECTIVE

From the point of view of the investor, what emerges is a complex set of relationships and ownership, some direct, some indirect. As shown in Figure 2.5, with every additional investment in a fund, fund of funds, or company, there are more connections, and there is more work.

DIFFERENT POINTS OF VIEW

What is private equity? Ask a manager of a fund of funds, and you will get a very different answer from the one an investor will give you.

Fundamentally, each perspective is that of an investor. You could put any of these entities at the center of the diagram, and the relationships shift. Put the GP at the center, and the importance and scale of each task change. And, of course, each perspective has the potential to change how work and success are measured.

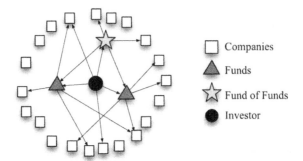

FIGURE 2.5   An investor's perspective is at the center of a complex web of relationships to funds, funds of funds, and companies.

In the coarser reality, capital flows in all directions, often at once. Capital may be called at the same time it is being distributed. In most portfolios, transactions occur in several currencies. There are other players in the mix, including placement agents, who help bring GP and LP together, specialized attorneys, investment banks, accounting firms, and data services. An LP with a sizeable portfolio can have relationships with hundreds of GPs and indirect relationships with thousands of portfolio companies. Funds of funds can have the same complexity and deal not only with hundreds of investors, but dozens of funds over their lives, making for a very complex business and view of their private equity world.

MEASURING FROM DIFFERENT PERSPECTIVES

Differences in perspective arise from different missions and agendas. The private equity portfolio of a typical endowment, foundation, or pension is usually a portion of their total assets. Traditional investment advisors and custodial banks are often at a loss as to how to measure in a meaningful way a mix of assets that includes substantial commitments to private equity.

In contrast, the track record of a GP stands alone. A key milestone for a GP is raising the next fund. Successful GPs raise fund after fund and may in time invest in hundreds of companies, each one of them a measure unto itself. On a simple level, both GPs and LPs can be said to succeed when they outperform other investment opportunities on a risk-adjusted basis and cover the added operational costs of investing in private equity.

CONCLUSIONS

As is so often the case, what you see depends on where you sit.

Private equity is not one thing, nor is one perspective necessarily dominant. Each participant, whether the owner of a company, the administrator of a fund of funds, an investor, a general partner, an attorney, or placement agent all work in private equity, but they do very different things and think very differently about what they do. Each point of view has a different scale of concerns, with different measures of success.

This book is focused on the limited partner, and so most of what we will write about going forward will have the concerns of the LP in mind.

CHAPTER 3

Managing the Investment Process

Fiorello	*Hey, wait, wait. What does this say here, this thing here?*
Driftwood	*Oh, that? Oh, that's the usual clause, that's in every contract. That just says, uh, it says, uh, if any of the parties participating in this contract are shown not to be in their right mind, the entire agreement is automatically nullified.*
Fiorello	*Well, I don't know . . .*
Driftwood	*It's all right. That's, that's in every contract. That's, that's what they call a sanity clause.*
Fiorello	*Ha-ha-ha-ha-ha! You can't fool me. There ain't no Sanity Clause!*

—Groucho and Chico Marx, *A Night at the Opera*

Building a portfolio of private equity assets takes time and patience. This chapter introduces a structured approach to build or build onto a portfolio of private equity assets, provides some guidance on contract terms, and concludes with some timeless advice to fund managers from the standpoint of an LP.

CYA OR PROCESS?

Private equity investing is a high-stakes pursuit.

How do you make an investment decision that ties up millions for years, offers little liquidity, and binds you as partner to a specialized investment team? The answers at times can seem bizarre: "We *re-up*." This shorthand lets you know that the speaker's next investment is a continuation of an existing relationship, often one developed over many funds and years. For many LPs with deep trust in their GPs, this may be a rational approach. Of course, teams change, economic conditions vary, different times create different opportunities, relationships can sour, and there is no guarantee that things will turn out as before.

Some investors answer the question by looking around the room: "Who has committed to the fund so far?" Other LPs piggyback on the due diligence of others: "What did *the big endowment* do? How much did they commit?" Others investors draw lines in the sand: "We only invest in top-quartile managers."

So, for some, the private equity investment process is about corroborating a decision already made. Yet there are many other investors with a disciplined approach to investing that can boast great track records based on repeatable processes. We strongly prefer the latter, an investment process grounded in a set of integrated quantitative and qualitative methods. Every commitment to a fund should be part of a plan that is continually measured and periodically reassessed.

We suspect that most investors are averse to wagering millions on private equity folklore, such as assumptions that top-quartile managers will remain so. But we also suspect that we are not alone in our belief that this craft needs more science added to its art.

GAINING ACCESS

Some might argue that the world of private equity is not truly open even to those of means, including accredited individuals and institutional investors. Instead they see this part of the investment world as full of barriers, with access to the inner circles open only to a chosen few. If you are new to private equity, it is true that there are barriers of knowledge, language, and process, but the most disturbing one may be the barrier of access. With some fund managers, the door for new entrants is closed, not partially closed, but closed and locked. Why is this so?

Shift perspective from being an LP, and think about the problem of access to a fund from the standpoint of a fund manager.

Say that you are a general partner raising your third fund. Your story is not unusual. When you started your private equity firm 10 years ago, you had difficulty raising your first fund, only barely reaching the fund size that you had targeted. Fortunately, a few intrepid limited partners stepped up and took a risk with you and your group. You stayed focused, worked hard, and earned a solid reputation with your LPs. You didn't vary from your initial strategy. This first fund returned its capital relatively quickly and made a tidy profit. Your LPs were nicely rewarded for their faith in you.

You were happy with your relationships with your investors. You remain especially loyal to those who made commitments to your fund early on. Without them, you might have failed altogether.

Because you had a modest, but good track record, raising money for the second fund was much easier than the first. Most of your investors from the first fund re-upped with you. A few new investors, who had been reluctant to invest when you and your team lacked a track record, made modest commitments to this second fund. This fund is still in progress, but it too has had early success. The fund has plenty of value left to return to its investors.

Recently, when you went out to raise your third fund, you found you had little work to do. When you announced the fund, your current investors said: "Where do we sign, and how much can I commit?" With this, the fund was fully subscribed. You are about to close the fund, but each of your limited partners is pleading for a bigger piece of the pie. You now have a choice of increasing the fund size or of disappointing loyal investors. To top it off, you are now being approached with referrals by a number of great new investors with reputations for being very discriminating. You would love to have them on your roster of investors. If you increase the size of the fund, you risk coming off your central strategy. You have an embarrassment of riches.

To the point: What would you say to other investors wanting to come into your fund about whom you know nothing?

This scenario is of course hypothetical, but it is symptomatic of an industry where growth can be constrained by talent and experience. Fundamentally, this is about supply and demand. The conclusion of course, is that some fund managers with great track records, experienced teams, and cachet do not need new investors. Don't take it personally.

The Hazards of an Access-Based Approach

Our advice (a little Zen-like, we admit) is to let go of the things that you cannot control. But before you accept this advice or not, understand how an obsession with access to a fund, or a specific set of funds, can harm your investment program. Consider this second scenario from the perspective of an LP.

You help manage a long-established investment program with a history of private equity investing. You are known as a reliable investor to GPs around the world. You are always asked to be on advisory boards. Your firm has a long-term focus and is patient. You have plenty of capital at your disposal. Your organization can suffer a few lean years without changing investment strategy. You, in fact, are an ideal limited partner.

Your portfolio consists of some the best fund managers that have walked the earth. You are always invited to participate in follow-on funds from these managers. But you have a problem.

The problem is that although you are getting into potentially very good funds, you cannot put enough of your capital to work because you no longer have a choice about how much money to commit to these funds. Instead of the good old days, when you let the GP know how much money you could commit, you now receive an *allocation* to a fund. You are grateful for these allocations, and you believe that if you do not take the allocation as offered, you will never be given another allocation again.

As a result, your portfolio is a patchwork of small (or less than ideal-sized) commitments to more funds than your team can manage. You are constantly on the prowl for places to put more capital to work.

At the end of the day, the most important question that you, as a portfolio manager, can ask is: "Does access matter?"

The knee-jerk reaction that we hear most from LPs is "Of course it matters!" The problem is that these small allocations distract you from critical decisions that you ought to be making about your portfolio. Your sense of obligation to maintain your relationship with certain fund managers can change your investment behavior. The same oft-cited rule applies here as it does in the public markets: "Do not fall in love with a stock." What we would like to convey most strongly in this text is that however a particular fund may matter to you, it may matter a lot less to your portfolio and the wealth that it generates.

That being said, quality matters, and firms that endure do so for a reason.

However, even the best private equity firms face problems of expansion, retention, succession, and the challenges of the daily grind. Even the best of firms have been known to dissolve, and it can be argued that some private equity firms have a natural lifespan. Any business that is dependent on the talents of a few individuals should gracefully go out of business when the time comes. Often, younger associates with experience, anxious to run their own show, will split off and form their own private equity firms.

Investors come and go as well. Fund managers who become too de-pendent on particular investors may set themselves up for disappointment. Many institutional investors are subject to the dictates and whims of invest-ment boards. Investment policies change for all sorts of reasons. If access is about anything, it is about being available when opportunities arise.

AN APPROACH TO PRIVATE EQUITY INVESTMENT

There is no single investment process—one size does not fit all. So keep in mind that what we describe here is an approach, something that has been successfully put into practice at a number of institutions, but ours is by no means the only valid approach.

In our view, once started, investing in private equity has neither beginning nor end. Instead it is a continuous cycle that follows a regular pattern. The elements are bound together. Figure 3.1 outlines this cycle as we see it.

1. Since there is no beginning or end, the logical place to begin is determining your objectives for your overall asset allocation. This is a complex exercise, potentially involving many other investment teams. The most important thing to determine from this phase is how large

FIGURE 3.1   A private equity process is built on a continuous cycle of assessment.

your private equity allocation should be as a percentage of your overall portfolio.

2. Determine your sub-asset allocation objectives. This means that you should apportion, ahead of time, the amounts that you plan to commit to each sub-asset class, including the likes of buyouts, venture capital, mezzanine, and distressed securities.

3. Get to work. Generate and screen deal flow for the best opportunities consistent with your investment objectives.

4. For each investment opportunity you have screened, verify and analyze the quantitative and qualitative information.

5. Negotiate and close a legal agreement that aligns your interests with those of the GP.

6. Monitor your portfolio with a view to optimizing its risk-adjusted returns.

THE PRIVATE EQUITY INVESTMENT POLICY

Your asset allocation and sub-asset allocation should be set out in some detail in an investment policy statement that is the product of interacting with your governing board of trustees, directors, regents, or the like. You let them know what to expect from private equity and what its risk, return, correlation, and liquidity characteristics are; they let you know what they are comfortable with. This is an iterative process that should ultimately result in a stable platform. All of the participants understand each other's roles and positions. Once your board adopts an investment policy, it becomes a kind of constitutional framework within which you can operate to implement the program.

An investment policy should include at least the following key items:

- Long-term investment strategy
- Asset allocation target and range
- Sub-asset allocation targets and ranges
- Investment objectives of the private equity portfolio
- Asset class (and perhaps sub-asset class) benchmarks
- Permitted and prohibited investments
- Risk management considerations
- Roles and responsibilities of staff, consultants, committees of the board, and so on
- Reporting requirements

GENERATING DEAL FLOW

It may seem counterintuitive to some that you would need to advertise your desire to invest large sums in private equity in the coming year, but unless you periodically make the market aware that you are shopping, you may lack for choice. In many cases, it is enough simply to announce your investment objectives in the financial press and let the marketing departments and marketing representatives of potential investment managers do the rest. However, if you have a relatively small investment program or if you have an interest in reaching out to minority managers, emerging managers, foreign managers, or managers with any combination of these or other highly specialized qualities, more effort is required.

The GPs at the smaller or more specialized end of the market require special attention and may require you to be more proactive. Many of these groups cannot afford a dedicated internal marketing department or a third-party marketing agent and are likely to reach out using telephone campaigns. As a result, you are less likely to see all that is available at the smaller or more specialized end of the market. To bridge this gap, you should devise your own marketing campaign to ensure that these GPs look upon you as receptive to their proposals. Your efforts will depend upon the market segments you are trying to reach. In addition, by cultivating relationships with like-minded investors, you are sure to get referrals for groups that you might not have seen.

SCREENING DEAL FLOW

Even without reaching out to minority, emerging, foreign, or other highly specialized managers, a major private equity investment program in the United States can receive 500 or more Private Placement Memoranda (PPMs) per year. Some institutional investors attempt to meet with as many managers as possible, scheduling as many as 300 interviews per year. We recommend that you winnow the initial pool down to 30 to 50 candidates in order to focus your efforts on managers most likely to add to your program.

Here we look ahead to quantitative measures and techniques we introduce in later chapters. To reduce the number of potential investment managers you meet with, it would be beneficial to take the following actions:

- Compare the track record of the prospective manager to a public market index using the Index Comparison Method (ICM). See Chapter 11, The IRR and the Public Markets.

- Measure the risk the manager has taken to produce these returns, and the correlation of these returns with the relevant public market index. See Appendix G.
- Determine performance attribution to ensure that the manager's returns have been the product of skill, rather than luck. See Chapter 12, Performance Attribution.
- Summarize these results in an easy-to-understand graphic format that allows for easy screening. See Chapter 10, Visualizing Private Equity Performance.

The candidates that make it through this gauntlet will make up your viable investment universe out of which you can select the best for your program.

Although we are skeptics of research based on commercially available databases, several studies have concluded that performance is persistent (Conner 2005; Phalippou & Gottschalg 2005), indicating that past success is an indicator of future success. If this is true, evaluating a manager's track record is critical.

Advantages of Quantitative Screening

Quantitative screening provides you with:

- *Responsiveness.* GPs like quick decisions. So should you. You will gain a lot of respect if you can say "no thank you" quickly rather than let a decision languish.
- *Objectivity.* A quantitative analysis will help you to state clearly why you have passed on opportunities to your senior management, board, advisers, or donors. With results in hand, you might share with GPs with whom you have relationships why you cannot, at this time, commit to their fund.
- *Control.* You will be better able to ensure that the funds you select comply with the overall risk/return profile approved by your board.
- *Sophistication.* The questions you ask of GPs and their staffs during the qualitative due diligence phase will be much more directed and effective.
- *Efficiency.* You will quickly screen out the vast majority of inferior investment opportunities.

Verifying a Track Record

Getting past the gloss of a marketing pitch of a new fund by a GP or placement agent takes work.

We recommend that you use quantitative screenings to check the accuracy of traditional marketing materials, such as PPMs. After their presentation in your offices, go to their offices, review their files, and conduct structured interviews. Check their references, but follow up by asking about them through your network of industry contacts. In Appendix B, you will find an on-site GP audit program guide; in Appendix C, we present a structured interview template; in Appendix D, a template for structured reference calls.

We suggest that you begin by auditing their cash flows and valuations. For instance, Messrs. Long and Nickels have been given false track records on three separate occasions. However improbable it may be that a GP would simply make up numbers, we believe that your fiduciary duties require that you verify cash flows and valuations to lay to rest any possibility that you have been or will be subjected to fraud or misrepresentation. Avoidance of fraud or misrepresentation is, after all, one of the primary goals of due diligence.

QUALITATIVE DUE DILIGENCE

Request for Information (RFI)

A PPM is designed to set out the best case for investment: it does not provide a suitable framework for decision making. To remedy this, we routinely request supplemental information through an RFI. There are model due diligence questionnaires available in the industry from institutional investors and consultants. The objective of the RFI is to get a more nuanced view of the GP's operations and track record. With an RFI, you get to ask the questions. GPs often dread its arrival, but they should not object to responding to an RFI that is well thought out. After studying their response, you can decline to proceed further or move on to the next step. See the Sample RFI in Appendix E.

Structured On-Site Interviews

A positive response to an RFI sets the stage for the more intensive process of interviewing the fund manager in their offices. These structured on-site interviews should ideally be with all of the principal investors on their team. If the fund has multiple offices, your interviews may require more time. On rare occasions, a particular fund manager may have either so many offices, so many principals or offices that are so far-flung that you will have to sample them instead of visiting them all.

The purpose of structuring a set of interviews is to enable you to repeat your process in exactly the same way each and every time. Repeatability is the essence of skill, and without structure interviews tend to become chummy sessions that allow GPs skilled at marketing to dominate the discussion and skip or cloud important issues.

Interviewing a fund manager is a skill in its own right. You should always ask: "What is the worst deal you have ever done?" The best responses are full of candor. We look for managers with an unusual combination of qualities, including candor, attention to detail, humility, and a passion for continuous learning and improvement.

Structured Reference Calls and Headline Risk

We recommend that you follow up interviews by talking to references who have invested in, or know the fund manager well and are willing to share an honest opinion with you. This is about give and take—one sure way to be able to get these useful opinions is for you to give them to other LPs when asked. The reference call is about the character and investment acumen of the members of their team. Money is at stake, usually a great deal of money, and all of it hinges on this evaluation.

From time to time you may have to dig deeper, and this may require considerable effort. We use the "front page of the newspaper" test to keep motivated in this research.

SCANDAL ROCKS INVESTMENT GROUP

Fourteen Indicted, Including You

This is common enough to have a name, "headline risk." The last thing that you want to be is the star in your own daytime legal drama.

Most matters can be put to rest with three or four phone calls to the right contacts. Occasionally something may require scarce resources, such as time and money, to investigate. Unless you are satisfied, your fiduciary duty of due care mandates that you decline to invest. We were once told by a disgruntled former partner that another partner had been involved in serious breaches of fiduciary duty. It took six weeks of phone calls and in-person interviews with third parties to determine that the allegations were groundless. The main point is that these are long-term relationships and should be able to withstand any test that makes you sure of your decision.

Negotiating and Closing an Agreement

The goal of every contract negotiation should be to align your interests as closely as possible with those of the fund manager. Here is the gist of it: the manager should not make money if you do not make money. Partnership agreements, however, are anything but plain in either language or content. Messrs. Long and Nickels have negotiated roughly 150 partnership agreements and have never seen two exactly alike. There are many legitimate reasons for this (not including the need for attorneys to justify their fees), but there are many complex and subtle legal issues involved that are not amenable to easy summarization or solution. The old saying applies: if you don't know diamonds, you should know your jeweler. You should get to know the very best partnership investment counsel you can find. Much is at stake in a partnership negotiation.

Following are some issues that we feel are important in these negotiations. Even if you are not directly involved in the negotiations for a contract, we think that it will help you understand the underpinnings of your investments with general partners.

Standards of Care and Fiduciary Duties   In 1916, the National Conference of Commissioners on Uniform State Laws (NCCUSL) promulgated the Uniform Limited Partnership Act (ULPA), which over the years, with insignificant variations, was enacted in almost every state in the United States. The ULPA adopted the common law view that general partners owed their limited partners fiduciary duties, including the duty of care, the duty of loyalty, the duty of fair dealing, the duty of candor, and so on.

In 1986, however, the American Law Institute issued the Revised Uniform Limited Partnership Act (RULPA), which has since been enacted by most of the states that figure prominently in the private equity industry. Perhaps the single most important difference between the original ULPA and the RULPA is that general partners no longer owe their limited partners any duties that are not explicitly spelled out in the partnership agreement.

This may seem dry and dull until you deal with a general partner unconstrained by duties under a lenient partnership agreement. It is then a fascinating topic that can save your investment or even your investment program.

The most frequently-cited description of fiduciary duty is *utmost good faith*. In turn, dealing in utmost good faith imposes the duty of the fiduciary to act for another's benefit while subordinating the fiduciary's own interest. This is the highest standard of duty implied by law. And the reason we included the history of the RULPA in the first paragraph is that the law of most states is that now you can't hold your GP to a fiduciary standard unless your partnership agreement says you can.

Why, you might wonder, does this matter? Well, consider the following hypothetical scenario:

Suppose that your GP has used borrowed capital to buy investments in advance of raising another fund. This is called "warehousing," and there is usually nothing wrong with it. However, in this case, there is still time remaining in the acquisition period of your GP's current fund, the one in which you have invested. These warehoused investments could therefore conceivably be acquired by your fund or, as the GP apparently intended, could be acquired by the next fund. Unfortunately, in this case the GP personally guaranteed the debt used to acquire these warehoused investments and a sudden market reversal has put them deeply underwater.

Since the large losses on the warehoused investments could be viewed to impeach the investment acumen of your GP, and since no LP would invest in a new fund that would buy these investments from the GP at cost, the GP has a couple of alternatives: leave the warehoused investments in a separate portfolio by liquidating personal wealth to satisfy the creditors whose loans were used to acquire them, thus taking a substantial personal loss; or, have your fund—your money—acquire these at cost, citing the open acquisition period in the current fund—your fund—and its valuation policy of holding investments at cost that are less than a year old, thus sticking you with the loss. Ouch.

Now, if this hypothetical GP owed you fiduciary duties under the current fund's partnership agreement, sticking you with the loss this way would be a clear breach of fiduciary duty. Whether the GP would back down voluntarily or would require a court order to act, in either case you would not get stuck with the loss. If, on the other hand, your current fund's partnership agreement was silent on fiduciary duties, there would be no such duties, and you would be stuck with the loss—without recourse in law or in equity. That's a big difference.

And that's why you always want to seek to include explicit fiduciary duties in your limited partnership agreement. The difference between having explicit fiduciary duties in the agreement and not having them can be literally billions of dollars at the partnership level, enough to threaten any individual investment or even an investment program.

No-Fault Divorce Clause   Especially in the case of new and emerging managers, LPs want the ability to simply call the whole thing off. GPs, of course, have an opposed interest in locking the LPs into the partnership. The usual compromise is that the LPs can force the end of the acquisition period and the liquidation of the fund by the vote of a supermajority in interest (say, 80 percent) for any reason or no reason. Cautious GPs try to make sure that their most stable and long-term relationships comprise a blocking interest.

No-Fault Removal of GP   Again, this provision is usually reserved for new and emerging managers. The idea is that a supermajority in interest of the LPs can remove the GP, for any reason or no reason, and replace the GP with a new one recruited from outside.

No-Fault Freeze of Commitments   This is a step down from no-fault removal. A supermajority in interest of the LPs can cause the GP to suspend the acquisition period in order to observe the portfolio or await other input indicating that it is safe and prudent to reinstate the investment program and allow the GP to call capital.

Removal of GP for Cause   This provision is almost always limited to a material breach of the agreement, but other considerations may apply. The definition of *cause* usually excludes ordinary negligence, which means that the material breach has to be the product of gross negligence, willful neglect, defalcation, fraud, and similar occurrences.

This provision is sometimes accompanied by language allowing for a termination of the partnership for cause in cases in which the GP is removed and no new GP becomes a replacement.

Advisory Board Seat   Whenever and wherever possible, we advise you to seek an advisory board seat. The advisory board is frequently the first to learn about important developments in the partnership, whether good or bad. Also, the advisory board almost always has approval rights over the GP's valuation of the partnership's investments. In certain circumstances, this approval role can become pivotal in partnership governance.

GP Committed Capital   Many LPs feel that the more capital a GP has committed to the partnership the better. Nothing speaks to alignment of interest more than the common exposure to personal economic risk of the GP and the LP. Some major LPs go so far as to require a specific threshold commitment from the GP, although we argue that a high threshold unfairly cuts many smaller and newer GPs completely out of the market. We believe that determining the effective alignment of interests is better determined by the size of the GP commitment relative to the GP's personal economic circumstances. Even here, there can be such a thing as too much—you want your GP to be watching over his money alongside yours, not obsessing about the personal leverage required to enable her to invest.

Legal Opinions   Request the GP to deliver formal legal opinions on organization, tax, and securities law aspects of the partnership. The organizational legal opinion should state that you, when serving on the advisory board, will not be deemed to be involved in management and control of Partnership pursuant to the law under which the partnership was formed (frequently Delaware law).

Purpose of the Partnership   The agreement should require the GP to cause the partnership to invest in a manner that is consistent with the contents of the PPM. This may seem obvious, but the collapse of the venture capital bubble in 2000 brought to light numerous high-profile departures from the investment strategy originally sold to investors.

Key Man Provision   If a designated principal or a designated combination of particular principals withdraws from the GP's organization, the GP should be required to give prompt written notice to the LPs. Depending upon the relative negotiating strengths of the parties, LPs can set a specific time period after the departure, commonly 120 days, during which the GP can only make new investments with the Advisory Board's approval. In the case of a designated combination of particular principals, agreements frequently require the approval of a majority in interest of the LPs to make any new investments (with exceptions for transactions subject to a letter of intent at the time of the departure and for follow-on investments in companies in the portfolio) with approval of the Advisory Board.

Capital Contributions   The agreement should state clearly that capital will not be called unless or until it is needed, either for administrative purposes (the management fee, for example) or for investment. Capital contributions should be strictly limited to the amount of your commitment, and the agreement should further provide that you do not waive any breach by responding to a capital call.

ERISA Provisions (If You Are a Corporate Pension Fund)   This is a complicated area of the law, but in general, corporate pension funds in order to protect their trustees from personal liability, must reserve the right not to answer a capital call if doing so would result in violating certain ERISA rules and regulations. Also, in the same vein, pension funds under ERISA must be allowed to withdraw from the partnership without penalty if remaining in the partnership would cause the pension fund to violate ERISA rules and regulations.

Later-Closing LPs   Unless the partnership will have a single closing, the LPs who close later in the process (later-closing LPs) can find themselves having to share with the earlier-closing LPs the investments made in the interim. The agreement should contain specific provisions on how these investments are to be shared. Frequently, the later-closing LPs will be required to pay interest on the capital contributed by the earlier-closing LPs whose positions are then diluted.

Restrictions on Partnership Borrowing in the United States One of the potential ramifications of partnership borrowing is what the tax law calls a debt-financed acquisition. Any partnership assets that are debt-financed acquisitions subject the LPs to unrelated business taxable income (UBTI) when they are sold, a potentially disastrous result from both an administrative and an economic perspective. Economically, UBTI is subjected to income tax at the prevailing corporate rate, thus creating a gulf between gross proceeds and net proceeds after tax.

Fees, Including Carried Interest, and How Transaction Fees (If Any) Will Be Shared Management fees usually decline over time to reflect the view that it takes much more time to buy things and run them than it does to sell them. In other words, many partnership agreements load the management fee up front to compensate the GP for the time and expense of finding, closing, and then managing investments. This assumes that the sale of the investment takes little or no time and, in any event, is coincident with the liquidity event everyone involved was waiting for. The usual formula is that after the investment period, usually three or four years, the management fee will decline from a percentage of commitments to a percentage of the net book value of assets remaining in the portfolio. Whether the percentage declines as well is a matter for negotiation.

There are two principal issues with regard to the carried interest: whether there will be a hurdle rate required in order to pay carried interest (and a related but subordinate issue, whether there will be a catch-up); and whether the carried interest will be paid deal by deal or whether the portfolio will be aggregated in determining payback. Proceeds are usually split different ways before and after the carry kicks in. Let us assume, for example, that the GP has committed 1 percent of the capital to the fund and has a carried interest of 20 percent. Before the carry kicks in, the LPs split 99 percent of the proceeds to the GP's 1 percent. After the carry kicks in, the split is 80 percent to the LPs and 20 percent to the GP.

Over time, the hurdle rate has come to center around 8 percent or so. This is usually a compound rate, but from time to time we still see hurdle rates that are calculated using simple interest. The idea is that the GP can't pay itself carried interest until the investors have received the hurdle rate of return.

Some older agreements simply change the split of profits to 80/20 from 99/1 after reaching the hurdle rate of return so that the GP does not receive a carried interest on the preceding amounts paid out. In the current market, however, most agreements provide that after the LPs have received the hurdle rate there is a catch-up period in which all or most of the proceeds of liquidated investments are paid to the GP in such a way as to leave the

GP with a carried interest on everything paid out before reaching the hurdle rate. After reaching the hurdle rate and paying out the catch-up, proceeds are split 80/20.

The aggregation of gains and losses is also a critical issue. If gains and losses are not aggregated, the GP pays itself carried interest in each investment that results in a realized gain. In extreme cases, that means that a GP could take a substantial carried interest payment on one investment and then lose all of the LPs' capital in, say, 12 investments. If gains and losses are aggregated under the same assumptions, however, that first carried interest payment would be subject to clawback because the total effect including all investments would be a substantial loss. We believe that deal-by-deal payment of carried interest gives the GP a free option that leads to riskier investments; we therefore recommend always requiring aggregation of gains and losses in calculating and paying the carried interest.

Clawback   Under certain circumstances, usually a portfolio with very successful early investments and very large and very unsuccessful late investments, it is possible for the early payments to the GP to wind up being more than 20 percent of all the capital paid out. In order to address this situation, most agreements impose a personal liability on the GPs to pay back into the partnership, for distribution pro rata to the LPs, an amount that results in the GP's receiving exactly 20 percent of total profits. This liability can be extremely substantial in very large partnerships.

MONITORING AS PART OF THE INVESTMENT PROCESS

The monitoring process is not usually thought of as part and parcel of the due diligence process. Yet the monitoring of your investments, including both quantitative and qualitative work, forms the basis for assessing and proving the skills of the manager. Quarter after quarter, year after year, the investment history builds. Along with it are daily interactions and shared experiences of working together.

Even with the best due diligence process possible, including unlimited time and an unlimited budget, there are some things you simply do not learn about people until you've known them for a while—and in particular until you've worked with them through stressful events. Put simply, people will surprise you—sometimes in a really good way and sometimes in a really bad way—and you never know for certain which way you'll be surprised until you've actually experienced it.

What you learn from those surprises will form part of the experience and expertise you bring to all of the other aspects of due diligence, even to the asset and sub-asset allocation processes. Some GPs will completely justify your confidence in them; others may make you reconsider your view of human nature. And since it is human nature that the due diligence process attempts to assess, the experience you gain through monitoring your portfolio will prove invaluable in gauging the attractiveness of future opportunities.

CONCLUSIONS

The investment process is a continuous activity that is best done with a structured approach. We are big fans of quantitative analysis for screening deal flow, and we introduce several approaches to help measure and organize this in later chapters in this text. We also regard it as your fiduciary duty to verify the track records that you are given. We believe in structured interviews to help keep the process fair.

Our basic philosophy on the investment process is "Trust, but verify!"

BONUS SECTION! ANNUAL MEETINGS

The annual meeting is one of the chief means for an LP to keep up with the activity of the GP. We cannot say it any better than Tom Judge did in 1992. We think that this is good reading for everyone interested in private equity.

ANNUAL MEETINGS NEED TO BE MADE MORE PRODUCTIVE

Tom Judge

What's on the Agenda?

In my view, the ideal agenda for an annual meeting would have the following items on it, in this order of priority:

(Continued)

(Continued)

Overview 10-20 percent of the meeting
- Strategy
- Market Environment
- The Firm

Partnerships 50-60 percent of the meeting
- Performance
- Problems
- Winners

CEO Presentations 20-30 percent of the meeting

Over the past 12 years, I have attended many annual partnership meetings. I can say from experience that the quality of these meetings is all over the lot, from highly productive to uninformative.

As the 1993 annual meeting season opens, I thought it would be useful to share some thoughts on how these meetings can be more productive. Some of my suggestions might seem to be minor. As a whole, however, they are intended to help the general partner who "gets stuck" with the job of organizing the annual meeting to make it more productive and a pleasant get-together.

Given the large number of partnerships in which the AT&T Master Pension Trust has invested, we typically meet with a firm's general partners at any length only once a year. That occasion is the firm's annual meeting. I suspect the same may be true for other large institutional investors. Hence, it is of the utmost importance that the annual meeting be as productive as possible.

To begin with, the meeting date should be set and communicated to the limited partners at least three or four months in advance, if the general partners expect a high level of attendance. You would be amazed at how many investment firms set a date just weeks before the meeting, and then are surprised that few limiteds can attend. You might even want to poll the LPs to find the most mutually convenient date.

You might also be surprised at how many conflicts arise because investment firms schedule meetings for the same date. Invariably, one meeting is in New York, and one is on the West Coast. (Many years ago, I suggested to the people then running the National Venture Capital Association that the NVCA should act as a clearing house for annual meeting dates. I have come to learn that the NVCA has a one track mind; if it doesn't concern the capital gains tax, forget it.)

My ideal annual meeting starts with a "refreshment" hour and dinner the evening before. This informal setting provides an opportunity for social amenities, such as greeting old friends, making new acquaintances, discussing the weather and complaining about lousy airlines.

The informal get-together also offers a place where a limited partner can discuss somewhat sensitive subjects with a general partner one-on-one, in private. Maybe it's the way the GPs are handling an investment that's gone bad. Maybe it's a personnel issue. The limited might not feel comfortable, for whatever reason, raising the point at the annual meeting. The general partner might be overjoyed that the item was raised privately.

When the gathered throng sits down to dinner, make sure that there is at least one member of the firm at each dining table. The GPs and associates shouldn't bunch up at one or two tables. You might even think about assigned seating for members of your firm.

Finally, provide name tags that people can read. Name tags that come out of a typewriter are worthless. Remember, I haven't seen most of these people in a year.

The sun rises and it's annual meeting day. Set a schedule and stick to it. If continental breakfast is at 8 A.M., start the meeting promptly at nine. The starting time should reflect the travel plans of your LPs. For example, local limiteds might need extra time to commute.

If your LPs are from out of town, don't hold the meeting at an airport hotel, or a resort that is a two-hour drive from the airport. You're not doing them any favors. Hold the entire affair at a downtown hotel. It is more convenient for your limited partners, who probably have scheduled other nearby business meetings around yours.

I have an ideal agenda in mind, which is outlined in the box at the beginning of this feature. Here's how I suggest you address each point.

Strategy: Reiterate the firm's strategy and talk about any changes you have made in the past year. I would hope that alterations are minor and have been made simply because general partners get smarter as each year passes. If it is a drastic change, the annual meeting is not the place to announce it. The general partners should visit each limited partner before putting any major strategy shift into action.

Why discuss strategy? It's a good discipline for the general partners. And it will put everything else that follows at the annual meeting into

(Continued)

(Continued)

context. Remember, I am trying to keep track of 85 strategies, and I haven't seen you for a year.

Environment: Describe the environment in which you operated during the past year. Discuss the quantity and quality of deal flow. Is the pricing better or worse? Has your competition for deals eased or intensified? Finally what is going on in the industry and how has this affected your firm?

The Firm: Don't forget to talk about any changes within the firm. As with strategy shifts, however, the annual meeting isn't the place to announce major staff changes. If a partner leaves the firm, tell your LPs immediately by letter. Same thing goes if you hire a new partner.

Okay, you have reminded us of your strategy and brought us up-to-date on the investment environment and internal developments. Now, we limiteds have a context for understanding what the general partners say about each partnership.

Partnership Performance: I know general partners don't like to talk about performance, but this is the bottom line and I do like to keep score as the game goes on. Once a partnership becomes five or six years old, performance must be discussed. And every year after that, it becomes more important. By the way, I am talking about internal rate of return to the limited partners after fees, expenses, and carry—net, net to LPs. Also discuss the return multiple that each fund has achieved so far.

Partnership Problems: Let's get the problems and the living dead out on the table and talk about them. What went wrong? Can it be reversed? What did you learn? No one likes to talk about their problems, but it is good to get them out in the open as soon as possible. This approach will pay off in your dealings with the limiteds down the road.

Partnership Winners: Everyone likes to talk about their winners, especially since they just finished talking about their problems. How better to end on a high note?

Now, you might think that since you have invited the CEOs of a few of your winners (who invites losers?) to speak at the meeting, it would be redundant for GPs to discuss the same companies. Not so. As a limited, I want the GPs' independent evaluation.

Also, if one of your partnerships is nearing liquidation, talk about this process before it begins, not after the fact.

CEO Presentations: You have invited your best and brightest, and that's good. But don't schedule so many CEOs that they have to rush their presentations, or go past your "stop" time. Chances are your meeting is going to take longer than you originally planned. So, make your cuts when you set the agenda.

An hour is too long to listen to one CEO. Twenty minutes is about right. Make sure he or she sticks to the time limit, and leave time for questions.

You might prefer to have an "industry discussion" by several invited experts, instead of CEO presentations. This is also fine. However, don't even think about putting CEO presentations or industry discussions on the agenda until you have covered strategy, environment, the firm and the partnerships.

By the way, don't just repeat what was in the last quarterly or annual report. Please assume that I read it before the meeting.

If your firm manages several partnerships, the annual meeting might take all day. A firm with only one or two partnerships might finish by around noon. Some LPs might rush to catch a plane. Others will want to stay and discuss agenda items or chat with CEOs. Provide lunch, so they can meet conveniently.

Some LPs might be interested in visiting nearby portfolio companies. Schedule such visits at the same time you're sending out invitations to the annual meeting—i.e., in advance.

Reserve any recreational activities, like golf, for after the entire annual meeting has ended. This way, people who have other things to do can leave and not miss anything.

An invitation to an informal dinner on the evening of the annual meeting is in order. You might not get any "takers," but you did extend the invitation.

Finally, in a few days follow up by phone with the attendees. Get their comments on the meeting. Maybe you can make next year's annual meeting even better than this year's.

(My thanks to Paul, Sandy, Tom, and Wendy for their generous contributions to this article.)

CHAPTER 4

Capturing a Portfolio

Measuring a portfolio starts with capturing and organizing data. Traditional accounting systems are generally ill-suited to capture the complexity of private equity. This chapter introduces a simple framework for capturing private equity fund transaction activity. But do not expect to run a portfolio from this model for long—for that you will need a real database system.

HUMAN TECHNOLOGY

We were at a private equity conference, and the subject turned to the use of technology. We complimented our colleague on his institution's reputation for stellar performance and wondered aloud what database system he used. He hesitated and then said, somewhat sheepishly, "Dan."

"Dan?"

"Yeah. Dan," he said. "Dan has a near-photographic memory for every fund we've ever invested in. Anybody's got a question, and they ask Dan."

We couldn't resist. "What's your job?"

"Mine?" he laughed. "Simple. To make sure that Dan doesn't get hit by a bus."

Memory is imperfect, but in many organizations, memory serves as a proxy for analysis. We have met few superhuman portfolio managers that live their data the way Dan obviously does. Accomplished private equity portfolio managers may know their investments intimately and not feel a need to further unravel how money was made. But as a portfolio grows in size and complexity, intuition may fail even the best of managers.

This chapter is not a blueprint for a private equity portfolio management system. Rather, it is meant to equip you with a basic understanding of some of the needs and complications of tracking private equity investments.

MONITORING INVESTMENTS

Congratulations. The due diligence is complete, the terms are negotiated, the commitment is made, the closing documents are signed, and you are now a limited partner in a private equity fund. But what is it that you have invested in? And just as important, what do you do to monitor the investment? The answers to these questions involve, in part, the scale of your ambitions. The first investment in a fund is usually the first of many in a portfolio. For the next 20 or so investments, the process of tracking and reporting on these funds may seem comparatively easy. You can think of this as the calm before the storm because, in our experience, the big practical problems begin when you have 30 or more fund investments.

The good news is that although all funds are different, most have a lot in common, which makes understanding what you have to capture to measure private equity fund investments fairly straightforward.

PERFORMANCE MONITORING OR ACCOUNTING?

Every organization has an accounting system. At some point, someone will suggest using the accounting team and the accounting system to record investment activity. If only life were that simple. One of the most important reasons not to do this has to do with auditing. Accounting systems are used to record activity between period closings. At quarter end, accountants lock down the state of the world by "closing the books." Mistakes discovered after a closing date rightly cannot be changed, but instead are "corrected" with adjusting entries in a following period. Without an ability to lock down accounting entries, auditing the books would be a nightmare.

One of the most critical aspects of capturing the performance of any investment is to get the timing right. If the date associated with a cash flow is wrong, the calculation of your return will be wrong. Performance-minded analysts and portfolio managers need both the numbers and the dates to be right, even if this means correcting entries long after they occur. As you will see in Chapter 7, some performance measurements rely on the value of money over time. Record the right amounts on the wrong dates, and your performance measures may be meaningless. For this reason alone, accounting and performance-based systems have to be separate.

We disagree with those who contend that this leads to double the work. In our experience, it is relatively easy to feed data from one system to another through structured exports and imports.

A Word on Standards

As you begin to think about capturing information, we suggest that you take some time to create standards of wording, capitalization, and punctuation. Spending time with this activity up front will save you a great deal of pain later on. Your rules about these entries go not only to the name of a fund and its suffixes, like "LP" and "IV," but to other abbreviations and identifiers that you employ. Is it "Capital Call," "Takedown," or "Funding"? It does not matter as long as you and your team agree.

RECORDING THE COMMITMENT

Begin by thinking of what you are tracking as a portfolio of investments. A portfolio is a collection of investments in funds that you think of as somewhat distinct. For example, some endowments have their investments divided into a set of operating assets and a set of long-term assets. A gatekeeper might have a portfolio for each of their clients.

Within these portfolios are commitments to funds. The bare essentials about a commitment might be the name of the fund and the commitment amount, but as shown in Table 4.1, we would suggest a few more

TABLE 4.1 Characteristics of a Private Equity Commitment That Are Useful to Capture for Ongoing Monitoring

The Commitment	
Fund Manager	Hilltopper Associates, LLC
Fund Name	Hilltopper Partners III, L.P.
Commitment Amount	10,000,000
Fund Size	200,000,000
Currency	USD
Closing Date	4 Apr 2008
Asset Class	Private Equity
Sub-Asset Class	Venture Capital
Vintage Year	2008

characteristics, including fund manager, fund size, currency of the fund, asset class, sub-asset class, and vintage year.

The fund manager is the name of the firm that raised the fund. The fund name is the legal name of the partnership. The commitment amount is in your portfolio currency, which we refer to as the base currency. We discuss currency in more detail later in this chapter. The fund manager is the legal name of the GP. The fund size can change and so at first be a moving target as additional investors come into the partnership. The currency that the fund reports in is the local currency. You can almost always expect the fund to provide financial information in local currency.

The closing date generally represents the date you officially signed into the fund. Asset class, sub-asset class, and vintage year are useful for classifying investments. Vintage is commonly thought of as the year in which capital is first drawn, but there are no hard-and-fast lines drawn on its assignment. It could be recorded as the year of the closing date, or if the first capital of a fund is drawn at the end of a year, some investors push this fund into the next vintage. Most importantly, the vintage year should be meaningful to you.

CAPTURING TRANSACTIONS

When a fund draws capital, it provides you advance warning with a capital call notice: a written request that provides, at minimum, the amount and the date that the amount is due.

If you have relatively few funds, you can use spreadsheets to record cash flow activity, typically recording the set of transactions for each fund in a separate spreadsheet. The only immediate drawback to this approach is the chore of aggregation: to measure the total activity of the portfolio, you will need to apply your spreadsheet skills to automate a few steps.

Alternatively, if you have some database expertise, you can employ a simple database ledger, with some form of linking, to record this activity. Contributions to the fund are often recorded as negative amounts; distributions as positive amounts. In a short time, this kind of transaction ledger for the fund might contain a series of entries for capital calls and distributions as shown in Table 4.2.

In Table 4.2, a descriptive *transaction type* is associated with each cash flow. Transaction types can be used for a variety of purposes. Be sure to set standards for their assignment.

TABLE 4.2 Basic Transaction Capture Format Includes Date, Amount, and Transaction Type

Fund ID	Date	Amount	Transaction Type
HP3	1 Jun 2008	−100,000	Management Fees
HP3	10 Oct 2008	−1,000,000	Capital Call
HP3	12 Jan 2009	−2,000,000	Capital Call
HP3	15 Feb 2009	500,000	Cash Distribution
HP3	31 Mar 2009	−2,000,000	Capital Call
HP3	15 Apr 2009	200,000	Stock Distribution

Note: We have included a Fund ID to link back to Hilltopper Partners III, L.P.

CALLING CAPITAL IS ABOUT PREDICTING THE FUTURE

Although the ledger as described allows you to capture basic cash flows, it does not allow you to record more complex transactions. For example, a capital call may consist of a combination of investment capital and fees, often with the investment capital for more than one company.

Our recommendation is to capture the transaction amount at the time of the capital call. If you know that a capital call is split between investment and fees, separate them into two transactions on the same day. With respect to splitting out investments in portfolio companies, leave the details for later. See Chapter 5, Tracking Portfolio Holdings.

Based on our experience, attempting to capture the precise use of a capital call, before the GP invests the money, is time and effort wasted. It is rare that a GP will give you exact details in advance on how your called capital is to be invested. Most GPs report this detail in their next quarterly report, when the transactions have been executed, exact amounts are known, and a longer narrative permits a precise reasoning to be drawn. Some fund managers provide rough predictions on how the capital is to be invested, while providing more precise accounting at quarter end.

Capturing Fees

Fees that fall within the commitment reduce the amount that can be called at any time, that which is known as the "unfunded commitment amount." There are also fees that are related to the investment activity but not included in the commitment amount, such as a late closing fee, or legal and due diligence fees. These are important costs of doing business with the fund and should be captured, but they have no effect on the unfunded amount and are not reported by the GP in performance calculations. Fees can be recorded in the simple transaction ledger as described before, with an appropriate transaction type.

Capturing Distributions

From an accounting standpoint, things get a bit more complicated with distributions of both cash and stock. A strict accounting of cash and stock requires you to break each distribution down into return of principal, capital gain, and income.

Many fund agreements permit the fund manager to recall capital that has been distributed for purposes of investment. This is termed "recallable capital." It is oftentimes associated with realizations that have occurred in the early years of the partnership.

Stock distributions present other complications. If the GP distributes stock to you, are these securities subject to restrictions that prevent you from selling them right away? If you have to hold these securities for any time, what measure of performance do you use? The GP's distribution price or the price at which you eventually dispose of them? These are normal issues faced by any LP that permits distributions of stock. Some LPs avoid this altogether by mandating that their GPs distribute only cash; others handle it by hiring a stock distribution manager.

WHAT IS IT WORTH?

On a regular basis, usually quarterly, the partnership reports the valuation of your portion of the fund. (See Table 4.3.) This comes in either a quarterly report, a direct notification, or with a separately published *schedule of partners capital*. Although you could commingle valuation data with the transaction data, putting this into a separate ledger allows you to create some basic fund performance measures with ease. Our recommendation is to keep these ledgers separate.

TABLE 4.3 Basic Valuation Data Capture Format

Commitment	Date	Amount
HP3	30 Jun 2008	80,000
HP3	30 Sep 2008	75,000
HP3	31 Dec 2008	943,000

PRE-EURO CONVERSION RULES

For funds raised prior to 1 January 1999 that were denominated in one of the pre-euro currencies, and then converted to a euro-denominated fund, there are special conversion rules that apply. For example, a fund raised in French francs (FRF) but now denominated in euros should have all cash flows converted to the euro. For audit purposes, the original cash flows should be kept. The European Commission sets rules that fix the number of decimal places used for each currency and dictates how conversions are done. The following is from Regulation 1103/97 of 11 September 1997.

ARTICLE 4; The conversion rates shall be adopted as one euro expressed in terms of each of the national currencies. They shall be adopted with six significant figures. The conversion rates themselves must not be rounded or truncated when making conversions. The conversion rates shall be used for conversions either way between the euro and the national currency units. Inverse rates derived from the conversion rates shall not be used. Monetary amounts to be converted from one national currency unit into another shall first be converted into a monetary amount expressed in the euro unit, which amount may be rounded to not less than three decimal places and shall then be converted into the other national currency unit. No alternative method of calculation may be used, unless it produces the same result.

ARTICLE 5; Monetary amounts to be paid or accounted for, when a rounding takes place after a conversion into the euro unit according to article 4, shall be rounded up or down to the nearest cent. Monetary amounts to be paid or accounted for which are converted into a national currency unit shall be rounded up or down to the nearest sub-unit, or in the absence of a sub-unit to the nearest unit or according to national law or practice to a multiple or fraction of the sub-unit or unit of the national currency unit. If the application of the conversion rates gives a result which is exactly half-way, the sum shall be rounded up.

Source: European Union, 1996.

CAPTURING CURRENCY EFFECTS

The challenges of investing in multiple currencies complicate the process of capturing appropriate data. Add just one investment denominated in a different currency to a portfolio, and tracking and measuring results get more challenging. Aside from cross-border tax, accounting, audit, and regulatory effects, mixing currencies means that you need to capture more data from the outset. Mixing currencies also means that you have more decisions to make about how you measure your private equity portfolio.

The simple fact is that an international private equity portfolio requires special attention. No investor wants an otherwise profitable investment or portfolio to show up as a loss due to currency fluctuations. In our discussion, we leave out consideration of currency hedging as beyond the scope of this book. We use the ISO standards for currency naming and abbreviation, thus United States dollars is USD; Singapore dollars are SGD; EUR is the euro.

BASE AND LOCAL CASH FLOWS

For each portfolio of investments picking a *base currency* creates a natural comparison currency and allows you to reference a mixture of currencies against a familiar one when measuring or reporting. The selection of a base currency is usually simple. A college endowment based in Indiana will have its portfolio denominated in USD. A Dutch pension fund will probably be in EUR. But an advisor or gatekeeper in New York, London, Zurich, or Singapore might be tracking client portfolios in many different base currencies.

The *local currency* is the currency of the partnership. Be sure to capture all cash flows in both base and local currencies. Cash flows in local currency are the purest representation of the activity of the fund. The GP of a euro-denominated fund will most likely ask for payment in euros, will pay you in euros and report to you in euros. A U.S.-based GP will do the same in USD. We have encountered GPs that depart from this practice and call capital or pay in the currency of the investment they are making. Pay them as you would. When convenient, take these GPs out in the woods and shoot them.

When a GP calculates a return or gives you a track record, the cash flows supplied will also likely be in local currency. If they are not, insist on getting them. The biases introduced by currency fluctuations should be absent from your due diligence analysis—your evaluations should be currency neutral.

We said that these local cash flows are the purest representations of the activity of the fund, not your activity. How you manage currency exposure is up to you. If you are drawing capital for a Singapore dollar (SGD) fund from an SGD bank account, the cost of the transaction may be minimized; the same transaction drawn in USD will have a different currency cost. Measuring currency effects involves many built-in and indirect transaction costs, including additional bank fees that may be embedded in the currency rates. Table 4.4 is an extension of our earlier design with both Local Amount and Foreign Exchange (FX) rate columns added.

TABLE 4.4 Valuation Capture with Local and Base Currency Amounts

Commitment	Date	Local Amount	Base Amount	FX Rate
HP3	30 Jun 2008	123,040	80,000	1.5380
HP3	30 Sep 2008	110,925	75,000	1.4790
HP3	31 Dec 2008	1,349,433	943,000	1.4310

CAPTURING EXCHANGE RATES

By capturing both local and base cash flows and valuations, you capture exact exchange rates. These rates are associated with specific bank rates used at the time of your transaction, including applicable fees; they are typically not average or end-of-day rates. Average or end-of-day rates are used when calculating the amount you owe in base currency, the *base unfunded amount*. See the sidebar on page 57 on conversion rules for converting pre-euro currencies to euros.

WHAT IS COMMITMENT DRIFT?

Obligations made in a foreign currency, one other than the currency in which you generally invest, can change dramatically and, if not monitored regularly, can catch investors by surprise.

For example, the weakening U.S. dollar from 2002 to the time of this writing affected investors in two ways. For U.S. investors, existing commitments to foreign funds increased significantly. For non-U.S. investors in U.S. funds, expected returns, measured in absolute terms, have weakened considerably.

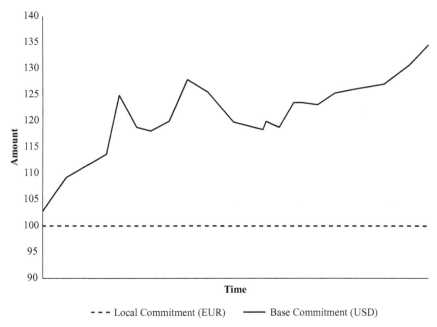

FIGURE 4.1 Commitment drift due to currency effects.

This movement away from your original commitment amount in your currency is called commitment drift. Figure 4.1 is a simple example that shows how quickly the base commitment can drift from the amount you pledged at closing.

A commitment amount, subject to the terms of your partnership agreement, is made in local currency and is more or less fixed. Complexity is introduced in the calculation of the *base commitment amount*. There is some debate over the best practices for computing the base commitment amount. The popular variations include the following:

- Keep the base commitment amount static by multiplying the local commitment amount by the exchange rate at the time the investment was made. This is the "head-in-the-sand" approach.
- Update the base commitment amount by multiplying the local commitment amount by the prevailing exchange rate at the time the analysis is completed.
- Update the base commitment amount by computing the sum of that which you have paid-in so far in base currency and then adding the base unfunded commitment amount.

We prefer the third technique because it takes into account both that which was actually paid and the outstanding balance. This approach was used in the Figure 4.1 to depict how quickly a commitment amount can grow.

THE SPREADSHEET PROBLEM

As we mentioned at the beginning of this chapter, many investors begin to track their private equity portfolios in spreadsheets. Spreadsheets are fine for capturing the basic activity of a few funds, but are poorly suited for large investment programs.

If you do use spreadsheets to start tracking a portfolio, keep in mind that you will encounter problems of scale early on. One of the main problems with using spreadsheets is aggregation. Even spreadsheet experts are challenged by the problems of creating the composite and portfolio IRRs that fund administrators, investment officers, or boards want to see on a routine basis.

Since they are lacking structure, spreadsheets also pose problems of data integrity, where careless keystrokes can alter or destroy results. Finally, spreadsheets may have maintenance and security problems.

CONCLUSIONS

In order to begin to measure the performance of a private equity investment, you need to take a systematic approach to identify and record data as it arrives. How you do this is important (and we may be biased) but we believe that accounting systems should be separate from performance measurement systems.

In this chapter we presented a brief discussion of the data elements that are essential for the most standard performance measures, including multiples and the IRR. Capturing investments in mixed currencies is a complicated subject, but we have discussed some of its most important aspects.

We think that new investors can survive by tracking their assets in spreadsheets, but only for a short time. That being said, without a proper data framework or a database system designed for private equity, you may find yourself challenged to conduct the analyses that we present in later chapters.

The next chapter addresses some of the challenges you will face in attempting to capture the underlying holdings of a portfolio of funds.

CHAPTER 5

Tracking Portfolio Holdings

In the early years figures are meaningless to anyone not very close to the company," said Doriot. "It's easier to pass judgement on a 24-year old man than a 3- or 4-year old child.
    —Georges Doriot quoted in Ante, *Creative Capital*, p. 193

Some private equity investors are content to know the minimum they can about how GPs invest their capital. Other LPs want to climb inside the heads of their GPs to learn everything they can. Most investors want to know as much as they can about the fund's portfolio holdings within limits. This chapter explores the challenges of capturing this second, deeper layer of private equity fund investing.

A BLIND POOL

Every private equity fund has a strategy, a general approach to investing in companies. This strategy can be most safely described as a statement of intent. At the outset, the strategy is known, but the actual companies that the fund will invest in are not. Thus investing in a private equity fund is committing to a blind pool of investments in companies. Over time, this pool, as it were, becomes clear and eventually you can see to its bottom. This chapter describes some of the challenges LPs face in capturing portfolio holdings data and how industry pressures are changing valuation processes.

FOREST AND TREES

You have responsibility for a large government pension fund with a 20-year history of investing in private equity. Today you have 250 active partnerships and indirectly hold 5,000 company positions. It's 8:00 A.M. and you arrive to work to a voice mail from a board member.

"Good morning. I was reading about the innovations at Spacely Sprockets in today's *Financial Times*. I remember something about them from our last board meeting. Can you give me our exposure to them? I am leaving on a flight to Singapore this evening. It would be great if I could have this by noon."

Or an urgent e-mail shows up:

"Representative Fife needs to know the early-stage biotech investments in the 22nd congressional district. She has a speech to constituents on this topic this afternoon. Please respond ASAP."

Or perhaps more routinely, you are asked to produce a report on your portfolio, describing stage, geography, and industry diversification down to the company level.

The bad news is that there are no shortcuts to the answers to these questions—they can only be answered from the bottom up. In other words, to be able to see the forest, you must identify and tag each tree. In a large private equity portfolio, this is a data collection and aggregation problem of a tall order, made all the more difficult by the piecemeal manner in which positions in companies are acquired by GPs. By now this should sound familiar, but to begin to measure the underlying holdings of a portfolio of private equity funds, you first need to know how to capture what you need.

NEEDED: FORENSIC ACCOUNTANTS

Data on portfolio holdings does not get assembled easily. First, do not look to transmittal documents, such as capital call and distribution notices, as reliable source material. A capital call notice is often short on details, with sufficient information to request funds but providing sketchy information on how that capital is to be invested. This is somewhat natural, as we will describe later. Distribution notices from GPs, where absolutely everything should be known about the realization or return of capital from an investment, can be cryptic as well.

To assess the health of the fund, most LPs look to the GPs' quarterly reports. These are usually written as summaries of periodic activity, with accompanying financial statements in snapshot format. These snapshots are great indicators of the health of a fund, but they tend to omit history. To reconstruct the complete chronology of a fund's investment activity, you will usually need all the reports from the fund's inception.

Capital Calls Are Predictive

We recommend that you not depend on transmittal documents for an accurate accounting of the underlying holdings for a number of reasons, the most important of which is their inability to accurately predict the future. By way of example, let's say that a fund draws capital with the intent to make an investment in a portfolio company. You are first made aware of this investment in a capital call notice. Table 5.1 is an example of a capital call notice, with a due date, an amount that is being called, an identification of what the capital is to be used for, and a pro rata share due from you.

You supply your share of the capital and record this information in the transaction ledgers we discussed in Chapter 4. Unfortunately, it is here, right at the beginning of the process that communication can begin to break down. A capital call notice is often only a guide to how funds are to be invested. In the quarterly report that follows this transaction by several months, you are given a true picture of how that capital was invested by reading a report. Table 5.2 provides the real picture of what happened in this circumstance.

As we said, these kinds of changes are natural as there is much that can intervene to change the best-laid plans. Stuff happens. While the GP and the owners of a company are in discussion, the market value of the company can be renegotiated. For a variety of reasons, the GP may have opted for a

TABLE 5.1 A Capital Call Notice May Not Accurately Reflect the Eventual Use of Funds

	The Space Fund III	
To:	All Investors in Space Fund III	
Subject:	Capital Call Notice	
Due:	22 May	
Amount:	25,000,000	
For Investment:	24,000,000	Spacely Sprockets, Aerospace Supplier
Fees:	1,000,000	
Your Pro Rata Share:	1,250,000	**5% of fund**
	Please remit to Account # ABC123	

TABLE 5.2 Final Disposition of Capital Call as Reported in a Quarterly Report May Differ Greatly from the Amounts Specified by an Earlier Capital Call Notice

The Space Fund III		
Date	Amount	Purpose
31 May	21,000,000	Spacely Sprockets, Series A
24 May	1,000,000	Management Fee
30 June	3,000,000	Cash Reserve for Future Investment
Total	25,000,000	

smaller position at the last moment. Other investors may have upped their contribution into a previously agreed-upon syndication. The rationale for this difference is often unexplained. In Table 5.2, the fund ends up with a temporary cash reserve—money that it may elect to hold or may shortly return back to you.

So the first practical problem an LP faces in recording ongoing information on a fund's investments in portfolio companies is that the capital call letter may be misleading or inaccurate. The second problem is that revisions may not be explained. As the fund matures, portfolio activity tends to get blended and becomes even more difficult to classify. If you have a large portfolio, the investments in a single company may be from two, three, four, or more funds. Finally, tracking what each company is worth is loaded with additional challenges.

At the beginning of a fund, the trail of bread crumbs that leads you from an investment in a portfolio company back to the initial capital call can be relatively easy to follow. As the portfolio gets larger and activity higher, this trail becomes harder to trace as funding commingles with other quarterly activity.

A Chinese Wall

Here we introduce a simple proven approach for tracking portfolio holdings.

- Cash is cash. Treat your transactions with the fund almost as if they have nothing to do with portfolio companies. Record your transactions of contributions, distributions, and valuations without explicitly tying them to portfolio company activity.
- Record portfolio holding information from quarterly reports at the full fund level, not as is often provided, as a pro rata share. Worry about calculating your pro rata share of companies separately.

THE POSSIBLE AND THE PRACTICAL

As noted in Chapter 4, the purpose of our modeling this data structure is to give you a sense of what to track, not as a prescription to a formal database design. To anyone who has studied the kind of information that GPs provide in quarterly reports, it should come as no surprise that we have opted for a simple model. This model is designed to hide unnecessary detail. Whether you find it useful may depend on what level of detail you find necessary.

For example, a GP may provide a bridge loan to a company in order to keep them in business while waiting for a planned funding round. The bridge loan and its repayment may occur within one reporting period. Some of the questions that LPs need to answer are "Do I care about the bridge loan?" and "If I did get information on that loan, would it be useful?" For LPs with hundreds of investments in funds, and thousands of investments in companies, questions of this sort become moot—our experience suggests that you will never be able to get consistent data at this level. This forces simplicity, and there is much to be gained from it.

This model, shown in Figure 5.1, has five parts including a list of holdings, three ledgers, and a list of companies and their characteristics.

The topmost layer, Positions in Companies, may be as simple as the list of companies a fund has invested in. The ledgers are used to record the funded amounts to a company (its *cost*), the market value of the position in the company at every period, and any proceeds from these company investments. The company characteristics include such things as location, industry, and stage.

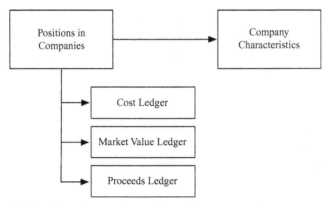

FIGURE 5.1   A simple data structure for portfolio holdings.

All amounts are captured at the full fund level, and no matter how many positions you own in the fund, the data is only recorded once. These separate ledgers can be as simple as transaction dates and amounts. When you record any kind of proceeds from an investment in the proceeds ledger, a simple negative entry in the cost ledger can be entered to reduce the total cost by any return of principal.

Currency

In a portfolio of mixed currencies, the most sensible approach is to record these entries in the currency of the partnership, the local currency, regardless of your base currency. This is sensible because the statement of partners' capital is almost always in local currency. This makes the work of reconciliation much easier. Combining these mixed currency cash flows can get done when reporting by looking up foreign exchange rates.

Company Characteristics

The typical attributes used to measure private equity portfolio company diversification are industry, geography, and stage of development. To consistently describe companies, you must be prepared to define what these terms mean. Here are some things you may want to think about:

- Industry codes used to classify companies vary in their level of consistency and detail. The Global Industry Classification Standard (GICS) codes were first promulgated by Morgan Stanley (MSCI Barra) and Standard & Poor's. The Industry Classification Benchmark (ICB) codes were put forth by Dow Jones and FTSE. The Venture Economics Industry Codes (VEIC) are another alternative.
- What is the location of a company? Is it the legal domicile of the legal entity, its headquarters, or the location of its principal operations?
- By stage, we mean terms such as "Seed," "Early-Stage," "Late-Stage," "Growth," "Expansion," and so on. Your list should be your own.

VALUATION CHALLENGES

The Market Value ledger is the place to assign a valuation to the position. What you choose to record there is an open question. We suggest that you use the market value that the fund provides.

Historically, private equity survived without valuation guidelines of any kind until 1990. At that time, the one-page valuation guidelines proposed by Tom Judge became the de facto standard. This document is in Appendix A. As we have indicated, there have been many attempts to create valuation standards, but partially due to the unregulated nature of the private equity industry and plain inertia, all of these attempts have ended up as guidelines. The International Private Equity and Venture Capital Guidelines (IPEV) were written by the European Private Equity and Venture Capital Association (EVCA), the British Venture Capital and Private Equity Association (BVCA), and the Association Française des Investisseurs en Capital (AFIC). The Private Equity Industry Guidelines Group (PEIGG) and others also recommend ways for valuing holdings—but participation is voluntary. This is changing.

On November 15, 2007, FAS 157, a new statement of the U.S. Financial Accounting Standards Boards, became mandatory for corporations that use U.S. GAAP reporting.

A single definition of fair value, together with a framework for measuring fair value, should result in increased consistency and comparability in fair value measurements.

At the time of this writing, the effects of this rule are being felt, with LPs and GPs alike experiencing increased anxiety, frustration, and confusion. We expect that this will lessen as the implications of this rule become clearer, clarifications are provided, and practices adapt.

CALCULATING PRO RATA OWNERSHIP

There are two means to calculate your exposure to underlying portfolio holdings.

1. The ratio of commitment to fund size

    The first method uses a percentage as a proxy for your ownership in the portfolio of companies that underlie it. Thus a $25 million commitment to a $250 million fund gives you a 10 percent share. This percentage is then applied to each portfolio holding in the fund.

    As shown in Table 5.3, cross-holdings, where two or more funds invest in the same company, can then be aggregated to give you total exposure to a company.

TABLE 5.3 Cross-Holdings Are Positions in a Company Held by Two or More Funds

	Cross-Holding Exposure to Company X		
Fund	Market Value of Position	Ownership Proxy	Your Exposure
The Space Fund II	2,480,000	10%	248,000
Rocket Partners	3,500,000	5%	175,000
Total			423,000

2. The ratio of commitment valuation to the fund valuation

The second method generally provides a more accurate result. This exposure methodology also uses a ratio, but the ratio can vary from quarter to quarter. This ratio is:

Commitment Valuation/Fund Valuation

This is a complex subject, but the gist of it is that the GP's share of the fund can be larger as the result of capital gain that is baked into the valuation of the fund at any time.

Protecting Public Exposure

Private equity portfolios can contain public (or quoted) companies. This is usually the result of strategic sales to public companies or IPOs. One of the more difficult tasks an LP can attempt to do is to monitor the public holdings in the private equity portfolio.

If you were an investor in any number of the venture funds that backed networking equipment or software companies in the dot-com era, you might have woken up to find yourself an indirect owner of Cisco Systems. The GP holds public securities, you indirectly own a portion of them, but the securities are not in your hands, and so you cannot sell them.

But what you do have is knowledge. In that heyday, a few forward-looking private equity investors hedged their public exposure to protect their gains. Lessons were learned.

Today, some LPs now take the trouble to monitor their portfolio holdings for significant positions in undistributed shares of public companies. This is difficult, as these positions are often in preferred shares, some of this activity is intra-quarter, and some of it is never directly reported. But for those willing to take the trouble to keep track of whatever public activity they can, there are potential rewards. Of course, there are costs associated with this work, and it generally pays off only with larger portfolios, where potential cross-holdings can make the size of these positions worth the trouble.

A Trend?

We see increasing demand for portfolio holding information on a variety of levels, whether it be from boards, auditors, or portfolio managers. With regulations looming large, there is increased pressure to collect this once-optional data. As well, with many LPs gaining control over their transactional data, this is a natural next step in the evolution of portfolio analytics.

CONCLUSIONS

In time, the blind pool of investments of a private equity fund is revealed to all concerned. Unfortunately, these investments are made and reported piecemeal. Trying to track them as they are made is difficult, time-consuming, and frustrating. A simpler approach is to use quarterly reports to build a fund-level portfolio holding history, with your pro rata share of these companies approximated in one of two proven ways.

This accretion of quarterly fund activity builds up the portfolio of companies. In order to get cross-holdings right, particular emphasis must be paid to standards, such as naming conventions. Companies must be classified according to geography, industry, and stage, in order to produce the kind of aggregations that most investment boards need to see to understand the kinds of risk the portfolio holds. As these companies are in constant flux, these characteristics need to be revisited often.

The work behind this effort is considerably more sophisticated than it may appear at first glance. Our final recommendation: do not take this task on unless you understand its costs and benefits.

BONUS SECTION! ADVICE TO GPs (JUDGE 1993)

Tom Judge wrote this article that first appeared in *Private Equity Analyst* in 1993. It is informative, and somewhat unfortunately, timeless. You'll see what we mean.

FINANCIAL REPORTS FROM GPs NEED TO BE IMPROVED

Tom Judge

The phone rings. A general partner of a firm with which we invested wants to come to see us. We set a time and date. I fax a map that shows how to get here.

Everything seems normal, except one thing. This is the first time in three years anyone from the firm has called. It doesn't take a brain surgeon to figure out that they're marketing their newest fund.

That's okay, but wouldn't it make for a better relationship if GPs regularly kept in touch with their limited partners? I'm not looking for more frequent visits, just better communications between fund raisings and annual meetings.

The best communication vehicles already exist: the quarterly and annual reports. However, there is room for improvement in content, format, and timing. Let's start with content.

Begin with a Balance Sheet for the total partnership, with both assets and liabilities, and a Profit & Loss statement in detail. Include my capital account in great detail. Yes, I am interested in how my capital account changed during the last quarter, but I am also interested in the composition of my capital account at the end of the most recent reporting period.

I want to know how much of my capital account is in public securities, private investments, other partnerships (I hope not any), cash, cash equivalents, accrued income, organizational costs, etc. Also, list any liabilities (other than my capital) that affect my account. All of these numbers should add up to my capital account.

Let's agree to use the same terminology. I prefer "capital account," rather than "partners' equity," "net asset value," or some other thing. But whatever term the industry agrees upon, let's be consistent.

Speaking of consistency, let's agree to include unrealized appreciation or depreciation in each LP's capital account. Some firms include this in the total partnership balance sheet and leave it out of an LP's capital account. I don't understand this!

When it comes to information about each investment, please refresh my memory. Remember, I am trying to keep track of 1,900 portfolio companies. Give me the town and state where each company is headquartered. Briefly remind me (10 words or less) of the business they are in. Then you can talk about how they are doing or not doing, prospects for the future, etc.

Portfolio company valuations and changes since the last report are not only helpful; they are vital. Valuing each investment shouldn't be difficult or time-consuming, based on the following assumptions.

1. Every venture capital firm has a written valuation policy that has been approved by the LPs or an advisory committee composed of LPs. (If you don't have a written valuation policy, I'd be delighted to provide one. It's only a one-pager, and it was proposed by a committee of general and limited partners back in 1990.)
2. A general partner acts as the "lead" person for each portfolio company, and is aware of every transaction and event that affects that company. Hence, at any point in time, the "lead" person can put a valuation on that company that is consistent with the valuation policy.

Assuming you have "bought into" the above, I shall proceed with more assumptions:

1. Every Monday morning, each "lead" provides the CFO of the venture capital firm with a list of his or her company valuations (based on the valuation policy) as of the preceding Friday close of business.
2. The CFO, via computer, assembles this data into one alphabetical list showing the current valuations and previous valuations, highlighting the valuations that have changed.
3. At the Monday morning partners' meeting, the changes are briefly discussed and altered, if necessary.
4. Abracadabra! We have updated valuations for two line items of the balance sheet (public and private investments), which is 95 percent of the work.
5. After a quick check of "other assets," the CFO pushes a button on the computer, and every limited partner instantly has an updated capital account valuation.

(Continued)

(Continued)

Actually, I'm only kidding about doing this every Monday morning. But, my point is this: If you have a written valuation policy and the right procedures in place, it should be relatively easy to produce portfolio valuation information in a timely manner.

Make the report format simple and "user friendly." Make it easy to find things, like my capital account balance, changes in investment valuations, etc. Don't bother to make it glitzy.

A good portfolio investment valuation summary is printed on one page and includes all investments in alphabetical order. The columns are devoted to cost, fair value last reporting period, fair value this reporting period, change in fair value, reasons for change (in a few words), and finally, which of your written valuation policy items applies to each current valuation.

The "reason for change" column can quickly explain that a valuation has changed because an additional investment was made, warrants were purchased, a loan was repaid, etc. Be brief.

The last column contains a symbol (alpha or numeric) that ties into an abbreviated valuation policy printed at the bottom of the page or, if necessary, on page two. An abbreviated valuation policy might include such items as "market price less 25 percent discount," or simply "written down." The abbreviated policy does not replace a written valuation policy. It is simplified solely to save space on the report.

We receive slightly more than half of the quarterly and annual reports on the 151 partnerships in which we are invested within 45 days of the end of the reporting weeks. But the last report arrives sometime during the fifth month after the end of the reporting period!

Well, if half can do it within 45 days, then everybody should be able to do it within 45 days. In fact, I think LPs should receive quarterly reports within 30 days and annual reports (not including the auditor's report) within 45 days.

Reports might be delayed because general partners have difficulty finding time to complete the "write-up" on each company for which they are the lead. This is understandable. The solution: Value the investments and get the "accounting" portion of the reports (including my capital account information and the "investment valuation summary") to me within 30 days. Send the write-ups within the next two weeks. Don't hold up the annual report because you're waiting for the K-1 or the annual audited statement. Send them under separate cover.

Some other thoughts about how to improve communications:

- Call every LP if a GP leaves the firm or you hire a GP. Follow up with a letter. After all, the LPs place their bets on people.
- Call your LPs to discuss any planned change in strategy. After all, the LPs place their bets on a certain strategy.
- Give you LPs more than a few days' notice of cash calls and distributions. If the LPs have provided you with instructions about how to make distributions, follow them. The last thing I want is a call from some broker asking me what to do with a stock that has been distributed.
- Some firms assign a specific GP to each LP. The GP is then responsible for "on-going communications" between fund raisings. This may or may not be a good idea: you decide.
- Some firms issue occasional newsletters that contain updates about people, investments, the market, etc. This is fine, but it may be too burdensome for some firms. I'd rather get my financial reports on time.

(My thanks to Wendy, Tom, Sandy and Paul for their generous contributions to this article.)

Measurements and Comparisons

Standard Measures

1. Get the cash. 2. Get the cash. 3. Get the cash.
—The Three Rules of Accounting

This chapter begins to introduce some of the standard measures of private equity. Multiples, which are ratios, are reliable measures of an investment's progress and performance. We discuss the challenges of consistent reporting with uneven sources of data. We end up with some challenges every portfolio manager faces and a common solution, the Adjusted Valuation.

Many investors regard private equity as a cash-on-cash business. What did I pay in? What did I get out? How long did it take? To these investors, the focus of the activity of private equity investing is on the cash, not the nuances of how the fund values the investments.

Money-in, money out, and money outstanding: this is what the standard measures of private equity are all about. For this discussion, we make few distinctions between interim and final results despite the fact that it is only at the end, when a fund is liquidated, that you can assess its overall performance.

MULTIPLES ARE RATIOS

Multiples are simple and powerful ratios of aspects of a private equity investment. They can be quick gauges of the health or overall return of an investment. Be careful, for the "multiple" is talked about as if it were one thing—in fact, there are many multiples. We are big fans of multiples.

For us multiples help gauge, without equivocation, the *wealth* created by a private equity investment. We define wealth as the sum of realized and unrealized gain from investments. For this and other reasons, we will be using multiples rather than the IRR in many of the examples we use to introduce more advanced concepts later in this text. However, multiples are missing an important element, the effect of time, and it is for this reason that they are usually used in conjunction with time- and money-weighted measures, particularly the IRR.

THE NAMING OF MULTIPLES

For convenience sake, multiples have both names and commonly used abbreviations. For example, the investment multiple is known as TVPI. This abbreviation is a mnemonic, meant to give you a clue about what it represents. In this case, TVPI stands for "Total Value to Paid In." Unfortunately, the names and abbreviations of multiples are a bit inconsistent.

The nomenclature we use is based on the abbreviations in Table 6.1. These are PI, D, RV, TV, and C. This table also has a column for sample data amounts used in the examples for each multiple.

The Realization Multiple—DPI

The realization multiple, DPI, is a good cash-on-cash measure. DPI is the ratio of distributions to the amount you paid-in. Instead of the more

TABLE 6.1 Abbreviation Definitions and Sample Data for the Examples Explaining Multiples

Name	Abbreviation	Description	Sample Data Amount
Paid-In	PI	Capital Invested + Fees	90
Distributions	D	Cash + Stock Returned	80
Valuation	RV	Also known as Residual Value	100
Total Value	TV	Valuation + Distributions	180
Commitment	C	Capital Pledged for Investment	100

Note: The valuation is represented by RV, for residual value.

mathematical D/PI it is simply referred to as DPI or "Distributions to Paid-In."

$$\text{Realization Multiple} = (\text{Distributions}/\text{Paid-In}) = D/PI$$

Using our sample data, DPI is 0.89:

$$\text{Realization Multiple} = (80/90) = 0.89$$

DPI is a gauge of cash flow activity only. It ignores the valuation. Investments without any distributions have a DPI of zero. A DPI of 1.00 means that a fund has broken even on a cash basis. In our example, this fund has a DPI of 0.89 and so it has not yet broken even on a cash basis. A DPI greater than 1.00 is a good start—the investment has returned more capital than has been paid in. Conversely, a DPI less than 1.00 means that the investment has not returned the capital you have put into it.

The Unrealized Multiple—RVPI

The Unrealized Multiple, RVPI, is an indicator of unrealized gain. The formula for the Unrealized Multiple is

$$\text{Unrealized Multiple} = (\text{Valuation}/\text{Paid-In}) = RV/PI$$

Using our sample data, RVPI is 1.11:

$$\text{Unrealized Multiple} = (100/90) = 1.11$$

The problem with this RVPI is that we can draw no conclusions from this measure alone. If there have been no distributions and an RVPI close to 1.00, it may indicate that the investments are being held at cost. A high RVPI may indicate that much of the gain on the investment is unrealized.

Since paid-in is a cumulative measure and valuation is not, we do not find much use for this multiple. We do, however, find it interesting to compare the valuation to the cost of the investment.

WEALTH

Performance as measured by the IRR is interesting, but ambiguous.

We like measures that have a direct relationship with the outcome for the investor. For private equity funds, this outcome can be measured at any time simply by adding its realized and unrealized gains. We call this wealth.

Like the IRR, wealth is a transient measure until the fund is liquidated. Unlike the IRR, wealth is always unambiguous, and in many ways it is the bottom line.

The Investment Multiple—TVPI

If there is a multiple that is *the multiple,* the one that is implied by many texts, it is the Investment Multiple, which is known as TVPI.

$$\text{Investment Multiple} = (\text{Total Value/Paid-In}) = \text{TV/PI}$$

Using our sample data, this fund has a TVPI of 2.00. The fund's combination of distributed and unrealized value is twice what you paid in:

$$\text{Investment Multiple} = (180/90) = 2.00$$

In general, TVPI lets you know what multiple of the overall cash you invested to expect back. If the investment is liquidated, TVPI is a definitive measure of the wealth it produced.

The Realization Ratio—RR

The realization ratio is the proportion of the total value of your investment that has been distributed. The realization ratio is commonly abbreviated RR rather than what might be more consistently abbreviated as DTV.

$$\text{Realization Ratio} = (\text{Distributions/Total Value}) = (\text{D/TV})$$

Using our sample data, the RR is 0.44:

$$\text{Realization Ratio} = (80/180) = 0.44$$

The realization ratio will always be a value from 0 and 1.00 At the end of the life of a fund, the fund is fully realized, and so the RR is 1.00. If the realization ratio is low, there is potentially much more cash to come from this investment. This RR of 0.44 quickly tells you that somewhat less than half of the current total value of your investment has been distributed. If the realization ratio is high, most of the value has been wrung from this investment.

The Paid-In Capital Multiple—PIC

The Paid-In Capital multiple, PIC, is

$$\text{Paid-In Capital Multiple} = (\text{Paid-In}/\text{Commitment}) = (\text{PI}/\text{C})$$

Using our sample data, the PIC is 0.90:

$$\text{Paid-In Capital Multiple} = (90/100) = 0.90$$

In this case it is 90 percent. The Paid-In number that is represented here is a simple value. In the event that the fund has the right to recall capital, the size of the commitment, and a PIC multiple based on it, may not be accurate.

Investment Multiple (TVPI) Time Series

Calculating the investment multiple at a point in time gives you a snapshot of the performance of an investment. If you plot TVPI over the lifetime of a fund, at every quarter valuation for example, trends may be seen. The chart in Figure 6.1 uses sample data from real funds over the course of 10 years to show the variation in the investment multiple.

MAKING CASH FLOWS COUNT ... OR NOT

Up until now, we have been making sweeping assumptions that you know what we're talking about when we use terms like "Paid-In" and "Distributions." Many of you do, but for the sake of clarity, we need to peel the layers off these assumptions.

In Chapter 3 we highlighted some of the challenges an LP faces in capturing data to measure performance. We urged you to consistently apply standards to naming and categorization.

Measuring what *you* want to measure takes a well-defined process. For example, a late closing fee should likely be excluded from your calculation of paid-in, otherwise it will affect the measures that use it. This requires that you create a calculation process that treats this type of transaction differently.

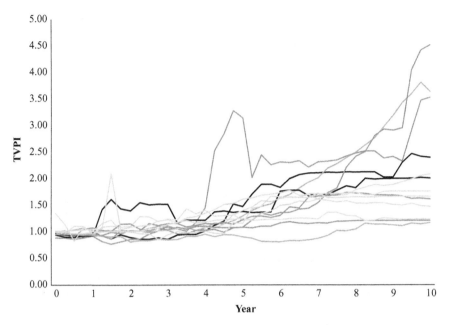

FIGURE 6.1   TVPI Time Series for a series of funds shows some variation.

You do this by first categorizing all of the types of cash flows you encounter. You should set up rules of inclusion and exclusion to create a uniform approach. To avoid confusion and misunderstanding, the rules should be written, agreed on, and understood. Only then can you report these measures with confidence. Standardizing on what you calculate *with* is as important as *how* you calculate measures. A consistent approach will make an enormous difference in how your portfolio measures up.

THE CHALLENGES OF MEASURING A PORTFOLIO

To an investor, one or two funds do not a portfolio make. With time and dedication to a continuous program of investing in private equity, a portfolio of funds emerges, and measurement becomes more interesting and more challenging.

The cash-on-cash measures that we have introduced so far primarily rely on your record of these transactions. You know when you contribute cash to the fund; you know when you get it back. The only thing preventing you from having the ability to calculate these multiples is one thing: the valuation of the fund.

The valuation is used in the calculation of the investment multiple (TVPI), the unrealized multiple (RVPI), and the realization multiple (RR). The valuation cannot be calculated by an LP—it is a number that can only be supplied by the GP. Fund managers do this quarterly, supplying the valuation of the entire fund along with the pro rata share of each limited partner.

One of the biggest challenges in preparing periodic reports on the state of a portfolio is getting valuations promptly.

This is so because LPs are at the top of a food chain of private equity information—they, in effect, get to eat after everyone else gets to eat. For fund managers to report results back to the LPs, the GPs have to gather current data from each of their portfolio companies. This takes time. The more companies a GP invests in, the longer it takes. Likewise, the more funds an LP is in, the longer the overall process takes. If an LP is invested in one or more funds of funds, the delay is even longer. Although most GPs report quarterly, some only report semi-annually.

Limited partners are the last ones to know complete information about their investments. Just how long is this delay?

Document Delays Impact on Reporting

Private Informant, a data service of the Burgiss Group that tracks portfolio holdings, receives partnership reports on the behalf of their clients. This service received over 10,000 documents from fund managers in 2006 (Burgiss Group 2008). Many of these were unaudited quarterly and audited annual financial reports.

The average time elapsed from quarter end to the date the report was received varied by investment type. In Table 6.2, these delays are broken out by sub-asset class. You can see from this data that reports from venture

TABLE 6.2 When Do Quarterly Reports Arrive?

Sub-Asset Class	Average Days Following Quarter End
Venture Capital	81
Buyout	111
Funds of funds	129

Source: The Burgiss Group.

capital firms took the least amount of time, on average 81 days after the quarter end. Reports from funds classified as buyouts took on average a month longer. Finally, reports from funds of funds took over four months to arrive after the quarter end. According to this sample study, you should not expect a June quarterly report for a fund of funds until mid October.

Some GPs will supply LPs with preliminary data sooner, including quarterly valuations, but not all do. As the reports come in, the hard work of entering and checking this information begins in preparation for final reporting. Yet no matter what deadline you set for reporting to your board or other stakeholders, there is almost always missing information. We know of few boards with the patience to wait six months or more to know the state of their portfolios.

When it comes to measuring and reporting on quarterly results, LPs with complex portfolios generally follow one of two approaches.

1. Report only when complete information for a quarter is available. Depending on the size of the portfolio, this can be from three to six months after a quarter closes.
2. Report with the best available information. For the calculation of the traditional measures including IRR and multiples, adjust prior valuations for interim cash flows where needed.

THE ADJUSTED VALUATION

The most common solution to the problem of consistent reporting has two steps. First, report what you know definitively, and second, fill in the gaps with a consistent, calculated value. What you know definitively is from reports and capital account statements that give you your pro rata valuation of the fund. That's the easy part. The more difficult part is to fill in the gaps with what you can reconstruct from the last reported valuation, and any interim cash flows to the date of the report. This result is a proxy for the valuation and is commonly referred to as the *adjusted valuation*. This type of valuation can be calculated at any time.

In the simplest form of this calculation, every capital call subsequent to the last valuation increases the adjusted valuation. Every distribution during this period, whether stock or cash, decreases the adjusted valuation.

Table 6.3 makes explicit the calculation of the adjusted valuation for a fund for 31 Mar 09. In this case a valuation on 31 Dec 08 is adjusted by a capital call and the full value of a distribution. This calculation allows a proxy for the valuation to be created on any date in order to facilitate reporting.

TABLE 6.3 Adjusted Valuation Calculation Using Full
Cash Flows

	Fund A	
Type	Date	Amount
Valuation	31 Dec 08	45
Capital Call	17 Jan 09	+12
Distribution	5 Feb 09	−3
Adjusted Valuation	31 Mar 09	54

Table 6.3 adjusts the valuation for the full amounts of each transaction, but there may be times when this adjustment can be fine-tuned to come to a better approximation of the valuation. Instead of adjusting the valuation for the full amount of the distribution, you could instead adjust it for only the amount of the return of principal. With this example in Table 6.4, notice that the distribution is changed from the full amount, 3 to 1, the return of principal only. The adjusted valuation is higher as a result.

Be wary of this as a general technique, for the practices of individual GPs vary. For example, since the value of a company is not known until it is sold, it is possible that the company was misvalued by the GP at the latest reporting period. This means that the entire fund would have been under- or overvalued. Our recommendation is to use this technique with discretion.

If no cash flows occur after the last reported valuation, there are no adjustments, and that prior residual value is used. The adjusted valuation can be calculated for all funds in a portfolio, creating an adjusted portfolio valuation. Using the adjusted valuation allows a portfolio of funds to be measured with a consistent methodology at any time.

As shown in Table 6.5, the adjusted valuation for a portfolio is calculated investment-by-investment and then totaled.

TABLE 6.4 Adjusted Valuation with Return of Principal Portion of a Distribution

	Fund A	
Type	Amount	Purpose
Reported Valuation	45	
Capital Call	+12	
Distribution	−1	Return of Principal Portion
Adjusted Valuation	56	

TABLE 6.5 Adjusted Valuation for Several Funds and a
Portfolio

Fund	Valuation	Adjustment	Adjusted Valuation
Fund A	10	1	11
Fund B	20	−5	15
Fund C	5	1	6
Fund D	10	0	10
Total	45	−3	42

With an adjusted valuation for the portfolio, you can calculate the
IRR or any set of performance multiples that makes sense. This technique
helps create a consistent approach to analysis and reporting, using the latest
available information.

NEGATIVE ADJUSTED VALUATIONS

With a large distribution, it is possible for the adjusted valuation to be
negative. For example, a holding held at cost was realized for a large gain.
For whatever reason, this individual gain exceeded the prior valuation of the
fund. For this intra-quarter period, the calculation of the adjusted valuation
results in a negative value. This is confusing at best, and there are three ways
to handle this scenario:

1. Use only return of principal to adjust the valuation downward.
2. Let the result be negative. Educate those that need to know that this
   situation is possible and temporary.
3. Cap the effect of distributions from the fund in your analysis so that the
   valuation of the fund is never negative. This is still a Band-Aid, because
   it is very unlikely that the valuation of the fund is being accurately
   portrayed.

CONCLUSIONS

Performance measurement always sounds simple at first, but inevitably ends
up entangled in nuance. Which flows should be included? What happens
if the fund hasn't reported the latest valuation? How are stock distributions treated? And so on. This chapter introduced some of this nuance, and
introduced the multiples used to describe performance of an investment.

CHAPTER 7

The IRR

Another measure, the IRR, turns out not to be so simple or reliable. We discuss the reasons this measurement has been used and has endured and provide an example-based tutorial on nonobvious flaws.

THE IRR CONUNDRUM

Time is a factor in measuring all investments. A private equity investment with a realization multiple (DPI) of 2.25 looks better than one with 1.75, but what if the former started six years ago, and the latter is only two years old? What if all the capital was invested at the beginning for one and the other called capital over time? When were distributions received? The internal rate of return (IRR) was designed to help measure the performance of a series of cash flows. Another measure, time-weighted rate of return (TWRR) is weighted only by time.

The CFA Institute's Global Investment Performance Standards (GIPS) and other standards bodies think that the IRR is an appropriate measure for private equity. But is it? It may be. But not everyone is happy with the IRR.

In his footnote from his hilarious tale of venture capitalists and their world, *The Silicon Boys and Their Valley of Dreams*, David Kaplan manages to get to the heart of the IRR conundrum in just a few paragraphs (see sidebar). As Mr. Kaplan suggests, the controversy begins with the peculiar math behind the calculation and extends well beyond, into the realm of the subjective. We begin with simple and then head into more peculiar math.

The nomenclature VCs use to describe their investment returns is somewhere between unfathomable and impenetrable. Rather than a simple term like "annual return"—how much your money, on average, appreciates in a given year—the VCs use "internal rate of return." IRR is an economic term of art that seeks to account for the fact that the $1 million you commit to a fund isn't actually all there on Day 1 (instead being "drawn down" by installments). You may have sent in $100,000 at the beginning, another $200,000 in six months, and gotten back $53,000 in dividends at the end of the year. IRR takes into account these different cash flows.

I still have no idea how to compute IRR. After talking to a business professor, an accountant, two VC financial officers, three investors in KP funds, and one of my neighbors, I'm convinced IRR cannot be explained in English, which is my first language. The trouble with IRR—a mathematical equation that a leading corporate finance textbook describes with eight variables—is that it doesn't indicate the bottom line. Invested a million dollars in KPCB VIII? Given an IRR of X percent, how much did you make? The correct answer is, "It depends."

Yet in describing VC returns, virtually every business publication—from the *Wall Street Journal* to *Business Week*—takes the IRR of venture firms and describes it as just "annual return," which is misleading. Because, while an IRR of, say, 80 percent sounds impressive, it probably isn't. If it's based on a single investment of a small chunk of your million dollars, then you haven't actually made many dollars, the high IRR notwithstanding. Some venture firms will go out of their way to front-load their wins—for example, by selling a stake in a company—so that early on in an investment fund's life they have a high IRR that, in turn, allows the firm to go out and round up new investors. IRR isn't part of some nefarious scheme to inflate VC success rates. Using it is standard practice in the industry. But its use does suggest that VCs can exaggerate their numbers by not forcefully distinguishing to investors and business journalists between IRR and the simpler measures of success—what did I make in total dollars over the life of my investment? I asked one of KP's investors whether he was frustrated by the nomenclature. He said, "I gave up years ago. All I know is I get back a lot more than I put in."

Kaplan (2000, 204)

MEASURE FOR MEASURE

For better or worse, the IRR is looked on as *the measure* of private equity performance. When people ask "What is your return?" in private equity they mean "What is your IRR?" Why? And is the IRR your return? If not, what does the IRR mean? Exactly what does the IRR measure?

One of the reasons that the IRR has risen to prominence is because no other relatively-simple-for-computers-to-calculate measure takes into account the timing and magnitude of cash flows into and out of your private equity investments. Unlike a public manager, who receives cash at your discretion, a private equity general partner calls capital when needed and distributes cash back somewhat randomly.

This timing is a natural reflection of the process. The fund asks for capital from investors opportunistically, as it finds and makes investments. In theory, if the money is not going to be put to work, it is not going to be called from you. As these portfolio investments make money, the GP is able to return capital and gains to the LPs. The IRR helps take this into account as it is both a cash- and time-weighted measurement.

We say that the IRR is relatively simple for computers to calculate, not necessarily for humans to calculate without their help. Microsoft Excel, with its IRR and XIRR functions, makes it easy to calculate an IRR. Yet when comparing IRRs from several different sources, you need to be careful to compare apples with apples. Although a daily-weighted IRR is the industry standard, it is not uncommon to run into legacy systems that churn out monthly- or quarterly-weighted IRRs, where cash flows within a month or a quarter are pushed to middle, end, or beginning of a month or quarter. Changing the dates associated with cash flows changes the IRR.

THE SINCE INCEPTION IRR

When we refer to the IRR, assume that we mean the IRR from the beginning of the investment. This is sometimes referred to in the literature as the "Since Inception IRR" (SI-IRR). This is a mouthful, and doesn't roll off the tongue particularly well. When we talk to our clients about performance, the IRR is assumed to be since inception, unless otherwise specified. We hold to this convention in this text.

THE IRR SMELL TEST

The IRR is wrapped in too much mystery. Before we get started in exploring problems of time, weight, quadratic equations, polynomials, and multiple solutions, we offer this simple test. When choosing between multiple mathematically correct solutions, follow these rules:

If a deal makes money, the IRR will be positive.
If a deal loses money, the IRR will be negative.
If a deal breaks even, the IRR will be zero.

This sounds intuitive because it is. Ignore it at your peril.

SIMPLE START

It would be nice if the formula to solve the IRR began with:

$$IRR =$$

But unfortunately it doesn't. That would be too easy. Instead, the IRR is a rate of return associated with a stream of cash flow activity and has to be solved in a more complex way. Here is how the formula might be described:

The sum of the discounted cash flows, weighted for time and value, plus the discounted valuation, weighted for time and value, is equal to zero.

Here is the formula.

$$\sum_{i=0}^{n} \frac{CF_i}{(1 + IRR)^i} + \frac{RV_n}{(1 + IRR)^n} = 0 \qquad (7.1)$$

Here CF is a cash flow, i is the time period associated with the cash flow and starts from zero, RV is the residual value (the valuation) of the investment and n is the total number of periods subsequent to the first cash flow.

Almost always, this equation must be solved iteratively. Sometimes this is easy. Sometimes it isn't. As we will explain shortly, sometimes there are multiple results. We begin with a trivial example and build up from there, into more complex permutations.

The Simplest IRR

If you were to invest $10 today and one year later it is worth $11, what is the IRR? In this example, no cash comes out. There is only one cash flow followed by a valuation.

When substituting these values into the formula, the signs of the cash flows always reflect their direction from your perspective: contributions are always negative; distributions and the valuation are positive.

$$0 = \frac{-10}{(1 + IRR)^0} + \frac{11}{(1 + IRR)^1}$$

$$10 = \frac{11}{(1 + IRR)}$$

$$1 + IRR = \frac{11}{10}$$

$$IRR = .10 = 10\% \tag{7.2}$$

This equation easily solves for the 10 percent return. What could be simpler?

A Quadratic Equation

Next we look at the complications of adding one more cash flow and extending the calculation by one year. In Table 7.1, we have added a distribution of $1 a year after an initial capital call of $10. At year two, the investment is still worth $10.

Before turning to the equation, guess the result. You contributed $10, got out $1 some time during the two years and still have the $10 remaining at the end of year two. That's intuitively about a 5 percent return on your money per year.

Since these cash flows are measured in years, the period, i, is 1 the first year and 2 the second year. The formula for two cash flows and a valuation

TABLE 7.1 Data for a Simple IRR Calculation

Year	Amount	Type
0	$10	Initial Capital Call
1	$1	Distribution
2	$10	Valuation

looks like this:

$$0 = \frac{CF_0}{(1+IRR)^0} + \frac{CF_1}{(1+IRR)^1} + \frac{RV_2}{(1+IRR)^2} \qquad (7.3)$$

Substituting cash flows and time and working this example:

$$0 = \frac{-10}{(1+IRR)^0} + \frac{1}{(1+IRR)^1} + \frac{10}{(1+IRR)^2}$$

$$10 = \frac{1}{(1+IRR)} + \frac{10}{(1+IRR)^2}$$

$$10(1+IRR)^2 = (1+IRR) + 10$$

$$10(IRR^2 + 2IRR + 1) = 11 + IRR$$

$$10IRR^2 + 20IRR + 10 = 11 + IRR$$

$$10IRR^2 + 19IRR - 1 = 0 \qquad (7.4)$$

This result is a classic quadratic equation, which can be solved with a little help from high school algebra.

$$ax^2 + bx + c = 0$$

$$x = \frac{-b \pm \sqrt{b^2 - 4ac}}{2a} \qquad (7.5)$$

We are solving for x, the IRR. As a, b, and c are 10, 19 and -1:

$$IRR = \frac{-19 \pm \sqrt{19^2 - 4(10)(-1)}}{2(10)}$$

$$IRR = \frac{-19 \pm \sqrt{401}}{20}$$

$$IRR = \frac{-19 \pm 20.024984}{20}$$

$$IRR_+ = 0.0512 = 5.12\%$$

$$IRR_- = -1.9512 = -195.12\% \qquad (7.6)$$

Quadratic equations have two possible outcomes. The "plus or minus" part of this formula results in two technically correct answers: .0512 (or 5.12 percent) and −1.9512 (or −195.12 percent). As we noted, we made money on this investment, the IRR must be positive, and so we rule out the −195.12 percent solution. The 0.12 percent extra above our guess of 5 percent has to do with the timing of the distribution. The $1 was received only one year into the investment.

PROVING THE RESULT

Take a moment to visualize the result within the formula:

$$0 = \frac{-10}{(1 + 0.0512)^0} + \frac{1}{(1 + 0.0512)^1} + \frac{10}{(1 + 0.0512)^2}$$

$$10 = \frac{1}{(1 + 0.0512)} + \frac{10}{(1 + 0.0512)^2}$$

$$10 = 0.951294 + 9.049598$$

$$10 = 10.000892 \tag{7.7}$$

This proves that the result, within the limits of our decimal places, is correct. The lesson is that IRR solves for an approximation that is within a tolerance of error. Solving for a closer tolerance means using more decimal places in the calculation. In general, most published results for private equity show an IRR to four decimal places, which appears to have two decimal places when formatted as a percent.

FOUR FLOWS: TIME FOR A COMPUTER

If we were to add another cash flow into this stream, the formula is not as easily solved.

$$0 = \frac{CF_0}{(1 + IRR)^0} + \frac{CF_1}{(1 + IRR)^1} + \frac{CF_2}{(1 + IRR)^2} + \frac{RV_2}{(1 + IRR)^3} \tag{7.8}$$

Three cash flows and a valuation create a third-order polynomial. In most real-life situations, where there are dozens of cash flows, pure mathematics is of little use. Here we resort to computers and brute force.

Commercial software generally uses iterative guessing and tolerances to arrive at a solution. The IRR can be solved for through an iterative process with a predetermined margin of error. Pick a rate. Is it close? Pick another. Has it resolved toward or away from a reasonable solution? Guess again with this improved information. Is the IRR within the tolerance we set for accuracy? No? Iterate again. Close enough? Done.

THE MICROSOFT EXCEL IRR AND XIRR FUNCTIONS

The simple Microsoft Excel IRR function assumes that your cash flows are paced at even intervals.

$$= IRR(Flows)$$

This formula works well for monthly, quarterly, or yearly aggregations of cash flows. For greater precision and flexibility, we favor the Excel XIRR function, which uses specific dates rather than implied intervals and results in a daily-weighted IRR. The XIRR formula requires a range of cash flows associated with a range of dates:

$$= XIRR(Flows, Dates)$$

In Excel, both the IRR and the XIRR functions have an option that allows you to set the first guess that the formula uses to solve for the result.

$$= XIRR(Flows, Dates, Guess)$$

In most situations, a guess is not needed. In rarer instances the guess you make can significantly alter the result.

IRR ASSUMPTIONS AND ANOMALIES

IRRs of Investments Held for Less than One Year

The IRR is most appropriately a long-term measure. Many argue that short-term IRRs mean nothing and let you know in no uncertain terms, with reports using "N/M" (Not Meaningful) for IRRs with terms shorter than three, four, or even five years.

This notwithstanding, you may need to calculate short-term IRRs for a variety of reasons. From Excel's help, the XIRR function is "based on a 365-day year." Excel always annualizes the result. This is generally reasonable, but what happens if the investment you are measuring is held in the portfolio for less than a year? In this case, the XIRR function uses an

TABLE 7.2 XIRR Calculation for an
Investment Held Less than One Year

Date	Amount
1 Jan 03	−10
1 Jun 03	5
30 Sep 03	4
XIRR	−10.00%

improper day count—this is an annualized IRR. To "unannualize" it, you
will have to perform the following steps.

1. Calculate the XIRR in Excel as shown in Table 7.2.
2. Calculate the total day count.

$$(30 \text{ Sep } 03) - (1 \text{ Jan } 03) = 272 \text{ Days}$$

3. The IRR using the correct day count.

$$IRR_{Unannualized} = (1 + IRR_{Annualized})^{(Days/365)} - 1$$
$$IRR_{Unannualized} = (1 - 0.10)^{272/365} - 1$$
$$IRR_{Unannualized} = (0.90)^{0.745205} - 1$$
$$IRR_{Unannualized} = -0.0755 = -7.55\% \tag{7.9}$$

The result is an unannualized IRR of −7.55 percent. Table 7.3 shows
annualized and unannualized the IRRs that differ significantly. In this

TABLE 7.3 Unannualized IRRs Can Significantly Differ from
Annualized IRRs

Date	Fund A	Fund B
1 Jan 01	−10	−10
31 Jan 01	15	5
Unannualized IRR	50.00%	−50.00%
Annualized IRR	13,781.73%	−99.98%

example, the unannualized IRRs of funds are 50 percent and −50 percent, but the annualized IRRs are close to 14,000 percent and −100 percent.

Annualizing the IRR, as Excel does, creates a gross misrepresentation in both cases. The annualized IRR for Fund A drastically inflates the IRR. The annualized IRR for Fund B implies that you have lost nearly all of your money, when in fact you have only lost half.

Large Positive IRRs and Later Cash Flows

With an existing positive IRR, each cash flow has less effect than might be expected. Large infusions of cash in the later life of a fund do not boost a positive IRR significantly. Since each cash flow carries a weight inversely proportional to its time in the investment, you can deliberately boost an IRR by giving cash back quickly. This is generally more easily said than done. Take a look at the example in Table 7.4 where we have set up an example to illustrate this effect.

Both funds have impressive IRRs, Fund A with 64 percent and Fund B with 73 percent. Only one cash flow differs: Fund B had a relatively large distribution seven years after inception. Their IRRs may be similar, but Fund B generated more than twice the wealth of Fund A. The lesson is simple—time is a factor. When the IRR is positive, the slower the payout, the less it changes the IRR.

TABLE 7.4 Large Positive IRRs and Later Cash Flows

Year	Fund A	Fund B
0	−5	−5
1	−10	−10
2	−15	−15
3	45	45
4	0	0
5	0	0
6	0	0
7	0	20
Paid-In	30	30
Total Value	45	65
Wealth	15	35
IRR	64%	73%
TVPI	1.50	2.17

TABLE 7.5 Large Negative IRRs and Later Cash Flows

Year	Fund A	Fund B
0	−5	−5
1	−10	−10
2	−15	−15
3	20	20
4	0	0
5	0	0
6	0	0
7	0	5
Paid-In	30	30
Total Value	20	25
Wealth	−10	−5
IRR	−55%	−10%
TVPI	0.67	0.83

Large Negative IRRs and Later Cash Flows

With an existing negative IRR, the denominator for each cash flow component is less than one and so later cash flows can make a greater difference to the outcome. As shown in Table 7.5, large cash flows in the later life of a fund can dramatically improve a negative IRR.

In this example, a distribution that is small relative to the contributions, made four years after the last distribution, dramatically reduces the negative IRR.

Multiple IRR Results

The IRR can have multiple correct mathematical solutions. The more cash flows involved, the greater the possibility of multiple correct solutions. The common wisdom is that this is where the guess that you supply in the IRR formula can make a difference. Here are the commonly cited circumstances when multiple solutions may result:

- Multiple changes in the sign of the sum of cumulative cash flows
- Large changes in the relative magnitudes of the cash flows

These rules are not a guarantee of an unstable IRR—they are merely indicators. The calculation of the IRR typically works well with private equity cash flows. In our experience, if you follow the "IRR smell test," you will rarely, if ever, encounter ambiguity in IRR calculation results.

THE IRR TRANSFORM

The formula for the IRR is unable to accommodate several unique circumstances:

1. All of the capital was lost. TVPI is zero.
2. All of the capital, and then some, was lost. TVPI is negative.
3. Any case where the first cash flow is positive.

Using the IRR formula to solve for the first case, where all capital is lost, ends up without a result because of division by zero. If you refer back to the IRR formula, every cash flow is being divided by (1 + IRR). When the IRR reaches −100 percent, the process breaks down. This is solved fairly simply, by adding another rule to our "IRR Smell Test." The IRR of an investment is −100 percent if and only if all of the capital invested has withered away.

The second case involves leverage, where you not only have your capital invested, but have tied some form of debt to the investment. This is problematic because the formula for the IRR breaks here as well. As a result, there is no standard way to handle circumstances where a leveraged position has gone sour.

The third case is certainly not common, but there are circumstances where it presents itself. Take for instance, the set of cash flows shown in Table 7.6, where you receive two cash distributions before you have to pay money out in Year two.

Many algorithms struggle with this type of cash flow sequence because the first flows are positive. But in this case, we know that the result must be positive because the investment was profitable. The challenge is how to derive an IRR based on this activity.

TABLE 7.6 It Is Possible to Compute an IRR Even When the Cash Flow Series Begins with Distributions

Year	Amount
0	10
1	5
2	−12
Wealth	3

TABLE 7.7 Computing the IRR with Unusual Cash Flow Patterns Using the IRR Transform

Year	Amount	Negated Amount
0	10	−10
1	5	−5
2	−12	12
	IRR	−12.62%
	Transformed IRR	12.62%

Here we suggest a rather simple and elegant innovation in the calculation of the IRR. The first step in this transformation is to reverse the signs of all the cash flows, including the valuation. Then simply calculate the IRR as you would normally. Finally, reverse the sign of the IRR for the result. This process is shown in Table 7.7.

As a closing note, this transformation has implications for the second case as well. The technical details are outside the purview of this text, but know that transformation can be applied in circumstances where the IRR ought to be less than −100 percent.

Total IRRs Exceeding Individual IRRs

Here is another IRR anomaly. Funds A and B in Table 7.8 share the characteristic that their cash flows all occurred within about a six-month period.

TABLE 7.8 Total IRRs Exceeding Individual IRRs

Month	Fund A	Fund B	Portfolio
0	0	−20	−20
1	−200	0	−200
2	−10	0	−10
3	−10	0	−10
4	−10	0	−10
5	300	18	318
Paid-In	230	20	250
Total Value	300	18	318
Wealth	70	−2	68
IRR (%)	137	−10	114
Unannualized IRR (%)	33	−4	37
TVPI	1.30	0.90	1.27

The unannualized IRR is an appropriate measure for each of them. Yet the unannualized IRR for the combination of Funds A and B is higher than the IRR for each fund separately. Why? Is there something wrong?

There is nothing wrong—this is simply the way these cash flows work. Here the timing and magnitude of the combined cash flows and the total day count can be a cause of confusion.

The IRR Fallacy

The IRR is only one way to measure performance. Take some time to look carefully at the four sets of cash flows in Table 7.9. All of these investments have the same outlay of capital. Three funds, A, B, and C have the same IRR. The fourth fund has a lower IRR. These scenarios present four very different outcomes for the investor, with an investment multiple (TVPI) that ranges from 1.20 to 5.16. There is huge variation in the wealth created from these investments.

Over a total of nine years, the Fund A turns around capital quickly, some might say, too quickly. Fund B requires a significant up-front investment, pays out small distributions yearly, and has a modest payout. Fund C has no interim cash flows at all, but produces the most wealth by dint of a very big payout.

TABLE 7.9 Stark Examples of How Four Capital Outlays of the Same Paid-In Can Have Four Very Different Outcomes

Year	Fund A	Fund B	Fund C	Fund D
0	−10	−50	−50	−50
1	12	10	0	0
2	−10	10	0	0
3	12	10	0	0
4	−10	10	0	0
5	12	10	0	0
6	−10	10	0	0
7	12	10	0	0
8	−10	10	0	0
9	12	60	258	85
Paid-In	50	50	50	50
Total Value	60	140	258	85
Wealth	10	90	208	35
IRR (%)	20.00	20.00	20.00	6.00
TVPI	1.20	2.80	5.16	1.70

Finally, for comparison, the 6 percent IRR that results from Fund D creates almost three-and-a-half times the wealth of Fund A, with its 20 percent IRR.

This should underscore that a 20 percent IRR is somewhat meaningless without context.

THE J-CURVE

Calculating the IRR at every quarter creates an IRR time series that helps reveal the evolution of the fund. The typical IRR time series, as shown in Figure 7.1, resembles a wide letter J, thus its name, the J-Curve.

The downward portion of the IRR series is typical of the start-up phase of the fund. Capital is called, often taking the form of fees that do not contribute appreciably to the valuation. The IRR is negative. Further, the practice of conservative valuation means that portfolio companies that are

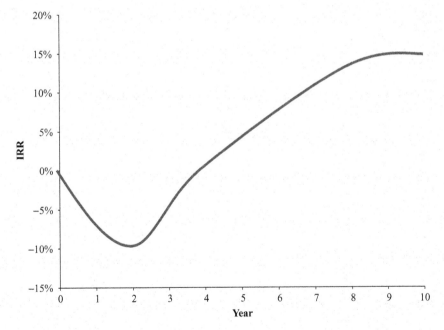

FIGURE 7.1 The J-curve is the IRR time-series of a fund. The shape of the J can vary, but typically shows a sharp drop-off in performance during the first few years of the fund's life.

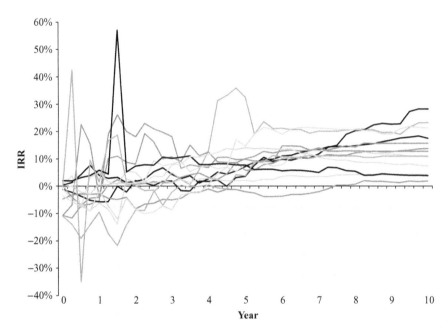

FIGURE 7.2 A chart of J-curves from a series of 13 funds illustrates the variability of the IRR over time.

not performing are written down or written off sooner rather than later. The depth of the J-curve, the zero-to-zero term in months or years, is a quick measure of the pace of the recovery of the value of the fund.

As might be inferred, the net cash flow also takes on the form of a J-Curve.

As the fund invests in stable and growing companies, value is built. As cash is distributed, the valuation drops, and the IRR rises and stabilizes. Figure 7.2 superimposes J-curves from 13 real funds over a 10-year period.

COMPOSITE CALCULATIONS

Measuring groups of investments within a portfolio provides additional insight. For example, grouping by vintage year may help compare funds that were raised, closed, and came to maturity under similar macroeconomic conditions. Grouping by type, such as venture capital or buyout, may be of interest. The totals for the group IRRs or multiples are based on a composite of all the cash flows and valuations from the investments in the group. These are commonly referred to as composite IRRs or composite multiples.

OTHER RELATED MEASURES

The Point-to-Point IRR

All of the IRR calculations we have been discussing have been from the inception of the investment to an ending date. As shown in Figure 7.3, a point-to-point IRR measures only part of the investment's life, from a point in time to another point in time. In the literature, this measure is sometimes referred to as a *horizon* or *end-to-end* IRR.

The first cash flow is the valuation of the investment on that date, and its sign is negative. Like a first capital call, you might think of this cash flow as buying into the investment on that date at the prevailing valuation.

-<Beginning Valuation> or <Adjusted Beginning Valuation>
Interim Cash Flow 1
Interim Cash Flow 2

. . .

<Valuation> or <Adjusted Valuation>

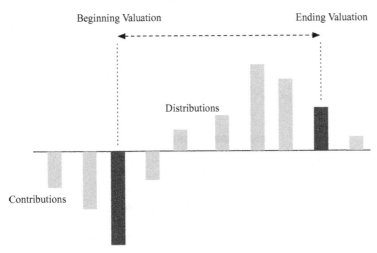

FIGURE 7.3   The point-to-point IRR measures performance between two dates.

The IRR is then calculated as if this interim series of cash flows was the entire cash flow stream.

Time-Zero IRR (IRR$_{TZ}$)

Previously, in Table 7.4, we showed how an early positive IRR can be sticky, creating a lasting measure that may not be representative of the total wealth created. We know of fund managers with IRRs exceeding 70 percent stemming mainly from early winners in their portfolios. A bonus to the GP for this early success is that all subsequent investments get a bit of a free ride, with only extraordinarily poor performance having a major impact on their IRR. The Time-Zero IRR (IRR$_{TZ}$) calculation can help reveal this unfair bias.

To create an IRR$_{TZ}$, you first have to prepare the cash-flow stream. You do this by aligning the beginning dates of all of the cash flow streams, in effect time-shifting the entire series as shown in Figure 7.4. These cash flows, with their modified dates, are then used to calculate an IRR. The result is the IRR$_{TZ}$.

Most importantly, the IRR$_{TZ}$ changes only the *portfolio IRR*—it has no effect on the IRR for each investment. As with other portfolio IRRs, the IRR$_{TZ}$ result may bear little resemblance to the IRRs of the individual funds.

Early Winner, Later Winner, Time-Zero IRR

With this concept in hand, we will walk through several examples to illustrate why this technique is interesting and valuable. Table 7.10 contains the

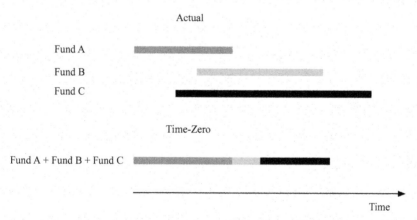

FIGURE 7.4 The time-zero IRR time-shifts cash flows to a common start date.

TABLE 7.10 When Fund A Is the Manager's First Fund, the Portfolio IRR is 23.89 Percent

	Actual Flows		
Year	Fund A	Fund B	Portfolio
0	−100	0	−100
1	−25	0	−25
2	200	0	200
3	−25	0	−25
4	0	0	0
5	115	0	115
6	0	−200	−200
7	0	0	0
8	0	0	0
9	0	0	0
10	0	0	0
11	0	200	200
Paid-In	150	200	350
Total Value	315	200	515
Wealth	165	0	165
IRR (%)	38.18	0.00	23.89
TVPI	2.10	1.00	1.47

cash flows of two hypothetical funds for a manager. In this scenario, Fund A begins first and lasts five years. Then Fund B begins and lasts five years.

Fund A is a clear winner with a 38.18 percent IRR. Fund B returns your money and nothing else; it has an IRR of 0 percent. Yet the track record of the manager, the portfolio IRR, is almost 23.89 percent, and this performance is primarily driven by the performance of Fund A.

To bring home our point, let us rewrite history. What if instead Fund B was the manager's first fund? If we reorder the cash flows so that Fund B occurs before Fund A, the early winner with its strong IRR goes away, and the manager's overall track record is dramatically reduced. This is shown in Table 7.11.

In this case the manager's track record changes from a lofty 23.89 percent to a lowly 8.24 percent as the first fund's 0 percent return drags the portfolio IRR down. As a reminder, since the magnitude of the cash flows are unchanged, the investment multiples and the individual IRRs are unaffected.

Let us now contrast this to a time-zero comparison, which re-imagines the funds as having the same start date. This is shown in Table 7.12.

TABLE 7.11 When Fund B Is the Manager's First Fund, the Portfolio IRR is 8.24 Percent

	Reversed Flows		
Year	Fund A	Fund B	Portfolio
0	0	−200	−200
1	0	0	0
2	0	0	0
3	0	0	0
4	0	0	0
5	0	200	200
6	−100	0	−100
7	−25	0	−25
8	200	0	200
9	−25	0	−25
10	0	0	0
11	115	0	115
Paid-In	150	200	350
Total Value	315	200	515
Wealth	165	0	165
IRR (%)	38.18	0.00	8.24
TVPI	2.10	1.00	1.47

TABLE 7.12 When Funds A and B Start at the Same Date the IRR Is 11.81

	Time Zero Flows		
Year	Fund A	Fund B	Portfolio
0	−100	−200	−300
1	−25	0	−25
2	200	0	200
3	−25	0	−25
4	0	0	0
5	115	200	315
6	0	0	0
7	0	0	0
8	0	0	0
9	0	0	0
10	0	0	0
11	0	0	0
Paid-In	150	200	350
Total Value	315	200	515
Wealth	165	0	165
IRR (%)	38.18	0.00	11.81
TVPI	2.10	1.00	1.47

TABLE 7.13 Summarized Results of Tables 7.10, 7.11, and 7.12.

Dates Are	Portfolio IRR (%)
Actual	23.89
Reversed	8.24
Time-Zero	11.81

By starting all of the investments at the same date, the time-zero IRR neutralizes the effect of the early winner. At the portfolio level, the time-zero IRR is the result of commingling the cash flows with the same start date. The results of this example are summarized in Table 7.13. If Fund A is the first fund, the portfolio has an IRR of 23.89 percent; if Fund B is the first fund, the portfolio IRR is 8.24 percent. By putting the funds together at a common starting point, the IRR_{TZ} is 11.81 percent.

This comparison is artificial and is meant to illustrate a point. Normally you simply compare the actual return of the portfolio of funds with the time-zero return. Note as well that this time shifting does not take into account other externalities, such as macro-economic conditions—it is only meant to compare the absolute performance of two or more portfolios. We will make additional use of the time-zero IRR in later chapters, and we will abbreviate it IRR_{TZ}.

PRIVATE EQUITY AND THE TIME-WEIGHTED RATE OF RETURN

In a mutual fund, the investor is responsible for the timing of cash additions and withdrawals. In private equity, the GP is responsible for calling and distributing capital, and so the IRR is generally the preferred measure for the LP. If the GP were to draw all capital committed to a fund at once and hold on to all distributions until the fund is liquidated, the timing of cash flows would play no special part. In this case, the IRR would be equal to the time-weighted rate of return (TWRR).

There are two prominent methodologies for the TWRR, the linked point-to-point IRR series and the Modified Dietz method. We do not cover them in this book. Many private equity investors question the appropriateness of a TWRR calculation in private equity. The reason is simple—the only way to remove the impact of interim cash flows is to revalue the investment at the time of every transaction. This is not pragmatic, or as some might say, possible in private equity.

However, the TWRR provides a way to report performance for the portfolio as a whole—particularly helpful in reporting on a large portfolio where private equity may only comprise a small portion of that portfolio. We often see the TWRR used this way, measuring the effects of private equity within an entire portfolio.

CONCLUSIONS

The IRR is extremely useful in gauging the progress and relative performance of one or a series of private equity investments. Beware these pitfalls:

- Investments that make money have positive IRRs. Investments that lose money have negative IRRs. Investments that break even have an IRR of zero.
- With a large positive IRR, cash flows later in the investment's life have little effect on the IRR.
- With a large negative IRR, cash flows later in the investment's life can have a dramatic effect on the IRR.
- Multiple IRR solutions are possible, but, in practice are usually a non-issue.
- A portfolio IRR may be higher than individual investment IRRs.
- A higher IRR does not mean higher profitability; higher profitability does not mean a higher IRR.
- The IRR needs to be supplemented with other measurements to gauge the true performance of the private equity investment. In Appendix F, we explore a concept called duration of performance, which attempts to draw a relationship between the IRR and TVPI.
- Calculating the Time-Zero IRR (abbreviated IRR_{TZ}) neutralizes the effects of early winners.

CHAPTER 8

Universe Comparisons

We introduce and discuss some available data on private equity performance. In light of our findings, we introduce simple methods to gauge individual fund and portfolio performance that are based on publicly available data.

HOOKED ON NUMBERS

A continuing challenge in evaluating performance for the private markets investments is establishing appropriate benchmarks. Since 2000, the Investment Board has changed or modified its private equity benchmarks five times as industry-wide performance data have become more available.
—State of Wisconsin Investment Board (2007, 3)

This guy goes to a psychiatrist and says, "Doc, my brother's crazy; he thinks he's a chicken." And the doctor says, "Well, why don't you turn him in?" The guy says, "I would, but I need the eggs."
—Woody Allen in *Annie Hall*

UNIVERSE? WHOSE UNIVERSE?

In the financial world, a universe is an attempt at representing related data completely. Of course, getting complete data on a private universe, such as private equity, is impractical or impossible. Getting a representative universe is possible, but difficult. Table 8.1 shows published first-quarter 2008

TABLE 8.1 First Quarter 2008 10-Year IRRs from Two Providers of Private Equity Benchmarks

Cambridge Associates	32.83%
Thomson Reuters	17.20%

10-year historical point-to-point IRRs (Cambridge Associates 2008; Thomson Reuters 2008) for venture capital from two of the industry's most cited providers of data.

In an industry where performance is measured in one-one hundredths of a percent, a basis point, this difference is staggering. What could account for it? Are these two firms measuring the same thing? Who would know? There are obvious culprits including timing of cash flows, participation or lack thereof, survivorship bias, and just bad data.

But a difference of this magnitude is a bit of a problem. To many investors, these industry measures are critical, helping justify the investment of hundreds of millions or even billions. To portfolio managers with compensation linked to performance, these numbers are the numbers to beat. To industry lobbying groups, they are numbers that help convince lawmakers that private equity is a vibrant part of the economy and deserves special treatment. Whatever their eventual use, the purpose of these numbers is to objectively present how venture capital has fared during this time.

Why do we accept this disparity? Some would say that we need the eggs.

WHY COMPARE?

There are four common uses for comparison universes, or what are also commonly referred to as private equity benchmarks.

1. *Periodic Indicators of Asset Class Performance.* There are many published measures of the health of private equity as an industry. These measures are usually calculated by firms that monitor large portfolios or that gather data from many sources, including both GPs and LPs. Examples of this are the performance results issued quarterly by Thomson Reuters in conjunction with the National Venture Capital Association (NVCA), a U.S. venture capital industry group, and the British Private Equity and Venture Capital Association (BVCA).
2. *Due Diligence.* When considering prospective investments, both the absolute and relative performance of a fund manager matter considerably.

Although historical performance measures are used as predictors of future results, they are also compared to vintage year and other group measures. In your own due diligence, we have a simple recommendation: get the fund manager's cash flows, and do your own analysis. Refer to our sections Generating Deal Flow and Screening Deal Flow in Chapter 3. How the manager achieved those results is the subject of a deeper discussion in Chapter 12, Performance Attribution.

3. *Performance-Based Compensation.* Some investment groups compensate staff with pay scales or bonuses that depend on beating a benchmark. This introduces an interesting dynamic into the investment process. Choosing the benchmark is obviously important: the benchmark needs to be appropriate. Those choosing the benchmark should be objective (the fox should not be guarding the chicken coop). Changing benchmarks can be fraught with problems, but sometimes not changing the benchmark is worse. Finally, calculating performance objectively and with the same methodology as the benchmark is critical.

4. *Ongoing Monitoring.* The reality check—"How is my private equity portfolio doing?"—may be the most difficult thing to measure. The problem is not only the availability of valid comparison sets, but more importantly matching the characteristics of an available universe to your portfolio. You may, for example, have had the widest possible opportunities to invest, but did not, for whatever reason, choose to participate in what became the best performing funds for a particular year. You may have been overcommitted to mid-size European buyout funds and so skipped on several opportunities. You may not have had the opportunity to invest the amounts you desired and so were under your target allocation to venture capital in a particular vintage year. This skews your plan, but more importantly, the actual commitments you made may make it more difficult to compare a benchmark without a custom comparison set prepared just for you.

WHAT IS SUCCESS?

Success is often measured in private equity investing by comparison to the best performing or *top quartile* funds. Yet, like the fictional above-average children of Lake Woebegone, nearly all fund managers we have met lay claim to being top-quartile. Despite its seemingly statistical improbability, there may be some truth to this. The ultimate performance of a fund is unknown until it is liquidated. Early on, or even midway through its life, a fund *may have been* within the top-quartile of some published universe for a time.

The lesson here is simple: *when* a fund is ranked makes a big difference (Wang and Conner 2004). And secondly, against what measure? If you were a GP coming to market, you might be more inclined to cite the lowest top quartile you could find. Beating 20 percent is much easier than beating 35 percent. Is a claim to be a top quartile fund truth or hyperbole? You need to be the judge.

Unfortunately, success for an LP is also caught up in this hype. We have attended industry conferences where limited partners publicly question why anyone without access to the "top quartile" fund managers would even think to invest in private equity. This is nonsense.

It is up to you to gauge success. If you are an endowment with a 20-year history of investing in private equity you will have different opportunities, expectations, and measures from an investor just getting started. If you manage a fund of funds, your fee structure may mean you will be measured differently by others. If your investment team has decided to establish new relationships with first-time funds, you will have your reasons. If you are paring down your relationships in a period of retrenchment, you may expect to sustain some short-term losses in your portfolio performance. If you are investing in a new region, your expectations should change. If you are investing in secondaries, you may have different criteria altogether.

In any event, it is up to you to ask important questions:

- Is my portfolio in line with my investment policy?
- Are my strategic reasons for investing in private equity being met?
- If pure return is my goal, does my private equity portfolio outperform the public markets? If it does, does it justify the risk?
- Is my private equity portfolio appropriately diversified?
- Is my total portfolio better diversified because of my investment in private equity?
- Is my track record of investing in private equity outperforming my peers? Is it among the best in the industry?

The last questions are in some ways the most difficult to answer.

THE HAVES AND HAVE NOTS

If you are just starting to develop a private equity portfolio, you are at an information disadvantage. In theory, larger, longer-term investors in private equity have a trove of their own data. Captured and exploited properly, this data is invaluable. With the benefit of a long-term history, investors have a better understanding of how these private assets behave under different conditions. Those without a long-term history have no choice but to rely on publicly or commercially available performance data.

Whether you have access to data or not, the world of private investing tends to be isolating. Not knowing how you are doing in comparison with others can increase your isolation. Most investors we know talk to their colleagues about the industry and subscribe to and read with interest available sources for performance data from a wide variety of producers. Most GPs also want to know how they rank (although some feign indifference). Funds of funds, advisors, and gatekeepers make their living in part by knowing how funds rank. In sum, only a few players are willing to show their cards, but everyone wants to know what cards everyone else is holding.

WHO ARE YOU GOING TO TRUST?

This section introduces the variety and variability of publicly available sources. We use public in its broadest sense. First, there are fee-based subscription-based data services and investor-only services that are open to anyone with money.

And then there is everything else, all of it on the Web. Search for "private equity benchmarks," and you will find loads of information. There are voluntary disclosures on the web sites of public institutions including state college endowments and state pension funds. There are PowerPoint presentations to be found from industry conferences around the world. There are press releases and published indexes.

As a result of our rigorous research, we can reliably report to you one fact: all of these sources are wrong. Or, uh, perhaps one is right. We just can't tell you which one.

QUARTILES ARE RANKINGS

To some, private equity investing is a job, to others it is more of a blood sport. There are few who doubt that private equity investing is competitive. GPs aggressively compete with each other for the next big thing. They compete with each other for the attention of the market and for the money of investors. A few GPs with outsized reputations command larger shares of the profit. LPs compete with each other for access to top-tier funds and then compete to get bigger slices of them. Larger LPs demand co-investment rights to get in on the action.

Most of this competitiveness is natural, but some of it is driven by what is published. And if you are part of this competitive private equity world,

TABLE 8.2 Quartile Names and Boundaries Are Often Confused

Quartile	Abbreviation	Begins	Ends
Fourth	Q4	75th Percentile	Maximum Value
Third	Q3	50th Percentile (Median)	75th Percentile
Second	Q2	25th Percentile	50th Percentile (Median)
First	Q1	Minimum Value	25th Percentile

Note: The fourth quartile is also known as the "top quartile."

much of what you hear is driven by talk of *quartiles*. We are not big fans of quartiles, but they are in broad use, and you should know about them.

Quartiles are rankings. Sort a list of funds by a measure, such as the IRR, from highest to lowest, and then divide the list into four equal portions. The first portion of this reverse-sorted list is the fourth quartile, most often referred to as the *top quartile*. The boundaries must be carefully referred to and the standards are shown in Table 8.2, with columns describing where a quartile begins and ends.

There is confusion on these standards. Several providers reverse this list, referring to the best performing funds as being in the first quartile.

Similarly, a *decile* ranking breaks the list into 10 portions. The top decile exceeds 90 percent of the observations below it.

As you can see, quartiles are easy to calculate, publish, and understand. There are valid criticisms to the quartile ranking approach, however. Most importantly, all you have to do to be in the top quartile is to be above the 75th percentile. For this and other reasons, some prefer ranking using actual percentiles; for example, you can say a fund was in the 63rd percentile. You have to have the data used for ranking to do this.

SUB-UNIVERSES

Earlier, we identified a universe as an attempt at representing related data completely. In the public markets, this is much more plausible, as the extent of a universe is known. In the private markets, the extent of the universe is unknown, and some might say, unknowable.

One of the most prominent providers of private equity data, Venture Economics, is now a division of the publisher Thomson Reuters. Its VentureXpert database is a subscription-based service. Cambridge Associates, an advisory firm, publishes a benchmark and has a portfolio analysis database. Private Equity Intelligence, or Preqin, is a publishing group that obtains much of its information from sources that are under forced disclosure, such as Freedom of Information Act (FOIA) requests. Sand Hill Econometrics, a consultancy, has a proprietary portfolio company database around which it bases its fee-based subscription and research. Sand Hill's efforts are directed toward modeling a more timely approximation of the valuation of holdings and so better calculate interim returns.

Some fund managers have gone public. In fact, a Swiss firm, LPX GmbH, publishes an index based on publicly traded private equity funds.

All of these providers are working with a subset of the universe of private equity funds. For this reason, we call them sub-universes. The most pressing problem we see is that no one knows the true extent of the private equity universe. As a result, attempting to represent any benchmark as definitive is problematic.

INDEXES THAT ARE NOT INDEXES

Indexes, such as the S&P 500, usually begin at an arbitrary value (such as 1,000) and increase or decrease this value according to the periodic returns. An index is not a return: it is derived from returns. There are groups publishing returns that they call indexes. Beware, for many of these published results are no more complicated than composite performance measures. Do not confuse these measures with an index like the S&P 500.

In contrast, what is commonly called a *benchmark* in private equity is a composite return, whether by vintage, sub-asset class, or any number of investment characteristics. This is not the only type of benchmark, as you will see in subsequent chapters.

HOW THE SAUSAGE GETS MADE

It's a bit like sausage, you don't want to see how it's made.
—Jesse Reyes on the subject of Private Equity Benchmarks

We agree with Jesse Reyes, formerly head of research at Venture Economics, that the process of gathering and cleaning data is ugly. We have seen our share of ugly data. But we think that people want to understand how a benchmark is calculated. In this section you will see that calculating a benchmark from data is straightforward. However, we believe that the current process of creating benchmarks is flawed and mostly a result of inertia that can be overcome. More on that later.

TABLE 8.3 Data for a Little Benchmark

Year	Fund A	Fund B	Fund C	Portfolio
0	−10	−15	−25	−50
1	−10	−25	−40	−75
2	−10	0	−30	−40
3	0	−20	y−20	−40
4	0	0	−5	−5
5	10	0	20	30
6	20	0	20	40
7	30	0	20	50
8	10	0	20	30
9	5	0	20	25
10	15	45	50	110
Paid-In	30	60	120	210
Total Value	90	45	150	285
Wealth	60	−15	30	75
IRR (%)	19.61	−5.00	3.51	6.10
TVPI	3.00	0.75	1.25	1.36

MAKING A BENCHMARK

Benchmarks are best made with significant amounts of data and perhaps best explained with only a little data. In Table 8.3 we have created cash flows for three funds and the combination of their cash flows as the portfolio. We use yearly cash flows only for the purposes of this simplified example.

A benchmark analysis typically creates three IRRs from this data: the median, the average, and the weighted average.

The Median IRR

In our tiny sample, the median value for the IRR, the one in the middle of a ranking of the three funds, is 3.51 percent, and comes from Fund C. The median is found by sorting and splitting the list. Table 8.2, which shows these rankings, intentionally omits the names of funds, as at this juncture, identifying the fund associated with these rankings is unnecessary.

If you were ranking, with hundreds or thousands of funds, you might find this middle value with the use of Excel's Median function.

The median IRR is a perfectly straightforward measure and well accepted for what it is.

TABLE 8.4 Calculation of Benchmark Median

IRR (%)	Rank	
19.61	1	
3.51	2	<– Median
−5.00	3	

The Average IRR

The benchmark average is the average of all of the IRRs in our list. With our list, this is

$$19.61 + 3.51 - 5.00 = 18.12$$
$$18.12/3 = 6.04$$

What does the average IRR measure? We think that the right answer is *nothing*. Averaging IRRs attempts to neutralize the relative weights of the size and timing of the underlying funds. As you will see later in Chapter 12, Performance Attribution, there is an appropriate way to do this.

The Weighted-Average IRR

Welcome to another flawed technique, the weighted-average IRR. The weight of an investment is the ratio of its paid-in capital to the total paid-in capital of the set of investments. Some choose to do this weighting by fund sizes. In this case, we use paid-in capital. The results are shown in Table 8.5. The weighted-average IRR multiplies the weight of each fund by its IRR and then adds them together. We think that this is a silly way to calculate a composite IRR.

As you can see from the portfolio IRR in Table 8.6, the correct result is 6.10 percent whereas this weighted-average IRR is 3.38 percent. The weighted-average IRR is a shortcut that is being used in place of the true IRR for the composite, which requires both the cash flow data and the infrastructure to complete the computation.

TABLE 8.5 Computation of Fund Weights for Weighted-Average IRR Calculation

	Fund A	Fund B	Fund C
	= 30/210	= 60/210	= 120/210
Weight	14.29%	28.57%	57.14%

TABLE 8.6   Calculation of Weighted-Average IRR

Fund	Weight * IRR		
A	14.29 * 19.61	=	2.80%
B	28.57 * (−5.00)	=	−1.43%
C	57.14 * 3.51	=	2.01%
Weighted Average IRR		=	3.38%

RETHINKING BENCHMARKS

There are other topics that would be useful to openly discuss and rethink. The characteristics used to create benchmarks should be clear and unambiguous, but should they be fixed? For example, as funds become bigger, do comparisons to past benchmarks lose validity? Call it a "large" buyout fund, and what does that mean? Should benchmarks be restated when better information is available? However, these technical and philosophical issues are secondary to the problem of getting good data, or even knowing what good data is.

EARTHLY MEASURES

So back on terra firma, we explore alternatives to this information in other, publicly-available data. We do not do this to supplant these sources, but to show what can be done with a little imagination and what is readily at hand.

FREEDOM OF INFORMATION EFFECTS

There is a common false belief in the United States that the Freedom of Information Act (FOIA) is one thing. In reality, there is a U.S. federal act and there are many separate acts promulgated by individual states. Most of the controversy involving private equity data stems from FOIA requests to state institutions.

The confidentiality of private equity data was first and most-publicly breached in 1999, when the *Houston Chronicle* had a FOIA-based lawsuit against the University of Texas Investment Management Company. Two of us, Messrs. Long and Nickels, were directly involved in this and learned much from the experience. Others lawsuits followed, including one brought by the *San Jose Mercury News* against the California Public Employees' Retirement System (Chaplinsky and Perry 2004). In their wake, a firestorm swept across the private equity industry, with long-standing relationships in embers. Both sides had compelling arguments. Public money was being put at risk. The prospects, plans, and finances of private companies were being exposed. For the most part, rational minds prevailed, and many government bodies enacted special exemptions for the kind of information that would have been ordinarily protected if regulated, for example, by the SEC.

To some of the parties involved in this drama, lines have been drawn that will not be crossed. Some funds continue to refuse investments by groups subject to FOIA, but for the most part laws are being amended to protect private equity data more appropriately. Typical is a statement from the California State Teachers Retirement System (CalSTRS), one of the largest state pension funds:

> ...*The extent of that disclosure consists of releasing the name of the partnership investment, CalSTRS' capital commitment to the partnership, capital contributed to the partnership, capital distribution to CalSTRS from the partnership, and the internal rate of return (IRR) calculated by CalSTRS pertaining to its investment in the partnership....*
> —California State Teachers' Retirement System (n.d.)

The important exclusion is that of any underlying portfolio holding data. The general rule is that the limited data that is supplied preserves the confidentiality of the current investment portfolio of the GPs.

PUBLICLY AVAILABLE SOURCES

One of the world's largest investors in private equity, the California Public Employees Retirement System (CalPERS) publishes performance data for its Alternative Investment Management (AIM) program quarterly. Performance is broken out by individual fund and vintage year performance. From its web site, Table 8.7 shows CalPERS vintage performance from the third quarter 2007 (California Public Employees' Retirement System n.d.). Note that this table uses CalPERS naming conventions.

This table is interesting reading. After a 2001 commitment of nearly $5 billion, CalPERS dramatically slowed their investment pace for several years. This is in line with the dot-com and technology bust. A period of retrenchment followed. However, from 2004 forward, the program began to aggressively expand. CalPERS reports that its private equity portfolio IRR from inception is 14.5 percent, with an investment multiple of 1.3. Their vintage year returns during this period range from 7.4 percent to 24.8 percent, with TVPI from 1.4 to 2.8. CalPERS does not supply aggregated

TABLE 8.7 Publicly-Available, Vintage Year Performance for CalPERS as of Third Quarter 2007

Vintage	Capital Committed	Cash In	Cash Out	Cash Out and Remaining Value	Net IRR	TVPI
1990	125.3	121.9	295.3	295.9	15.8	2.4
1991	171.7	179.6	509.3	509.5	27.6	2.8
1992	160.0	156.6	340.2	341.9	20.6	2.2
1993	563.0	560.0	1,041.4	1,076.7	20.0	1.9
1994	1,507.6	1,416.9	2,326.3	2,437.3	14.7	1.7
1995	1,197.9	1,141.3	1,791.2	1,922.7	15.8	1.7
1996	1,155.9	1,133.7	1,458.3	1,533.4	9.0	1.4
1997	1,111.9	1,090.0	1,399.1	1,592.1	9.1	1.5
1998	2,216.7	2,175.7	2,561.6	3,050.6	8.0	1.4
1999	1,207.4	1,149.4	1,176.8	1,550.1	7.4	1.3
2000	3,977.9	3,647.7	2,986.7	4,979.6	9.2	1.4
2001	4,816.8	4,225.1	3,667.7	7,669.5	21.5	1.8
2002	1,092.6	958.6	766.5	1,551.0	24.8	1.6
2003	1,496.2	1,235.5	1,025.7	2,303.1	N/M	N/M
2004	2,014.6	1,471.0	580.1	2,219.3	N/M	N/M
2005	3,932.0	2,519.7	418.1	2,940.1	N/M	N/M
2006	9,317.2	3,440.5	132.2	3,590.1	N/M	N/M
2007	13,002.9	2,931.0	8.9	2,860.5	N/M	N/M
Total	49,067.5	29,554.3	22,485.5	42,423.5	14.5	1.4

Source: CalPERS web site.

performance measures (N/M for "Not Meaningful") for the latest five years, regarding these vintages as too young to be reliable.

From additional reading on their web site, we learn that the weighted average age of the portfolio is only 3.5 years. How can this be so? If you look at the investments from 2003 forward, you will see commitments of nearly $30 billion which makes their portfolio very young on a weighted average age basis.

To benchmark themselves, CalPERS does the following:

> To address the young age of the partnership portfolio, CalPERS adopted a short-term benchmark, the Venture Economics Custom Young Fund Universe. The benchmark measures performance of the AIM Partnerships in the first four years of life against a similarly-aged universe of Venture Economics data.
> —California Public Employees' Retirement System (n.d.)

So even CalPERS, one of the largest private equity investors in the world with a large and mature data set, compares its own portfolio not to a published benchmark, but to a very specific performance benchmark from Venture Economics.

INDIVIDUAL FUND MEASURES

Many investment groups subject to FOIA publish performance for each commitment on a periodic basis. Table 8.8 shows the first 10 funds of published data from third quarter 2007 CalPERS data from their web site.

The first fund, 1818 Fund II, LP, is from vintage year 1993, has a net IRR of 11.2 percent and a multiple of 1.70. The next seven of eight funds listed show interim results but footnoted as "N/M" for *not meaningful*. From the complete list, we learn that CalPERS has invested in 356 funds from the inception of their private equity program in 1990. Of these, they consider 181 funds to be *not meaningful*. The remaining 175 funds have

TABLE 8.8 Publicly-Available, Vintage Year Performance for CalPERS as of Third Quarter 2007

Fund Description	Vintage Year	Net IRR	Investment Multiple	Footnotes
1818 Fund II, L.P.	1993	11.2	1.70×	
Aberdare III	2005	−2.5	1.00×	N/M
Acon-Bastion Partners II, L.P.	2006	−15.7	0.90×	N/M
Advent Global Private Equity IV-A, L.P.	2002	53.5	3.10×	
Advent International GPE V-D, L.P.	2005	136.2	1.70×	N/M
Advent Latin America Private Equity IV-D	2007	−5.0	0.90×	N/M
Advent Latin America Private Equity III	2006	18.2	1.20×	N/M
Affinity Asia Pacific Fund III, LP	2007	−83.1	0.60×	N/M
Aisling Capital II, LP	2006	13.9	1.10×	N/M
Alta BioPharma Partners I, L.P.	1998	22.2	1.50×	
...	...	...	...	...

Source: CalPERS web site.

TABLE 8.9 IRR Quartiles from 175 Mature Commitments from CalPERS

CalPERS IRR Quartiles From Public 3rd Quarter 2007 Data		
Quartile	Begins (%)	Ends (%)
Q4	23.65	103.50
Q3	11.30	23.65
Q2	0.95	11.30
Q1	−49.90	0.95

produced IRRs from −49.9 percent to 103.5 percent, with TVPIs from 0.10 to 5.60.

SUMMARIZING PERFORMANCE FROM PUBLIC DATA

For the purposes of illustration, we take this publicly available data and create quartiles, shown in Tables 8.9 and 8.10. Creating measures at this level will only give you a sense of the range of outcomes for the entire portfolio. In practice, it is most common to see quartiles based on vintages.

The top quartile IRR begins at 23.65 percent. The top quartile TVPI begins at 2.05. If you were to use CalPERS as a proxy for the industry, you would have IRR quartiles with known funds. CalPERS is a big investor, but this is a small portion of the private equity universe. Let us add another publicly available source, the Washington State Investment Board (2008). This group started investing in 1981. Following the same exclusions for funds younger than 2003, this adds 152 funds to our quartile charts and

TABLE 8.10 TVPI Quartiles from 175 Mature Commitments from CalPERS

CalPERS TVPI Quartiles From Public 3rd Quarter 2007 Data		
Quartile	Begins	Ends
Q4	2.05	5.60
Q3	1.50	2.05
Q2	1.05	1.50
Q1	0.10	1.05

TABLE 8.11 Combining CalPERS and WSIB Quartiles as of Third Quarter 2007 for Mature Commitments

	Quartile	CalPERS		WSIB		Combined	
		Begin	End	Begin	End	Begin	End
IRR (%)	Q4	23.65	103.50	22.03	135.60	23.05	135.60
	Q3	11.30	23.65	10.85	22.03	11.20	23.05
	Q2	0.95	11.30	4.50	10.85	3.30	11.20
	Q1	−49.90	0.95	−42.10	4.50	−49.90	3.30
TVPI	Q4	2.05	5.60	2.15	8.41	2.10	8.41
	Q3	1.50	2.05	1.60	2.15	1.52	2.10
	Q2	1.05	1.50	1.21	1.60	1.15	1.52
	Q1	0.10	1.05	0.04	1.21	0.04	1.15

is shown in Table 8.11. Keep in mind that this is an example exercise, not necessarily something that we would recommend in practice.

The combination of these two portfolios shifts the range of these values only slightly. Both the lowest and the highest quartiles were similar, and the combination of their overall performance did not change appreciably. Of course, we do not question or delve too deeply into the specific means that these organizations use to calculate their measures. We expect that with enough of a sample, we would have the ability to better corroborate the results. As it stands, these two large investors had an overlap of 16 funds in our reduced sample. Of these, only two funds, which are shown in Table 8.12, had substantial differences.

The different vintages may help explain the variances between the published performance for these funds, but without further specific information,

TABLE 8.12 Overlapping Funds with Variances from the CalPERS and WSIB Portfolios

Fund	Vintage	IRR	TVPI	Portfolio
Doughty Hanson Fund II	1996	49.00	2.05	WSIB
Doughty Hanson Fund II, L.P.	1995	46.30	2.00	CalPERS
KKR European Fund	1999	23.10	1.96	WSIB
KKR European Fund I, L.P.	2001	31.40	2.40	CalPERS

we can do little but accept these numbers at face value. Also note that there is a variance in the naming conventions for the funds.

This exercise only begins to create a comparison set, and it is only meant to illustrate what can be done with publicly available data. In the absence of a subscription to a trusted set of data, or a portfolio large enough to be thought of as its own sub-universe, this little sampling represents a start.

HOW BIG IS BIG ENOUGH?

You have just seen a range of outcomes for two U.S.-based public portfolios. Despite their sizes, their combination of funds is a tiny fraction of the universe. Both Thomson Reuters and Cambridge have a sample size of about 2,000 funds, but we know that the universe is much larger.

How much data is enough? If you are studying the history of private equity investing or are doing advanced analysis that requires industrywide data, you will need to get your hands on all the data you can. If your portfolio began in the last five years, you may be most interested in the performance of funds over that period. You may be focusing your investment in Latin America or Asia and so need as much data on that geographic sector as you can find. Your program may have a greater emphasis on buyouts. The point is that your need depends on your purpose.

Using publicly available data has advantages and limitations. Public data lives in daylight, and its accuracy can be openly questioned and compared. A big disadvantage with public data is that it is by nature a summary—to our knowledge, no one is or should be making cash flow data from private investments public. This limits its use for deeper analysis. As we have argued, comparisons are most useful when they mirror the opportunities you have had. In contrast, proprietary data, no matter how good, lives in darkness. This secrecy cloaks errors and omissions but affords opportunities to create customized benchmarks.

SAMPLE VERSUS CENSUS

In the beginning of this book, we said:

> *From our vantage, the current state of commercially available information about private equity is a mess. We are acutely aware that universe data about private equity is rightly hard to get, assemble, maintain, and audit. We believe that the industry is currently poorly served, and we are not alone in our criticism.*

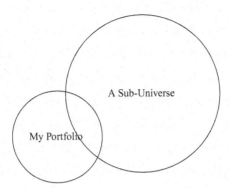

FIGURE 8.1 Overlap of a portfolio and a sub-universe.

Sample size inevitably forces us to demote the collection of funds known as universes to sub-universes. Estimates of the size of the known universe of private equity funds are several times the sample size of Cambridge and Thomson Reuters and so they both qualify for the sub-universe designation. As we depict in Figure 8.1, how your private equity portfolio compares with a particular sub-universe is an open question. Every portfolio is likely to have some kind of overlap with a sub-universe of size, but given the blinded nature of the comparison, the extent of this overlap is unknowable.

As well, given the current sample sizes, some larger LPs, gatekeepers, funds of funds, or custodians consider their in-house databases "universes" unto themselves. We think that they have a point, but we think this is largely irrelevant. Before laying claim to significance, what is first needed is better information about the entire private equity universe and until then what we will have may look like Figure 8.2.

We are in support of industry efforts to create independent, reliable, and durable benchmarks based on clear and consistent methodologies. But before creating yet-another-benchmark, what is first needed is a census, a more complete identification of the private equity universe. A census of course has its limits, as the universe continues to expand every day. Once the approximate extent is known, however, we encourage all parties to pool their data in order to obtain the largest and most diverse database of private equity cash flows and valuations, an outcome that should eliminate the survivorship bias.

We also realize that the implications of all of this are a bit unsettling. Much of the industry research and literature is built on these so-called

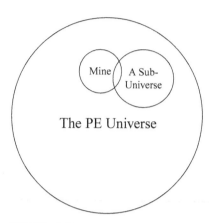

FIGURE 8.2 The universe compared
to a sub-universe and portfolio.

universes. We regard this as all the more reason to move forward with
industry-wide data aggregation efforts.

CONCLUSIONS

Collecting and assembling the data necessary to create a representative universe is a massive undertaking. It certainly is not for the fainthearted. At
present there are two main groups attempting to serve the industry's need
for the type of information that can be extracted from a representative
universe; Thomson Reuters and Cambridge Associates. Despite their best
intentions, the industry still feels underserved. This is partly due to the fact
that their performance numbers are radically different from one another
(see Table 8.1). Moreover, their sample sizes are not all that impressive.
As a result, the industry's dissatisfaction has created opportunities for new
providers to enter the space. We suspect that much will change within the
next five years.

CHAPTER 9

Flawed Research Methodologies

Much of the currently available research on private equity uses measures and approaches designed for the public markets. We believe that without modification, most of this analysis leads to questionable results. This chapter provides a framework for understanding some more advanced measures we introduce later in the text.

ANALYTICAL RUTS

Oh pity the plight of the private equity researcher, toiling to devise new measures when most of the available data is held in small scattered silos. It is no wonder that creativity is stifled and so much of this research uses practices from public markets. We think that some public market techniques are useful when analyzing private markets, but they have to be carefully applied.

In this chapter we highlight some of the challenges associated with time series analysis. We demonstrate that measuring the variability of returns is not as simple as computing the standard deviation of interim returns. Moreover, we again reinforce the necessity of incorporating wealth and magnitude into measures. The major ideas in this chapter are:

- Be wary of analysis that relies heavily upon interim returns and interim valuations.
- Be skeptical when an analysis uses TWRRs. We have seen many papers that use this as a shortcut to compute relationships between public and private markets. Methodologies must take into account that this is a money-weighted asset class.

- Be critical of analyses that exclude investment multiples and other measures of wealth creation.
- You never know the final outcome until the investment is fully exited. Investments come back to life, cash is found, and capital can be released from escrow. All of these have the potential to drastically impact the final outcome. With that said, do not be surprised when an analysis excludes active investments. There is always a burning desire to incorporate newer information, but it may end up diminishing the quality of the analysis.
- Question methodologies. There are no standards when it comes to time series analysis in this asset class. Read papers in journals, working papers on the Web, and explore on your own. We explore some new methodologies for computing standard deviation and correlation in later chapters.

WHAT DOES THE STANDARD DEVIATION OF AN IRR SERIES MEASURE?

A typical analysis of a private equity fund measures the standard deviation of the IRR over time, likening this measure to that of the more traditional time-weighted rate of return. We test the validity of this approach with a real-life example, a private equity fund with 12 years of activity. For our purposes, the fund's type, vintage, and other attributes are unimportant. Figure 9.1 plots the fund's IRR at each quarter end.

This fund exhibits a typical J-Curve. The early years of the fund are mostly negative, middle years are break-even, and then the return becomes positive and eventually flattens out. In this case, the final IRR is 7.32 percent, and the final Investment Multiple is 1.69.

PLAINS, FOOTHILLS, AND MOUNTAINS

If you chop this time series up into quarterly point-to-point IRRs, you can get a sense of their variability over time. As discussed in Chapter 6, you compute a point-to-point IRR by, in effect, buying the investment at the beginning of a period and selling it at the end of a period. In Figure 9.2, which shows unannualized point-to-point IRRs for every quarter for this fund, note the increasing variability of the quarterly returns.

For the first three years of the fund, this variability, its volatility, is relatively small. However, in its midlife and especially in later years, these IRRs make somewhat wild swings. Had these IRRs been annualized, these returns

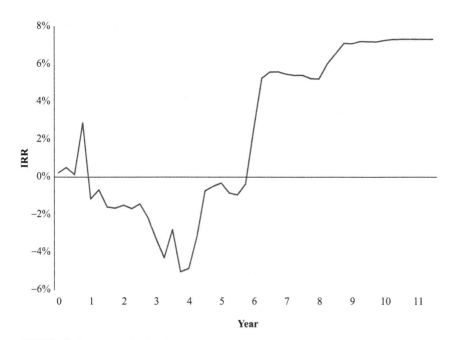

FIGURE 9.1 IRRs of a fund.

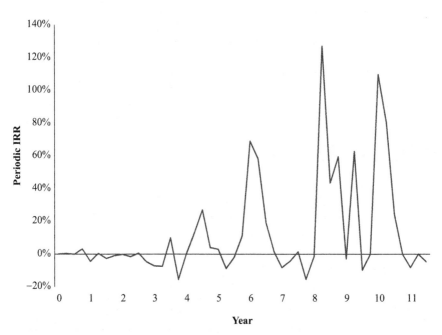

FIGURE 9.2 Point-to-point unannualized IRRs of the fund.

would have been much larger. The standard deviation, a measure of dispersion, is 32.01 percent, enough to frighten most investors. Of course, the good news in this particular fund is that most of the variability is upward. But why are the periodic returns so variable?

EXPLAINING IRR VOLATILITY

Without getting bogged down in detail, we attribute the variability of the periodic returns of most private equity funds to the following:

- Staleness of valuations. Valuations for private equity funds are conservative and are often delayed. It is common for companies in a private equity fund to be held at cost until there is a significant external event, such as another round of financing, an impairment, or the like. Here is its narrative: "Nothing is happening, nothing is happening, nothing is happening, this company is valuable, we sold this company." This, of course, leads to big spikes.
- For later periods, there is less and less capital at work, which means that it takes less and less movement to have a major effect on return.
- Over the short term, legitimate IRRs can seem whacky, and so many investors treat them as not material until their investments are at least five years old. In this example, we are always computing quarterly point-to-point IRRs.
- There may be a natural momentum to realizations. The companies within the fund may have a similar focus or strategy and it may happen that more than one will be sold off within a short time period.

VOLATILITY OF THE MULTIPLE

Now let us contrast the IRR of this fund with the investment multiple, TVPI. Figure 9.3 presents TVPI for the same fund at each quarter end and shows that it is relatively well-behaved, and has a similar shape to a J-curve. There are really no surprises here.

TVPI Volatility

To determine the volatility of TVPI, we calculate its quarterly percent change. We do this so that we can compare TVPI to the periodic IRRs. The results, shown in Figure 9.4, indicates that the percent change of TVPI is also volatile, but less so than the periodic IRR.

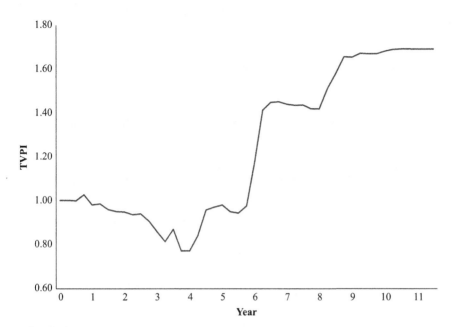

FIGURE 9.3 Investment Multiples of the Fund

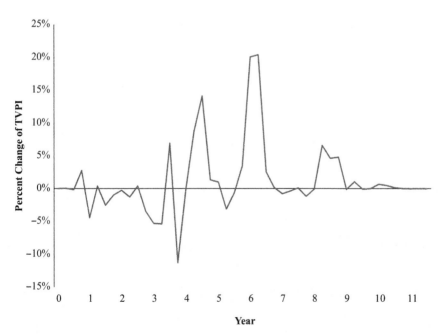

FIGURE 9.4 Periodic Percent Change of TVPI of the Fund

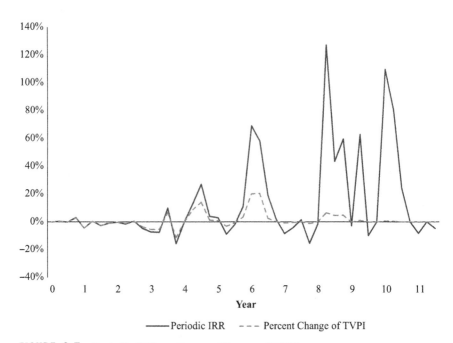

FIGURE 9.5   Periodic IRR vs. Percent Change of TVPI

This lessening of volatility is understandable, since the investment multiple reflects the impact on wealth as opposed to a raw return for the period. To put this into perspective, Figure 9.5 plots the periodic IRR and the percentage change of TVPI on the same chart.

What is particularly interesting about Figure 9.5 is that the lines are more or less in unison until year 7. Thereafter, the huge spikes in IRR have almost no influence on the TVPI, and the reason is not obvious. In later years the fund will, on average, have relatively little capital. As a result, the returns generated during this time will have very little impact on TVPI. The exception is an occasional outlier success. The huge spikes in the periodic IRRs in years 8 through 10 have almost no impact on TVPI. Here again, the wealth effect is not evident when you look at IRR alone.

Standard Deviation: Periodic IRR versus TVPI

We can take this analysis one step further by simply comparing the standard deviation of the periodic IRR and TVPI. Figure 9.6 illustrates the dramatic difference between them.

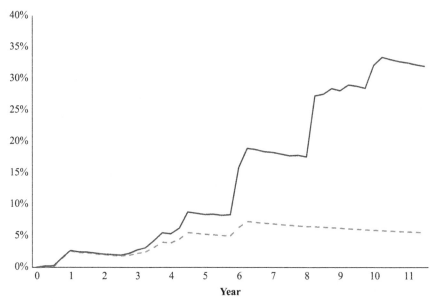

———— Standard Deviation of Periodic IRR   – – Standard Deviation of Percent Change of TVPI

FIGURE 9.6 Standard Deviation of the Periodic IRR and Percent Change of TVPI.

The periodic IRR's standard deviation is nearly six times greater than the standard deviation of the percent change of TVPI. The standard deviation of the periodic IRR line is pretty wild and continues to grow in value because of the spikes in later years. The TVPI line is much more well behaved.

Our point is that how you measure volatility is important. In fact, we present an entirely different way of measuring variability in Appendix G, Correlation and Opportunity Costs.

THE TIME-WEIGHTED COMPARISON

Another way of illustrating the challenges associated with using shorter-term return measures in private equity is to compare the IRR to TWRR. Figure 9.7 shows the enormous disparity between these two measures.

The TWRR is the average rate of return since inception—all periods are weighted equally. As a result, the performance spikes in the later years drove performance higher and higher. In contrast, the money-weighted IRR was

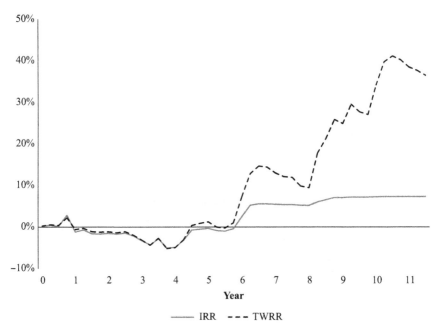

FIGURE 9.7   IRR vs. TWRR of the Fund

less affected because the magnitude of the cash activity was less significant than earlier activity.

CONCLUSION

After reading this chapter, we hope that you become a skeptic. Be skeptical of analysis that relies heavily upon interim returns and valuations. Be skeptical when an analysis uses TWRRs. Be skeptical when there is no discussion of wealth in the analysis. This is a money-weighted asset class, which means that it needs to be looked at differently from the public markets.

Private equity research is still in its infancy. Nothing is set in stone. Question proposed methodologies. Challenge assumptions. And most importantly, don't just accept the conclusions of articles because they were published in a journal or trade publication.

CHAPTER 10

Visualizing Private Equity Performance

A picture can be worth a thousand hours. We are big fans of charting, but we've been bar-charted to death. Here we introduce, through tutorials, some overlooked techniques. We show the use of radar charts as a means to quickly summarize quantitative aspects of a private equity investment. We introduce the bubble chart, to represent a third dimension to charting. Finally, we overlay fund performance over area charts for a more vivid means of quartile comparison.

PROSPECTING AND WORKING THE MINE

We were in the investment office of a major U.S. college endowment. "Where are your PPMs?" we asked. "On my desk are the ones I'm interested in. In the corner are the ones I might be interested in. I throw the rest away." We looked to the corner to see not one, but several knee-high stacks of bound proposals. On her desk were 20 or so private placement memoranda, also known as PPMs. "They come in every day. This is my way of dealing with it."

Private equity investments begin with relationships, both old and new, but as we described in Chapter 3, Managing the Investment Process, few investments should be made without a systematic approach to screening and due diligence. The Offering or Private Placement Memorandum (PPM) is an invitation and a marketing piece from fund managers in the process of raising new funds. Whittling down the piles of PPMs into the few that you seriously consider involves quantitative and qualitative work. Once investments are made, the ongoing process of monitoring the health of a set of investments, a portfolio, also takes work.

Much of this work involves performance numbers and comparisons, whether to other investments, standards, or universes. In this chapter, we introduce a visual shortcut to quantitative comparison that we have successfully used to screen investments and monitor the health of portfolios. We think that this technique has broad application in a variety of situations where multiple measures need to be compared. We also introduce two other charting techniques that we favor for representing complex data.

DRAW A PICTURE

Above all else show the data.
—Edward R. Tufte, The Visual Display of Quantitative
Information, p. 92

As you have seen, you cannot measure private equity with just one characteristic, such as its IRR. But trying to make sense of too many numbers can be error-prone and mind-numbing. For simplicity in presentation and analysis, make good use of graphics. You need not employ a graphic artist, but follow Tufte's rule as much as you can with off-the-shelf packages.

RADAR CHARTS

One of the simplest and most interesting means to display and contrast heterogeneous data is with a radar chart. If used well, a radar chart is a template for representing a great deal of data all at once, but its general purpose and limitations must be well understood. Radar charts paint data with broad strokes that are best seen from afar. In other words, do not use a radar chart for precise rendering. Instead use it for broad comparison.

One of the best uses that we have found for radar charts is quantitative screening during due diligence. When you have the track record of a fund manager distilled to a single radar chart it can be very interesting. When you have a dozen track records of fund managers on radar charts scattered about a conference table, and you've removed all names to hide who they are, you and your investment team are probably in for some lively discussion.

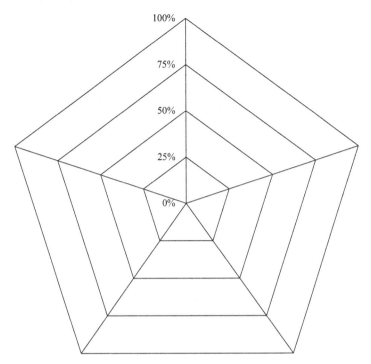

FIGURE 10.1   Radar Chart

A Short Tutorial

A radar chart, available in Excel and other popular graphing packages, looks like a spider web, with axes radiating from a center point. Each axis is an attribute you want to plot and is segmented by equidistant grid lines that create repeating geometric shapes. Figure 10.1 shows a radar chart with four unnamed attributes and no data.

Before you can plot attributes, you need to decide on the scale that each axis represents. The radar chart is symmetrical, and so each axis has the same length. The center of the chart represents, in all cases, the minimum value that you want to represent for each attribute. The outer edge of the axis represents the maximum value that you want to represent for a particular attribute.

Most published radar charts we see look too busy, and so are confusing to many readers. The common mistake many people make is to think that the background of the chart is as important as the data. As you can see in Figure 10.1, a radar chart can look busy without any data. Fortunately,

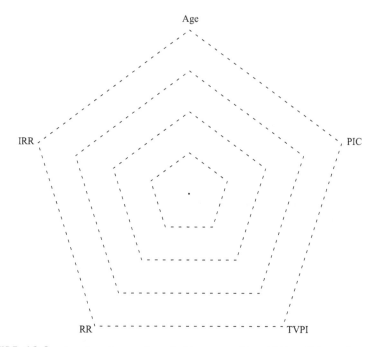

FIGURE 10.2 A radar chart stripped of its axes with grid lines lightened.

there are a few things you can do to help let the data stand out. As shown in Figure 10.2, we prefer to remove the axes and give the grid less emphasis (which can be done by formatting the grid lines and choosing a line style, such as dashed, that is less bold). Our recommendation is to leave only the aspects of the chart that give it general form so that data stands out.

The number of attributes that you choose to plot creates the basic geometry of the chart. Add another attribute to the pentagon and it becomes the hexagon in Figure 10.3.

PLOTTING OVERALL PRIVATE EQUITY PERFORMANCE

For active private equity investments, we have chosen to start with five attributes: Age, Paid-In to Commitment (PIC), the Investment Multiple (TVPI), the Realization Ratio (RR), and the IRR. If you were studying only liquidated investments, you might leave out Age and the PIC multiple, as these only have bearing on active funds.

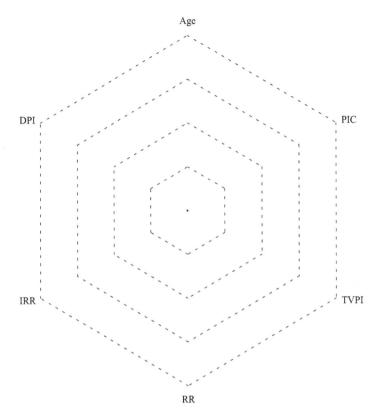

FIGURE 10.3 Adding an attribute changes the geometry of a radar chart.

To simplify our examples, we will use a linear scale for all attributes. We start by creating a table of reasonable minimums and maximums for values. Some attributes, such as the Age, are easy. For example, although many contracts extend several years beyond their initial term, the standard contract term for a fund is 10 years. We thus plot the Age attribute on a scale from 0 to 10. For another easy example, the Realization Ratio is about how much of the fund has been realized, and can only be within the range of 0 percent to 100 percent.

Creating sensible scales for the remaining attributes is more difficult. For example, due to the effects of recallable capital, the amount a fund has called can exceed the fund size. Is calling 110 percent of capital within a normal range for the PIC multiple absurdly high? With the IRR, some might choose to start its scale with −100 percent, but how often do you lose all of your money in a private equity fund? Perhaps a minimum value that signals that there is a problem is more appropriate. At the top of the range, how high an IRR should you represent? If one fund out of several hundred in your portfolio returns 135 percent, as it did with the Washington State Investment Board (see Chapter 8), you should probably consider this an outlier, and limit the maximum you use for the IRR.

In general, we recommend that you use the smallest range that displays the greatest precision without compromising clarity. For these charts to be most effective, you will most likely want to create a set of standard scales that everyone in your organization understands and adheres to, changing it only when it no longer meets your purpose.

SAMPLE SCALING

In the examples that follow, we set the scale of our axes based on Table 10.1, which represents a sample of a range of outcomes for funds. A simple measure, the Age, helps put interim results into perspective. The other four measures require scales that ultimately make sense to you.

When plotted, all values greater than the maximum are deemed to be the maximum and those lower than the minimum, the minimum. For example, by using the values in Table 10.1 as our scale, an investment with a TVPI of 6 is 100 percent, not 120 percent.

PLOTTING A PRIVATE EQUITY FUND

We will use the data in Table 10.2 for our example. This fund is mature, with most of its capital paid in, an investment multiple of 1.82, with most of the fund realized and IRR of 24.35 percent.

TABLE 10.1 Ranges for Radar Chart Attributes

Attribute	Low Value	High Value	Range
Age	0	10	10
PIC	0%	110%	1.1
TVPI	0	4	4
RR	0%	100%	1
IRR	−50%	75%	1.25

TABLE 10.2 Sample Data for a Hypothetical Fund

Attribute	Value
Age	7.75
PIC	0.91%
TVPI	1.82
RR	0.92%
IRR	24.35%

TABLE 10.3 Calculating Axis Values for a Hypothetical Fund

Attribute		Calculation	Axis Value
Age	=	7.75 / 10	78%
PIC	=	0 .91 / 1.1	83%
TVPI	=	1.82 / 4	46%
RR	=	0.92 / 1	92%
IRR	=	(50% + 24.35%) / 125%	60%

By dividing these values by the range of each scale, these values can be represented as a percentile. This is represented in Table 10.3. Note that because the IRR scale is −50 percent to +50 percent, you need to add 50 percent to the 24.35 percent to get its range correct.

Now plot each point on a radar chart.

Here's the payoff: we can describe all of the attributes of this fund with one chart. By looking at Figure 10.4, you can easily see that this is a mature fund—both the age and PIC are near their maximums. The position of the Realization Ratio shows that the fund has returned most of the value it created. The IRR is good, its Investment Multiple decent.

ORDERING AXES

Although the order of these points can be arbitrary, we plot these five measures clockwise starting with the age at high noon, and attempt to follow a natural order of the life cycle of a fund. As we expand on this initial representation later in this book, we add measures that help tell a story in an order that makes sense. We make no claim to a monopoly on a good ordering or selection of these measures. If consistency is applied, what

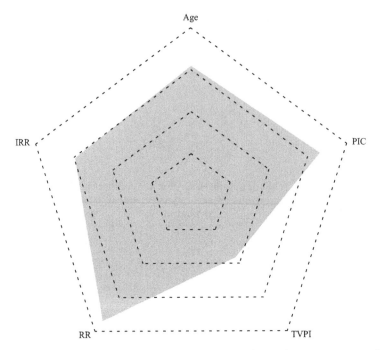

FIGURE 10.4   A radar chart of a hypothetical fund shows that it is a mature fund, almost fully paid-in, with most of its realizations accounted for.

may evolve is a common visual vocabulary that can significantly reduce time spent on comparative quantitative analysis.

Contrasting Two Funds

As we pointed out, radar charts show their power with comparison, whether between the nodes of a single chart, or between charts. Figure 10.5 shows a radar chart with two series overlaid, and it is easy to see that comparing a very young fund with a more mature fund can be of little value. Both these funds are shown with interim fund results. Their differences are stark.

Rendering Four Funds

As shown in Figure 10.6, plotting four funds is a matter of overlaying additional data and setting some transparency options.

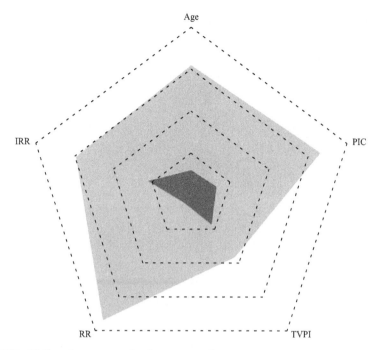

FIGURE 10.5 Plotting two funds as an overlay.

Unfortunately, the chart as shown in Figure 10.6 becomes almost impossible to read. In Figure 10.7, we present this data in individual charts, one per fund, which makes comparison clearer.

Describing these funds in maturity and performance is now a simple matter. We already know Fund A in detail. Fund B is simply immature. Fund C is mature, has a rotten IRR, has returned most of its value, but hardly any value above paid-in—it is a mess. Fund D is a mature winner. We generally recommend that when you have more than two funds to represent, you should avoid overlaying them and instead create separate charts.

Charting the Life Cycle of a Fund

This charting technique can be applied to the different life stages of a fund, creating a moving picture of its evolution. Figure 10.8 shows a fund from start to finish.

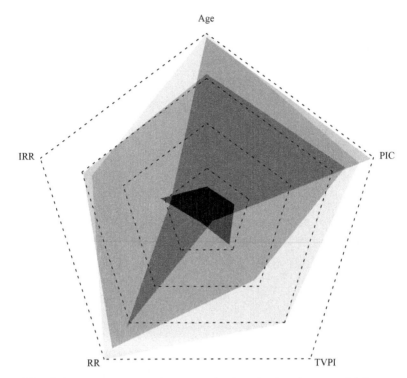

FIGURE 10.6 Overlaying the data series for four funds reduces readability.

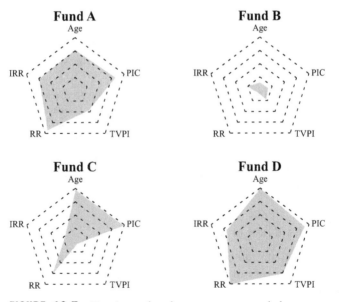

FIGURE 10.7 Keeping radar charts separate may help comparison with three or more funds.

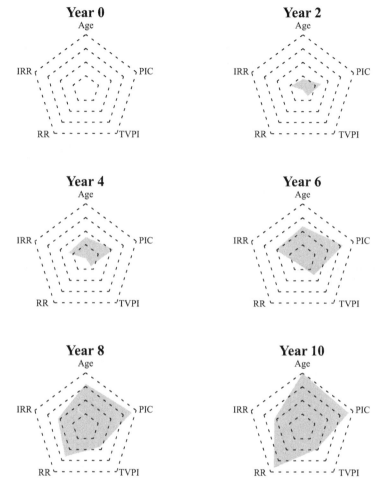

FIGURE 10.8 The life cycle of a fund.

We will be adding attributes to this pentagonal radar chart in coming chapters.

A Short Bubble Chart Tutorial

A bubble chart is a form of x-y chart, with the data point, a circle, that varies in size according to a third data element. Table 10.4 shows three columns, year, IRR, and valuation, that can be easily plotted. Figure 10.9 plots this data, which shows up as a variation on the theme of a J-curve.

TABLE 10.4 Sample Data for Bubble Chart of an IRR Time-Series

Year	IRR (%)	Valuation
0	0	0
1	−10	10
2	−30	40
3	−10	60
4	12	100
5	34	180
6	38	110
7	37	50
8	36	20
9	36	10
10	36	5

Of course, since there is no scale for size, the bubble is only meant to convey proportionality.

Two or more funds can be plotted together for easy comparison. Table 10.5 contains two funds, each with their own IRRs and valuations.

Figure 10.10 adds the second series to the chart.

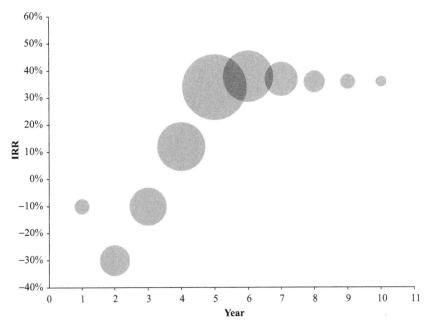

FIGURE 10.9 A bubble chart of an IRR time-series, showing a J-Curve.

TABLE 10.5 Data for a Bubble Chart that Includes Two Funds

Year	Fund A		Fund B	
	IRR (%)	Valuation	IRR (%)	Valuation
0	0	0	0	0
1	−10	10	−4	3
2	−30	40	−20	20
3	−10	60	−5	30
4	12	100	3	60
5	34	180	12	55
6	38	110	15	42
7	37	50	14	12
8	36	20	14	4
9	36	10	12	2
10	36	5	12	0

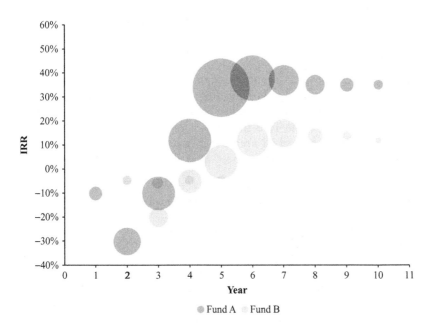

FIGURE 10.10 Bubble chart for two IRR time-series.

TABLE 10.6 Hypothetical Quartile Data

Vintage	1st Quartile (%)	2nd Quartile (%)	3rd Quartile (%)
2000	1	14	18
2001	5	15	23
2002	7	17	26
2003	6	12	24
2004	5	18	31
2005	9	19	27
2006	10	17	25

OVERLAYING CHART SERIES

In Chapter 8 you were introduced to quartiles, which are frequently used to compare funds. Charting quartile results can be a little challenging, but we present techniques here that we have found to be straightforward. The general approach is to combine two types of charts into one.

1. First lay down a background that represents quartile performance using Stacked Area charts.
2. Overlay these with scatter charts with the IRR values of your funds.

Plotting Quartiles

We begin with the following hypothetical data for quartile performance. Table 10.6 shows the upper boundary for these quartiles. The fourth quartile is anything above the third quartile and so is implied.

To put the data in Table 10.6 to work, it needs to be transformed a bit. The reason is that a stacked area chart is additive, and so we need to calculate the differences between these quartiles. For example, the 2nd

TABLE 10.7 Hypothetical Quartile Data Transformed for Plotting as a Stacked Area Chart

Vintage	1st Quartile Stack (%)	2nd Quartile Stack (%)	3rd Quartile Stack (%)
2000	1	13	4
2001	5	10	8
2002	7	10	9
2003	6	6	12
2004	5	13	13
2005	9	10	8
2006	10	7	8

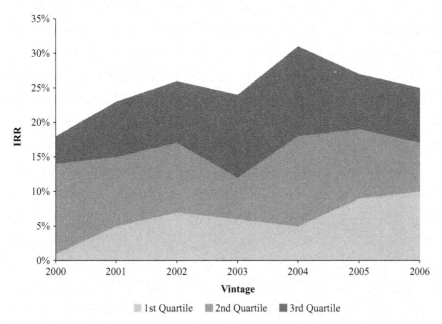

FIGURE 10.11 Plotting quartiles as stacked area charts as background.

quartile for vintage 2000 is stacked on top of the 1st quartile value. We need to compute the differences between the quartiles for the stacking to be accurate. The results are summarized in Table 10.7.

Plotting this is now straightforward. Figure 10.11 is not unlike a painting of quartile mountains in the mist, with the sky, appropriately, being the top quartile.

Next, we add in our vintage performance values separately. This data in Table 10.8 should be plotted as a scatter chart.

TABLE 10.8 Hypothetical Performance of a Portfolio to be Overlaid onto Quartiles

Vintage	My Return (%)
2000	19
2001	15
2002	12
2003	6
2004	19
2005	28
2006	35

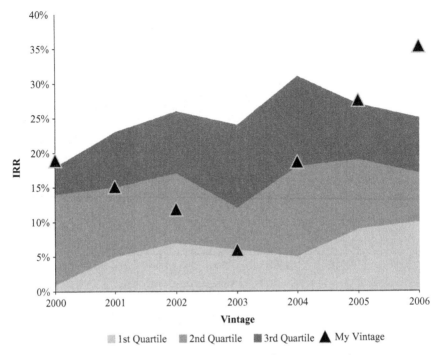

FIGURE 10.12   Portfolio performance data plotted against quartiles.

The final result, shown in Figure 10.12, is a composite chart, with the quartiles in the background and the values plotted against them.

Chapter 15 discusses how the number of funds in your portfolio affects how you ought to compare it to quartiles.

CONCLUSIONS

This chapter was all about empowering you to be creative with tabular data. Radar, bubble, and stacked area charts are just a few ways to visually summarize data in a meaningful way. These charts serve a very real purpose. They make the important data points stand out.

We will use some of these techniques to help simplify the presentation of data in coming chapters.

CHAPTER 11

The IRR and the Public Markets

Measuring and evaluating the performance of opportunistic investments requires techniques not commonly applied to more traditional continuous investments. The focus of performance analysis for opportunistic investments should be on the creation of value-added wealth relative to an appropriately specified benchmark. Solely relying on rates of return can produce misleading analysis and even provide managers not to act in the best long-term interest of their clients.
— Richards and Tierney, *Opportunistic Investing*, p. 20

This chapter introduces two measures: the Modified IRR, which removes the reinvestment rate assumption of the traditional IRR and has a conclusive result; and the Index Comparison Method, which computes an opportunity cost for private market investments.

MEASUREMENT INNOVATION

Standard measures, like multiples and the IRR, help you get a handle on the basic health of your private equity investments. This chapter builds on these measures to answer some deeper questions, without relying on external data.

In 1987, when Tom Judge of AT&T Investment Management Company was looking to compare private equity funds in his portfolio, he proposed grouping funds that started in the same year into the same comparison pool. Thus the *vintage year* comparison was born. The vintage year of a fund helps ground comparisons of its performance with funds that experienced the same economic conditions. A vintage year 2005 fund is likely to be very different from a vintage year 2000 fund. Grouping by vintage year helps avoid the traps we uncovered in Chapter 6 in the discussion of the time-zero IRR.

In 1992, when two of us (Messrs. Long and Nickels) were with The University of Texas Investment Management Company, we went looking for more objective measures for the private equity portfolio of the University. After not finding any we liked, we developed, presented to our colleagues, and published a new innovative technique that made public- and private-market returns comparable (Long and Nickels 1996).

Innovation born of necessity.

THE MODIFIED IRR

We start this discussion with some background into a particular technique that has more standing in academic circles than it does by practitioners. The modified IRR introduces the concept of modifying cash flow streams using specified rates to reduce complexity and arrive at a realistic and certain result. We then move on to more mainstream techniques.

Calculating a Modified IRR

Here is the process in a nutshell: shrink the contributions to a single capital outlay at time-zero. Grow the distributions to a single value, and add the valuation at the end date. Calculate the IRR, which because you are only dealing with two flows, is unambiguous.

Table 11.1 contains sample cash flows and the normal measures for a fund for this example. This fund has an IRR of 21.81 percent and TVPI of 1.67.

TABLE 11.1 Sample Data for a Fund

Fund A	
Year	Amount
0	−10
1	−15
2	−5
3	30
4	20
Paid-In	30
Total Value	50
Wealth	20
IRR	21.81%
TVPI	1.67

TABLE 11.2 Calculation of the Two Flows of a Modified IRR

Year	Flows	Present Value Factor	Future Value Factor	Present Value of Contributions	Future Value of Total Value
0	−10	1.0000		−10.00	
1	−15	0.9524		−14.29	
2	−5	0.9070		−4.54	
3	30		1.080		32.40
4	20		1.000		20.00
			Total	−28.82	52.40

If you have multiple contributions, they can be shrunk to a single outflow at time-zero by calculating their present value using a discount rate. The rate you choose to grow distributions is the reinvestment rate. In our example, we have chosen to use a discount rate of 5 percent and a reinvestment rate of 8 percent.

For the sake of illustration, we break down the calculation into the discrete steps shown in Table 11.2. For each contribution, we first calculate a present value factor. The present value factor is the number used to discount the contribution back to time zero. The future value factor is used to grow the distributions to the end date.

With these two modified cash flows in hand, it is a simple matter to create an IRR, the *modified IRR,* shown in Table 11.3.

In our example, the modified IRR of 16.11 percent is well below the IRR of 21.81 percent because the modified IRR assumes that distributions are reinvested at a lower rate.

INDEX RETURN COMPARISON METHOD (ICM)

With public equity, it is common to compare performance to an index. For Large Cap U.S. Stock Funds, the benchmark is often the S&P 500. For more

TABLE 11.3 Calculation of the Modified IRR

Year	Amount
0	−28.82
4	52.40
MIRR	16.11%

niche funds, the comparable index may be something like the NASDAQ 100 Technology Sector Index or the Dow Jones Consumer Goods Index. In private equity, the process of performance appraisal and comparison is cumbersome because there is no true standard against which performance can be compared.

First formalized in 1993 by Long and Nickels, the Index Comparison Method (ICM) is

> *a direct opportunity cost comparison of how net funds invested in the private investment portfolio would have performed had they been invested in the applicable stock index over the life of the particular investment.*

The ICM is also known as the Public Market Equivalent (PME). We prefer the term ICM because it better describes the methodology, which is not limited to the use of a public market index to calculate its results.

With the ICM, you model how a fund would have fared if its cash had been invested in a different investment vehicle. For example, what would have been the performance if the cash flows instead were invested in an index like the S&P 500 or Russell 3000? This measure and its variations can help you justify the existence of a private equity program.

THROW THE VALUATION FROM THE TRAIN

The only difference in the cash flows that are included in the calculation of the IRR and the IRR for the ICM (IRR_{ICM}) is the valuation. The valuation supplied by the GP is used in the calculation of the IRR. In calculating the IRR_{ICM}, the valuation supplied by the GP is ignored. Instead, we build up a valuation using only the cash flows and the index.

Build the ICM Valuation

Table 11.4 reflects cash flows and the IRR for a hypothetical fund. In keeping with our practice, we have intentionally simplified the dates and cash flows.

TABLE 11.4 Sample Data for the ICM Calculation

Date	Fund A Flow Type	Cash Flow
1 Jan 00	Capital Call	−10.00
1 Jan 01	Distribution	1.00
1 Jan 02	Valuation	10.00
	IRR	5.12%

TABLE 11.5 Sample Index for the ICM Calculation

Date	Index
1 Jan 00	100
1 Jan 01	105
1 Jan 02	120

TABLE 11.6 Calculation of the Valuation for the ICM Calculation

Cash Activity			Valuation$_{ICM}$			
Date	Amount	Index	Index Ratio Calculation	Index Ratio	Calculation	Valuation
1 Jan 00	−10	100		100%		10
1 Jan 01	1	105	(105/100)	105%	(105% * 10) −1	9.5
1 Jan 02		120	(120/105)	114%	114% * 9.5	10.86

But as you will see, we will need to use this data, particularly the dates, in new ways.

This example uses a hypothetical index that starts at 100 on 1 Jan 2000 and rises to 120 on 1 Jan 2002. This is shown in Table 11.5.

There are several ways to approach this process of creating the ICM valuation (Valuation$_{ICM}$). For simplicity, we have elected to use a running balance of the valuation at each cash flow date. Table 11.6 illustrates how you grow the Valuation$_{ICM}$ with every transaction.

As a reminder, contributions increase the valuation, and distributions decrease the valuation. When you have the Valuation$_{ICM}$, you calculate the IRR normally, but this is now the IRR$_{ICM}$. Table 11.7 compares the IRR and the IRR$_{ICM}$ using the actual cash flows and the new valuation.

The IRR of 5.12 percent is 4.18 percent lower than the IRR$_{ICM}$ of 9.30 percent. The market, as defined by the index we chose, did better with these

TABLE 11.7 Calculation of the IRR and the IRR$_{ICM}$

Date	Flow Type	Actual Amount	ICM Amount
1 Jan 00	Capital Call	−10.00	−10.00
1 Jan 01	Distribution	1.00	1.00
1 Jan 02	Valuation	10.00	10.86
	IRR	5.12%	9.30%

cash flows on these dates than did our manager. We call the difference between these two values the "IRR spread."

The IRR spread is comparable across funds and so allows you to objectively compare them. The IRR spread has been likened to a Rosetta Stone that can be used to compare two or more private equity investments to a common standard. The ICM methodology, an apples-to-apples comparison, is the only method that tells you whether the fund manager is beating the public market or the index of your choosing.

END OF INVESTMENT LIFE

To the simple question of "When does a private equity investment end?" the obvious answer is "When it is liquidated, of course." Here is a related question. When should the measurement of an investment end? When it is liquidated? Experience has taught us that you probably want to carefully consider this assumption.

Although a private equity partnership may carry assets on its books for a full term of 10 years (or longer if the partnership term is extended), the carrying value of the small amounts of remaining assets is important to the problem of performance measurement. Because it affects the $\text{Valuation}_{\text{ICM}}$, the end date is particularly important. With mature funds that report a small valuation, the index value continues to change and so changes the $\text{Valuation}_{\text{ICM}}$.

Figure 11.1, a chart based on an actual fund, illustrates the challenge. The solid line shows the IRR. The dotted line shows the IRR_{ICM} derived with the method just discussed.

The IRR_{ICM} exceeds the IRR at first, but at about year 3 they are approximately equal. The investment IRR then begins to outperform the IRR_{ICM} by a wide margin, but is gradually dragged down. Eventually, the IRR_{ICM} rises above the investment IRR, creating a negative IRR spread.

Supporting this, Figure 11.2 shows that after six and a half years into the partnership, the ratio of the valuation to paid-in is comparatively small, less than 20 percent. At that point the IRR spread begins to close. Without imposing a rule of some kind, the IRR spread will become negative, leaving a very different impression of the overall performance of the fund.

An approach to solving this is to pick a means to end the comparison. For example, you could end the exercise when the valuation becomes a small defined percentage of contributions or distributions (say 5 percent). In this example, an end of life rule would change the sign of the IRR spread. If the clock is stopped early, the IRR spread, measuring a more significant portion of assets, may be positive. It is up to you to decide how to end the comparison.

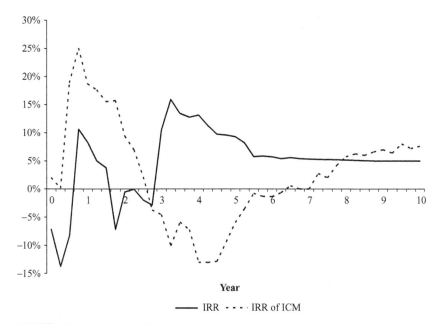

FIGURE 11.1 IRR and IRR$_{ICM}$ performance over time can reverse.

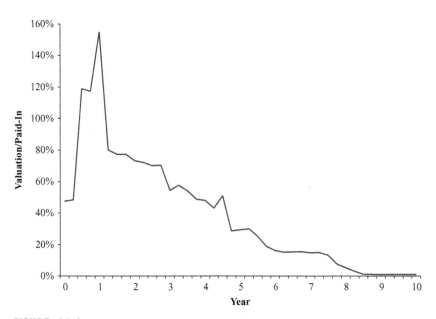

FIGURE 11.2 The ratio of valuation to paid-in (RVPI) capital over time diminishes.

NEGATIVE VALUATIONS

An index-based calculation can result in a negative Valuation$_{ICM}$. The Long and Nickels paper on the ICM (1996, p. 8) explains:

> *If a private investment greatly outperforms the index because it makes frequent, large distributions, it is possible for the final value determined by the index comparison to be negative. In effect, the frequent large withdrawals from the index result in a net short position in the index comparison.*

The ICM allows the Valuation$_{ICM}$ to be less than zero. This will happen when a distribution is greater than the Valuation$_{ICM}$ on the date of the cash flow, and this is relatively common when a very successful deal is exited.

For example, if an investment of $500 is made during the first year and the company is then liquidated for $4,000 during year 3, the Valuation$_{ICM}$ will likely be negative. More specifically, the $500 would not have been able to grow to $4,000 by year 3 (a TVPI of 8) in the public markets. This results in a negative (in other words, a short) position in the index because the massive liquidation is treated as a sale and the size of the sale exceeds the Valuation$_{ICM}$. In effect, you are selling more than you have.

This is understandable but problematic—particularly when you have two minutes to explain it to a board of directors at a quarterly meeting. Our recommendation is to be informed of the possibility of negative valuations as an issue and be ready to pull out a one-page explanation at presentation time when questioned.

There are people who have produced variations on this theme (Rouvinez 2004; Kaplan and Schoar 2005). Some have specifically attempted to address the negative valuation problem. There are also people who have studied the relationship between the original and the variations (Long 2008).

ANOTHER RADAR MEASURE

Of all of the measurements we have introduced, one of the most telling is the IRR spread. To recap, calculate the IRR, calculate the IRR$_{ICM}$, and subtract the two. This difference is the IRR spread. Now we can add this important measure to the radar chart that we built in Chapter 9.

As we have noted, picking the right scale for any measure is important. In the case of an individual fund, the IRR spread can be quite large. For example, if you are measuring a private equity fund with a modest return

TABLE 11.8 Range of IRR Spreads for a Radar Chart

Criteria	Low Value	High Value
IRR Spread	−30%	+30%

when the quoted markets are declining, the IRR spread can be a chasm. If you are measuring the performance of a group or portfolio of funds, you would expect that the spread to be relatively small.

Table 11.8 provides a reasonable range for many IRR spreads that we have encountered.

For instance, for individual funds a reasonable spread is from −30 percent to +30 percent. Adding a sixth attribute to our chart, as shown in Figure 11.3, makes the radar chart in the shape of a hexagon.

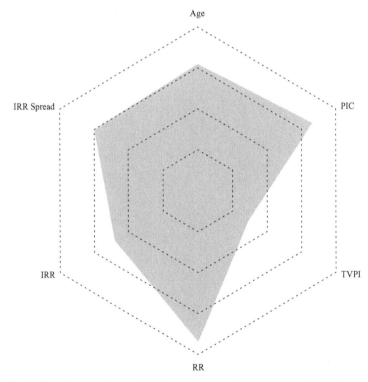

FIGURE 11.3 The IRR Spread adds another very important attribute for assessing the performance of a manager.

For purposes of illustration, we used an IRR spread that shows that the investment beats the IRR_{ICM} by 15 percent, outperforming the opportunity cost return of the same amounts invested in the public market by a wide margin.

CONCLUSIONS

The term "benchmark" is very ambiguous in this asset class. Some think of it as a universe comparison, others think of it as the Index Comparison Method, and some others have completely different approaches. Regardless of your stance on this subject, the ICM has a place in your analytical toolbox. We are big fans of the ICM, not just because two of us created it, but because it has many practical applications and it provides a strong foundation for measuring opportunity cost.

To see how the ICM can be used in more complex analyses, see Appendix G, Correlation and Opportunity Costs.

Topics on Risk

Performance Attribution

We combine time-zero and neutral weighting as a means to assess how timing and the size of commitments have affected the portfolio's performance.

WHAT ABOUT HARRY?

The day had arrived. A few members of the team from the Burgiss Group were at a new client, the investment arm of a U.S.-based consumer products company. For several weeks, we had worked at converting a jumble of spreadsheets into our database format. The job was done, and we had just finished installing our private equity portfolio management system onto their network. They were particularly anxious to get a look at the overall portfolio performance—for the first time. It seemed that no one had been able to figure out how to get a portfolio IRR from these spreadsheets.

At their urging, we fired up the reporting module and ran a performance report that showed the IRR of their entire private equity program. When the report came off the printer, they all stared at it. Silence. The result was clearly not what they were expecting. "This can't be right," one investment officer said. "We can check it," we said. "Wait," another intervened. "What if we run it without Harry?" she asked. "Great idea," someone else responded. "Can you run the portfolio again without Harry's investments?" We did. And their overall return, and their spirits, sank further.

The bad performance of the portfolio clearly wasn't only Harry's fault. Whose was it?

WEIGHTING DECISIONS

Constructing a portfolio takes time. Along the way are thousands of decisions. What opportunities came your way? Which deals did you pass on? Why? More importantly, which did you choose? How much did you commit to each of them? Again, why? Some portfolios have hundreds of investments spanning 20 years or more. An archaeological dig might reveal layers upon layers of decisions. Who did what and why?

Public market research provides inspiration in our attempts to answer these questions. There has been for some time the idea of measuring how investment selection and timing have affected portfolio performance (Brinson, Hood, and Beebower 1986). Investment selection involves your choices of the positions you have elected to take. Timing is a matter of when you get in and out of these investments. We believe this discussion to be the first application of these types of ideas to the private markets.

Performance attribution is a quantitative approach to assessing the impact of these kinds of decisions—but it won't answer all of your questions about how a portfolio was constructed.

Still, the first of the questions it can answer is how much of the return is attributable to the sizes of the positions, the commitment amounts, chosen by the portfolio manager. The *weighting effect* can be calculated at various levels (company, fund investment, vintage, sub-asset class, asset class, and so on) of the portfolio (Long and Nickels 2002). Take note that this is a departure from our previous discussions. This exercise will focus primarily on the amounts you committed to funds, not the direct effects of their cash flows.

As usual, we start with a simple example.

Example of Neutral Weighting

You are overseeing a private equity portfolio that made two investments six years ago. Their cash flows are shown in Table 12.1.

Your little portfolio consists of investments in two funds. You invested €10 over the course of five years in Fund A. You invested €30 all at once in Fund B, for a total of €40 for the portfolio. To neutrally weight these investments is in effect to pretend that the amounts you invested in both funds were the same, and so proportionally adjust the cash flows that occurred over their lives.

For this portfolio, one way to neutrally weight it is to meet somewhere in the middle. In this case, instead of commitments of €10 and €30, each would have a commitment of €20.

TABLE 12.1 Cash Flows and Performance for Two Hypothetical Funds and Portfolio

Year	Fund A	Fund B	Portfolio
0	−2	−30	−32
1	−2	0	−2
2	−2	0	−2
3	−2	0	−2
4	−2	0	−2
5	30	39	69
Paid-In	10	30	40
Total Value	30	39	69
Wealth	20	9	29
IRR (%)	39.18	5.39	12.08
TVPI	3.00	1.30	1.73

Note: The commitment to Fund B is three times the size of Fund A.

The second step is to change the cash flows of each fund to reflect their neutral weight. Since Fund A was doubled, double all of its cash flows; since Fund B was divided by 1.5, divide all of its cash flows by 1.5. These changes, and the effects that they have on the portfolio, are shown in Table 12.2.

By neutrally weighting the portfolio, the IRR would have been 20.17 percent, which is significantly higher than its actual performance of

TABLE 12.2 Neutral Weighting Adjusts Scale of Cash Flows

Year	Fund A	Fund B	Portfolio
0	−4	−20	−24
1	−4	0	−4
2	−4	0	−4
3	−4	0	−4
4	−4	0	−4
5	60	26	86
Paid-In	20	20	40
Total Value	60	26	86
Wealth	40	6	46
IRR (%)	39.18	5.39	20.17
TVPI	3.00	1.30	2.15

12.08 percent. This is bad news, and you could argue that wrong choices were made. For whatever reason, your investment team made different-size bets on these two funds, and they lost the bets, right?

Hold on. This is one of the principal dangers of this analysis—a conclusion like this is valid only if your team had the opportunity to invest equal amounts into these funds and there were no other constraining factors. Of course, there are always many factors, big and small, that play into final decisions about how much to commit to any fund. Some of these factors are clearly beyond the control of the investment team.

Notice that this doubling, tripling, or halving of any complete set of cash flows for a commitment has no effect whatsoever on the performance of a single commitment. The TVPI and the IRR of your individual commitments are unchanged after the neutral weighting. This should make intuitive sense because we have multiplied or divided everything proportionally. This also should make sense because these raw performance measures are the same for all investors in a fund, whether they have committed €10 or €20 or €100. Realize, too, that the amount that you choose to scale the funds to neutralize them is arbitrary. We chose to make it €20, but we could have made each commitment €100 or €2.

Since the weighting of funds is based on paid-in capital, in the case of partially-realized funds you should exclude funds that are too young or others that may skew the results. For example, you might want to exclude a new $100 million commitment to a fund which has called only $5 million of capital. Use your judgment.

In Chapter 8, we stated that averaging the IRR in any capacity is a mistake. We alluded to a better way to neutralize relative magnitude of the underlying funds. This scaling process is it.

PORTFOLIO CHANGES

Table 12.3 summarizes the differences between the actual and the neutrally weighted portfolio. This difference is called the *weighting effect*.

TABLE 12.3   The Performance Difference between Actual Weights and Neutral Weights Is Called the Weighting Effect

	Actual Weights	Neutral Weights	Weighting Effect
Wealth	29	46	−17
IRR (%)	12.68	20.17	−7.48
TVPI	1.73	2.15	−0.43

Had your portfolio been neutrally weighted, the portfolio's IRR would have been 7.48 percent higher, TVPI would have been 0.43 percent higher, and wealth would have been 17 higher. The rough conclusion is that although this portfolio made money, it could have made more money if it was neutrally weighted.

FOR THE SKEPTICS

Broadly speaking, this type of analysis is meant to help investment professionals understand how relative weighting affects the outcome of a portfolio. Neutrally weighting the portfolio helps identify strengths and weaknesses of a portion of the decision-making process. By running this analysis, the portfolio manager may be able to see how those decisions have benefited or harmed performance. Analysis of this kind may take courage, for it has the potential to expose weakness in areas where only strength is perceived. If your performance record is stellar, why would you want anyone to know that it could have been better? This is dangerous thinking. As hard as objective information is to take at times, it is almost always valuable.

Some professionals will argue that it is impossible in practice to neutrally weight the portfolio. We do not disagree. Going back to the example, assume that Fund A was a small venture fund, Fund B was a buyout fund, and the numbers in the table are in millions. You could argue that you fought just to get a €10 million allocation to the venture fund and you could not have gotten a bigger slice. It also might be argued that the high minimums of some of the buyout funds would preclude you from being able to make smaller commitments.

There are a couple of answers to this concern. The first is straightforward. If it is impossible to make neutrally weighted commitments across the various asset classes, then perform the analysis on each class separately. More specifically, compare the actual buyout portfolio to a neutrally-weighted buyout portfolio. Do this with all classes in your portfolio. Grouping by investment type or sub-asset class makes the argument moot.

The second answer is more abstract. Neutrally weighting a portfolio allows you to calculate the cost (or value) of *access*. In private equity terms, access is the entree to the fund that doesn't take on new investors, or the one that may grant smaller and smaller allocations to their long-standing investors. Access is needed if a fund is oversubscribed or has the same investor list time after time. In short, these are funds that have draw, but many investors tend to forget that although some funds are popular, not all popular funds are good.

If you have small allocations to these funds and they perform as expected, neutrally weighting your portfolio will likely tell you that you are doing a bad job, and you will be faced with the question: "What can I do to convince these managers that I deserve a bigger slice?" Yet if the performance of your portfolio is little changed by neutrally weighting it, you may discover that these small allocations to "top-tier" funds play very little part in creating wealth. And since all funds have administrative costs associated with them, you may decide, without sentimentality, that the prestige of these small allocations is simply not worth the trouble.

MULTIDIMENSIONAL ANALYSIS

We have thus far looked at weighting a portfolio by a single dimension. This offers the advantage of simplicity. There is no reason that prevents you from applying this technique at several levels at once. Often the difficulty of this approach is presenting it well and then understanding its implications.

For example, you can do a neutrally weighted analysis of a portfolio of funds by sub-asset allocation. If your portfolio has 70 percent in buyouts and 30 percent in venture, you could scale the portfolio so that you have 50 percent buyout and 50 percent venture. What would the portfolio performance look like then?

One way of approaching this analysis is to treat each vintage year as a separate composite. After you have performed this analysis, there will be two data points from the neutral weighting for each vintage year. The first data point is how investment weightings have affected the vintage's performance. The second data point is how sub-asset class weightings affect the vintage's performance.

The challenge is in representing this information, and this is where your knowledge of bubble charts, introduced in Chapter 10, comes in handy. Figure 12.1 shows a chart of vintages that illustrates weighting effects at the investment and sub-asset class levels.

In Figure 12.1 each vintage year is represented by a bubble that is proportional to the capital invested. The horizontal position of each bubble is determined by how much investment weighting benefited or harmed that vintage's IRR. Similarly, the vintage year bubble's vertical position is determined by how much sub-asset class weighting benefited or harmed the IRR of the vintage.

The ideal outcome would be that every vintage would appear in the upper right, quadrant I. In this example, there are only a handful of vintages that end up in that quadrant. Quadrants II and IV represent mixed results. If the analysis uncovers a large number of vintages in quadrant III, the portfolio manager knows that relative weightings are adversely impacting

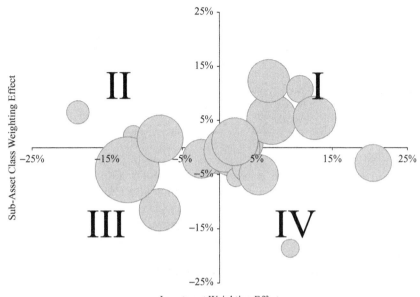

FIGURE 12.1 A bubble chart of vintages that illustrates weighting effects at the investment and sub-asset class levels for the IRR.

performance. Specifically, the vintages in quadrant III reflect poor sub-asset allocation (more capital invested in the vintage's lower-performing sub-asset classes) and poor investment selection (more money invested in the vintage's underperforming funds).

NEUTRALLY-WEIGHTED, TIME-ZERO IRR ANALYSIS (LONG AND NICKELS 2002)

Neutrally weighting a portfolio helps isolate the causes of successful or unsuccessful performance. In Chapter 7, we introduced the time-zero IRR to help remove the bias that may result from early winners or losers. We represented this type of IRR as IRR_{TZ}.

Another measure, the neutrally-weighted, time-zero IRR (IRR_{NWTZ}) isn't just a result—it is part of an analytical method that calculates the permutations of neutral weighting and time-zero and uses them to isolate the effects of timing and weighting on an investment or portfolio.

The sequence, or the order in which investments occur, is a matter of luck, not repeatable skill. If you recall from Chapter 7, the sequence does

TABLE 12.4 Hypothetical Results of Various Permutations of Time-Zero and Neutral Weighting of the IRR

Weight	Time	Abbreviation	IRR (%)
Neutral	Zero	IRR_{NWTZ}	30
Actual	Zero	IRR_{TZ}	24
Neutral	Actual	IRR_{NW}	31
Actual	Actual	IRR	35

not have an effect on wealth outcome of a portfolio, but it does affect its IRR (see Table 7.13). In contrast, the amounts you choose to commit to particular investments, vintages, or sub-asset classes is something over which you have control. Allocating these weights is a skill. The IRR_{NWTZ} analysis can be used for both internal and external comparisons. Within a portfolio, this measure serves as a mechanism to determine a portfolio manager's contribution to performance and further breaks it down into the sequence and weighting effects.

IRR Comparisons

Let's do an example using the results for a hypothetical portfolio in Table 12.4 for which we have four measures, the neutrally-weighted, time-zero IRR, the time-zero IRR, the neutrally weighted IRR, and the actual IRR.

Once you have all of these measures in hand, it is a matter of subtraction to come up with several key measures. The first, the Weighting Effect, is the difference between the time-zero and the neutrally-weighted time-zero IRRs. This measure takes out the effect of the timing bias of the IRR so it can exclusively focus on the weightings. The Sequence Effect is a measure of the manager's luck, in that luck is the order in which events have occurred. The Sequence Effect is the difference between the actual IRR and the time-zero IRR.

With subtraction, we are able to determine the results in Table 12.5.

TABLE 12.5 Summarized Results of Weighting and Sequencing Effects

Measure	Measure of	Formula	Result (%)
Weighting Effect	Skill	$IRR_{TZ} - IRR_{NWTZ}$	−6
Sequence Effect	Luck	$IRR - IRR_{TZ}$	11
Manager's Contribution			5

Although the contribution of this manager is positive, the added return was from the sequence of the investments, which was out of the manager's control. Moreover, the weighting effect, something that the manager can control, is negative.

This analytical method, which is built on the various permutations of time-zero and neutrally-weighted IRRs, can serve as a means to compare portfolios in their purest forms. More specifically, this type of IRR analysis makes it possible to isolate the effects of weighting and timing, thus stripping away much of the noise resulting from the nature of the IRR computation itself.

CONCLUSIONS

Analyzing the determinants of portfolio performance has long been available to public market portfolio managers. The methodology we put forth in this chapter is the first attempt that we are aware of to apply similar principles to the private markets. It is particularly useful because portfolio managers are able to deconstruct how the sequence and weighting of investments have affected the portfolio's outcome. Most importantly, measuring the weighting effect will inform portfolio managers whether the sizes of the commitments that they are making are effective.

CHAPTER 13

The Concentration of Wealth

This chapter introduces simple techniques to uncover how wealth was generated in a portfolio.

WHERE IS THE WEALTH?

As we have seen, measuring wealth on individual funds can be enlightening, but in this chapter we introduce and focus on techniques that help you discover the concentration of wealth in your portfolio.

A fund may have a great IRR and superb investment multiple, but what effect did the fund have on your portfolio? If the commitment was for $5 million and your portfolio is $2 billion, did it create significant wealth? These questions are answerable. With some simple techniques, you can compute how concentrated the wealth of the portfolio has been to help shape your decisions going forward (Conner 2006).

In its simplest form, concentration analysis focuses on the percentage of investments that made money, that is, where the total value is greater than the amount paid in. This process becomes more interesting when you break it down further to uncover how wealth was accumulated. Did a handful of investments carry the entire portfolio? If they did, what does that mean about the risk of the portfolio? As with nearly everything we have discussed thus far, this type of analysis can then be extended to companies, managers, vintages, and sub-asset classes.

DISTILLING PERFORMANCE

Our task is to determine which investments in a private equity portfolio contributed the most value and which investments destroyed value. As a reminder, we refer to this value simply as *wealth*, the total value less the amount you paid in.

$$\text{Wealth} = \text{Total Value} - \text{Paid-In}$$

Early on in this book we described the wealth of a private equity investment as simply the sum of its realized and unrealized gains—what you have received and are likely to receive above your cost. Some may feel uncomfortable defining wealth as anything but that which you have received. This analysis is indifferent to how you define wealth and can as easily be used on only the amounts you have realized.

This type of analysis is built on the belief that the more sources of wealth the better. We introduce this analysis with the simplest form, actual wealth. We then complicate things a bit by employing the ICM to understand how opportunity costs affected the generation of wealth.

When analyzing the concentration of wealth, you are looking to answer several fundamental questions:

- What percentage of investments made money? Lost money?
- What percentage of investments beat the index? Lost to it?
- How diverse are the drivers of wealth?
- Was the portfolio consistent over time?

THE LORENZ CURVE

The best way to visualize the result is with help from Max Otto Lorenz, who developed his namesake chart in 1905 to plot income distribution. Figure 13.1 shows perfect equality, with each axis being a percentage.

Lorenz contrasted the actual distribution of income in the United States to one of "perfect equality" which represents all conditions where y = x on a graph. In his case, an example of perfect equality might be "the bottom 30 percent of households have 30 percent of the total income." For our purposes, it would be "the top-performing 10 percent of investments generated 10 percent of the total wealth generated by the portfolio." The

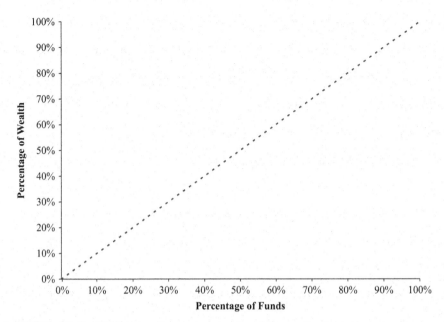

FIGURE 13.1 The Lorenz Curve showing "perfect equality."

perfect equality curve serves as a reference against which to compare actual results.

To plot a Lorenz curve that represents the cumulative distribution of wealth for your private equity investments, start with a spreadsheet with up-to-date contributions, distributions, and valuations for each investment. From there it is a matter of simple addition and sorting. Here are the preparatory steps:

1. Compute Wealth: Subtract Paid-In from Total Value for each investment.
2. Sum the wealth generated by all investments: This is the *Total Wealth* for the portfolio.
3. Add a column to compute *Percent of Total Wealth*: For each investment simply divide wealth by total wealth.
4. Sort the results in descending order on the *Percent of Total Wealth*.
5. Compute *Cumulative Wealth* by creating a running total of the *Percent of Total Wealth* for each investment.

CONCENTRATION OF WEALTH

The following topics provide a detailed example of how to perform this analysis. In keeping with presenting simple examples, following is a hypothetical portfolio of 20 funds that we made conveniently add up to a total wealth of 100. The 20 funds are shown in Table 13.1. We compute wealth and then sort the funds by wealth from highest to lowest. We also made the fund names anonymous, assigning them numbers.

From here we sum the wealth, add a percent of wealth column, dividing wealth by total wealth. Then we add a column with the running total of cumulative wealth and finally add a column for a perfect equality portfolio where each investment contributed the same amount to the total wealth. For this example, we made calculations easy. Since there are 20 investments, each fund should represent $100/20 = 5$ percent of total wealth in the perfect equality case. Table 13.2 shows the completed calculations.

The cumulative distribution of wealth in your portfolio can and probably will exceed 100 percent, which occurs when your portfolio contains investments that lost or (if interim results are computed) show signs of losing money. This is in effect, negative wealth, where you have contributed more to a fund than the total value it has generated.

Graphing this with a line chart is straightforward. A count of the funds plotted in percentiles is along the x-axis. The two data series correspond to the cumulative distribution and perfect equality column. The result is shown in Figure 13.2. Our example portfolio is fairly typical and shows that 75 percent of the wealth of the portfolio was generated by only 25 percent of the funds, and that 15 percent of the funds actually destroy wealth.

TABLE 13.1 Data for Concentration of Wealth Analysis

Fund	Wealth (TV – PI)	Fund	Wealth (TV – PI)
1	18	11	5
2	16	12	3
3	15	13	2
4	15	14	1
5	11	15	0
6	9	16	0
7	9	17	−1
8	7	18	−5
9	6	19	−7
10	5	20	−9

TABLE 13.2   Concentration of Wealth Example Data

Fund	Actual Wealth (TV − PI)	% of Total Wealth	Cumulative Distribution (%)	Perfect Equality Portfolio (%)
1	18	18	18	5
2	16	16	34	10
3	15	15	49	15
4	15	15	64	20
5	11	11	75	25
6	9	9	84	30
7	9	9	93	35
8	7	7	100	40
9	6	6	106	45
10	5	5	111	50
11	5	5	116	55
12	3	3	119	60
13	2	2	121	65
14	1	1	122	70
15	0	0	122	75
16	0	0	122	80
17	−1	−1	121	85
18	−5	−5	116	90
19	−7	−7	109	95
20	−9	−9	100	100

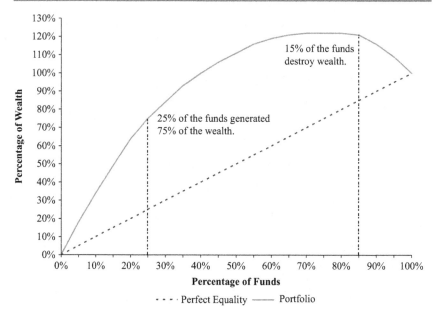

FIGURE 13.2   Concentration of wealth for a hypothetical portfolio of funds.

As you can see, working through this exercise can be revealing, high-lighting the real drivers of wealth of a portfolio. We said at the outset that this exercise used funds, but how would this work if we wanted to analyze vintage years? The analysis would be precisely the same. Instead of this data representing funds, you would aggregate these measures by vintage year.

We recommend you do the vintage year analysis as an exercise. Early on in this book we noted that the commitment to a consistent program of investing in private equity is one of the ingredients to success. Here is what we said:

Get cold feet, skip a year, and you may destroy all of your hard work.

This is what we meant: often one or two vintage years can drive the performance of an entire private equity portfolio. By measuring concentration of wealth, you determine the extent to which this is true for your portfolio.

ADDING A PUBLIC MARKET COMPARISON

This next step takes us a little deeper. We want to measure the concentration of the wealth that was generated above and beyond its opportunity cost. As you saw in Chapter 10, the Index Comparison Method (ICM) calculates an opportunity cost for investments. In that analysis, we focused on the IRR and the IRR_{ICM}. We introduced the IRR Spread, the difference between the two, to inform you how well you fared against the public markets. In this analysis, we compare the wealth generated in the private market to the public market and then summarize how that wealth is distributed across a portfolio.

Concentration of Wealth Using the ICM

For purposes of illustration, we use the same 20 funds as before. For the sake of comparison, we will need to differentiate between the wealth created for each fund, the Actual Wealth, and the $Wealth_{ICM}$.

To simplify this narrative, we will not walk through the creation of the $Wealth_{ICM}$, calculated with $(Valuation_{ICM} + D - PI)$. Simply accept these hypothetical results at face value. Table 13.3 shows the result and Figure 13.3 is a graphical representation.

These hypothetical funds are an undefined mix. They could be from different vintage years, be venture or buyout, or have different strategies. Our ICM reference indexes could be, for example, the S&P 500 or the Russell 3000. The difference between the actual wealth created and the wealth calculated with the ICM is the *incremental wealth*. Table 13.4 shows the incremental wealth for each fund.

TABLE 13.3 Actual Wealth and Wealth
Calculated with the ICM

Fund	Wealth	Wealth$_{ICM}$
1	18	14
2	16	−5
3	15	12
4	15	5
5	11	4
6	9	−3
7	9	−4
8	7	3
9	6	−1
10	5	1
11	5	−3
12	3	2
13	2	9
14	1	4
15	0	−2
16	0	−3
17	−1	−4
18	−5	3
19	−7	10
20	−9	−2

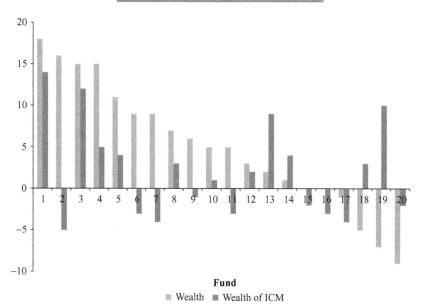

Fund

▨ Wealth   ▧ Wealth of ICM

FIGURE 13.3 Actual Wealth vs. Wealth$_{ICM}$ for 20 hypothetical funds.

TABLE 13.4 Data for Concentration of Wealth Calculated with the ICM

Fund	Incremental Wealth	% of Total Wealth	Cumulative Distribution (%)	Perfect Equality (%)
1	14	35	35	5
3	12	30	65	10
19	10	25	90	15
13	9	23	113	20
4	5	13	125	25
5	4	10	135	30
14	4	10	145	35
8	3	8	153	40
18	3	8	160	45
12	2	5	165	50
10	1	3	168	55
9	−1	−3	165	60
15	−2	−5	160	65
20	−2	−5	155	70
6	−3	−8	148	75
11	−3	−8	140	80
16	−3	−8	133	85
7	−4	−10	123	90
17	−4	−10	113	95
2	−5	−13	100	100

The chart shown in Figure 13.4 has a steeper ascent and a longer, steeper drop-off—fewer funds contributed to incremental wealth and more detracted from it. Once the ICM is applied, the concentration of wealth in our portfolio changed for the worse. Fully 75 percent of the incremental wealth originates from just 12 percent of the funds, more than halving the previous result. And 45 percent of the funds now destroy incremental wealth.

CONCLUSIONS

Knowing how your portfolio's wealth is concentrated enables you to quantify the costs of missed opportunities. Missed opportunities come in many forms. Maybe you didn't re-up with a top-tier manager, or your board prohibited you from investing during a market downturn, or you didn't take a

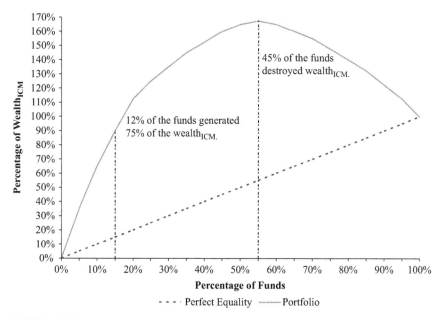

FIGURE 13.4 Concentration of Wealth using the ICM for a hypothetical portfolio of 20 funds.

meeting with an emerging manager. These things happen. But it is valuable to reveal how these types of events can affect the portfolio.

We suspect that some portfolio managers may become alarmed by the concentration that exists within their portfolios, but by uncovering these details you will be better able to structure the portfolio so that it generates wealth from more sources. In our experience, less-concentrated portfolios tend to be better diversified.

CHAPTER 14

The Diversification of Portfolios

The Count has an obsessive love of counting (arithmomania); he will count anything and everything, regardless of size, amount, or how much annoyance he is causing the other Muppets or human cast.
—Wikipedia

This chapter introduces an overlooked attribute of a portfolio of funds, its diversification as measured by the number of funds, and discusses why this matters.

COUNT MATTERS

Building a portfolio takes on a rhythm all its own. At first this tempo is halting, as the team invests in its first funds. Closings occur. The first capital is called. Reports arrive. Annual meetings are announced. The beat picks up as new investments are made, layering activity on activity. Calendars begin to fill, tasks demand daily attention, and the more you invest, the faster the tempo and the more the work. But beyond this operational activity, there are other more subtle differences that the sheer number of funds create.

Is a portfolio of 20 investments fundamentally different from a portfolio of 200? How does the number of strategies, vintages, and other characteristics of a portfolio affect your overall return? We believe that the count of investments matters but that most private equity practitioners simply lack awareness about this topic. However, there have been some attempts at studying how the number of funds affects performance outcomes (Rouvinez and Kubr 2003). This chapter explores a methodology to perform an analysis of diversification with your own data, but its applicability extends much further. The question we begin with is this:

Should the number of funds in the portfolio impact how you compare it to a universe?

WARNING: SOME PROGRAMMING AHEAD

This chapter departs from our do-it-yourself theme a bit. To simply understand why we think that counts are important, read on. But if you are interested in attempting to do what we illustrate here, you will want to brush up on your programming skills. As well, for the first time in this text, we are tapping into a database we have assembled. We do not believe that the composition of this data makes a difference in the overall points we are trying to illustrate.

ONE FUND, TWO FUNDS, THREE FUNDS, FOUR

A relatively easy starting point for a diversification analysis is to perform a simulation to understand how the number of investments affects outcomes. Before launching headlong into this analysis, it is good to first get an idea of how many combinations, that is, unique sets of funds, there are for a given sample.

How Many Hands in a Deck?

To give our exercise this scope, we introduce another little-used function from Excel, COMBIN, which computes the number of combinations of a pair of two integers. Let's first use COMBIN to get a useless fact with which to impress your friends at parties. If you draw five cards from a 52 card deck, the COMBIN function gives you the number of possible hands:

$$COMBIN(52,5) = 2,598,960$$

Each hand is equally likely.

If you want to simulate a portfolio that contains 2 funds, and your own data sample has 25 funds to choose from, there are 300 possible portfolio-of-two combinations from your data.

$$COMBIN(25,2) = 300$$

TABLE 14.1 The Possible Combinations of a "Portfolio" of Two Funds Drawn from Different Sample Sizes

Sample Size	Possible Combinations
25	300
50	1,225
100	4,950
200	19,900
400	79,800
800	319,600
1,600	1,279,200

This is manageable, but this manageability doesn't last. To give you some perspective, Table 14.1 shows how many unique portfolios of only two funds exist in different-sized data samples.

The numbers get exponentially larger when you start to ask questions about larger portfolios. For example, if you want all of the combinations from sampling 25 unique funds from a database of 800 funds, the number of combinations is:

$$\text{COMBIN}(800,25) = 166,745,878,313,166,000,000,000,000,000,000,000,000,000,000$$

Until supercomputing lends us sufficient processing power, most portfolios should use a reasonable threshold for the sampling size. We typically limit our sampling of the various combinations to 1,000, but for this example we've simulated 65,000 portfolios.

Step 1: Construct Portfolios

To begin, randomly sample two funds from a data set, store those cash flows, and repeat this process until your sampling limit is reached. Then, randomly sample three funds, store, and repeat. You get the picture.

Step 2: Compute Outcomes

The next step is to create measurements: that is, the outcomes for each simulated portfolio. Since this exercise is for illustration, we use representative data that we have assembled, and measure the investment multiple (TVPI).

TABLE 14.2 Quartiles Based on Simulation of Portfolios Containing Different Counts of Funds

Count of Funds	Min	Q1	Median	Q3	Max	Standard Deviation
1	0.00	0.90	1.25	1.85	42.36	2.82
2	0.00	1.01	1.34	1.82	40.54	1.98
3	0.01	1.08	1.39	1.81	37.05	1.51
4	0.07	1.13	1.41	1.80	25.91	1.20
5	0.13	1.17	1.43	1.80	21.67	1.00
6	0.23	1.19	1.45	1.79	16.85	0.87
7	0.31	1.22	1.46	1.78	12.57	0.76
8	0.33	1.24	1.47	1.78	11.76	0.70
9	0.38	1.26	1.48	1.78	10.35	0.65
10	0.43	1.27	1.49	1.78	9.32	0.60
11	0.52	1.28	1.49	1.77	8.91	0.57
12	0.52	1.29	1.50	1.77	8.60	0.53
13	0.58	1.31	1.50	1.76	7.90	0.50
14	0.55	1.31	1.51	1.76	7.64	0.48
15	0.57	1.32	1.51	1.76	7.29	0.46
16	0.64	1.33	1.52	1.76	7.05	0.44
17	0.66	1.34	1.52	1.75	6.83	0.42
18	0.67	1.34	1.52	1.75	7.03	0.41
19	0.68	1.35	1.52	1.75	5.87	0.39
20	0.72	1.36	1.53	1.75	5.84	0.38

Our simulation created portfolios containing up to 20 funds from a database of over 1,200 funds, sampling each count of funds 65,000 times.

Step 3: Create Quartiles

We of course are not interested in plotting or attempting to discern trends from over a million data points. Instead, we took these outcomes and created quartiles from them by sorting and ranking. We also computed standard deviations (see Table 14.2).

Step 4: Plot Results

Figure 14.1 plots these TVPI quartiles against the number of funds sampled and a picture of how the count of funds influenced return emerges.

As can easily be seen from Figure 14.1, the fewer funds sampled, the higher the top quartile. This should be enough incentive for you to compare your portfolio to universes based on this methodology. Why? If you

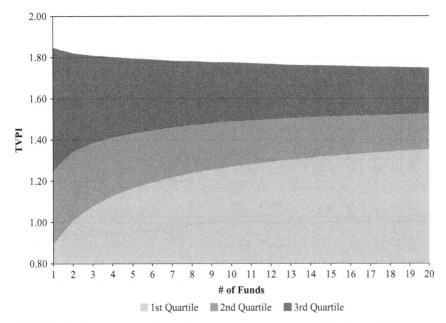

FIGURE 14.1 TVPI quartile performance for each count of funds sampled.

compare your portfolio to the one-asset portfolio that Thomson Reuters or Cambridge provide, you are setting yourself up to disappoint your board. Why make life harder on yourself?

Maximums

The conclusion that the top quartile threshold decreases with the count of the funds is also supported by plotting the maximum TVPI achievable against the fund count, as shown in Figure 14.2.

The highest achievable performance drops precipitously as you add funds and eventually the slope of the curve begins to flatten out. The lowest quartile rises as you add more funds into the portfolio indicating that you can never be as bad as the worst portfolio in the single fund case. Figure 14.3 plots the minimum TVPI at each count.

What About Variability?

Variability of outcomes is an important area to explore in private equity. By using the data we collected from this exercise, we are able to compute

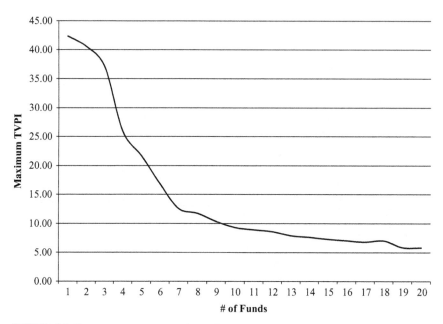

FIGURE 14.2   Maximum TVPI of portfolio decreases when count increases.

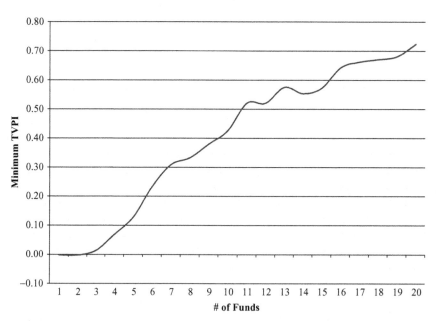

FIGURE 14.3   Minimum TVPI of portfolio rises when count increases.

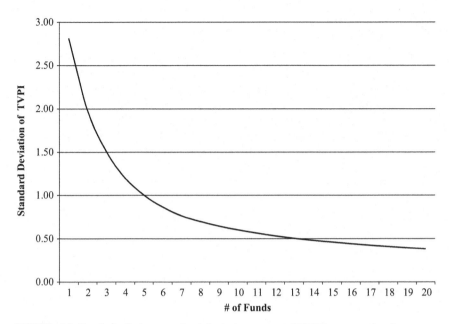

FIGURE 14.4 A declining standard deviation curve of TVPI as more funds are added to a portfolio.

standard deviations of the TVPIs for each of the counts. The results are shown in Figure 14.4.

As you would expect, the standard deviation of the outcomes drops off dramatically as more funds are added and eventually flattens out. This mimics much of what has been documented in the public markets. Here we see that a portfolio containing 20 funds is quite different from a two-fund portfolio.

THE OUTCOME OF A PORTFOLIO OF ONE

This simple approach allows you to compare your pick of a single fund to the rest of the herd with ease and is great for comparing the track record of a manager for the usual purposes of due diligence. However, as you have seen, a portfolio of funds is not comparable to a single-fund universe. With a portfolio, you are not betting on one horse, you are betting on a group of horses. The bet you spread on 25 funds will never pay out like a single bet on a top quartile fund.

ADVANCING THE ART

There are many different variations worth exploring on this front. Our dataset included various vintages, asset classes, and dramatically different-sized funds. We recommend exploring this analysis by using different samples. It may be interesting to look at individual vintages, compare the results, and draw conclusions about the benefits of temporal diversification. In a similar vein, it may be interesting to perform this analysis on neutrally weighted funds (as opposed to actual weights) to get an understanding about how position sizes impact volatility.

The important takeaway is that the diverse structure and composition of private equity portfolios does not lend itself well to a one-for-all universe comparison. Universe comparisons are only valuable if they are comparable to the original portfolio. This, of course, adds complication during board meetings.

CONCLUSIONS

The number of funds in a portfolio should to be considered whenever a private equity portfolio is being analyzed. The behavior and expectation of a portfolio containing 10 funds is much different from one containing 25, 50, 100, or more. This conclusion has implications for the way you should compare yourself to universes and your peers.

CHAPTER 15

Cash Management Models

Statistically sophisticated or complex methods do not necessarily provide more accurate forecasts than simpler ones.
—Makridakis and Hibon (2000, p. 470)

We introduce two different modeling techniques for cash management. Nonprobabilistic models are straightforward and relatively easy to implement. Probabilistic models require both substantial industry data and expertise in statistics.

ALL THAT GLISTERS IS NOT GOLD

You can spend all of your days and nights circling the globe attending private equity conferences. Over the clinking of water glasses and the unwrapping of throat lozenges, you will hear keynote speakers complain of too much money chasing too few deals, the burden of capital overhang, and the importance of being top quartile (while pitching their next megafund). This speech has changed little in 20 years. The cocktail party is done stand-up, wait staff in black offering finger food, chatter filled with references to big deals, outlier successes, allocations, and the latest industry gossip. In these venues, LPs are easily identified, with GPs and placement agents affixed to them like burrs. Oh the glamour.

There are many important ingredients to building a successful portfolio, but attending industry conferences is rarely at the top of anyone's list. Back at the office, prudent portfolio managers know that there is a great deal more to the private equity business than gaining access to and picking investments. In this chapter we explore why *cash management* and *commitment pacing* are critical to the successful construction of a portfolio.

WHY NOT CASH FLOW *FORECASTING*?

We intentionally use the term *cash management* here to represent the function commonly known as cash flow projections or cash flow forecasting. The reason is simple: there is nothing you can know about the future—we assure you that we do not. Unforeseeable events have and will continue to shape the private equity landscape. The run-up of the public markets to the year 2000 and its subsequent collapse; $10 billion buyout funds; oil at $140 a barrel then $50; the collapse of Lehman Brothers. Not one of these events was foreseeable.

The other term we introduce here is *commitment pacing*. Commitment pacing is the process by which the portfolio manager reaches the desired allocation to this asset class. As we have emphasized, private equity investments typically take on the form of self-liquidating funds that draw down and distribute capital opportunistically. The opportunistic nature of this asset class makes the portfolio manager's responsibility of hitting and maintaining a target allocation particularly difficult.

We liken these two portfolio management functions to budgetary planning. What is my budget? How much money will be going out? How much will be coming in? How much will be unrealized? These may seem like basic requests, but the responses cannot and will not be precise, and instead are presented as broad strokes about potential outcomes. Can you imagine a life where you do not know how much you will earn next month? How much your bills will be? Welcome to the world of private equity portfolio management.

Cash management and commitment pacing are inextricably linked. In fact, understanding and analyzing them requires an iterative process. Changes in asset allocation impact the number and size of commitments that will be made, which then impacts how cash ought to be managed. So what is a portfolio manager to do?

- The first step is to acknowledge that building and maintaining an asset allocation to private equity is a perpetual effort: it does not lend itself well to frequent changes.
- Because asset allocation decisions are often influenced by many stakeholders (other portfolio managers, committees, and board members), you should make sure that they all understand that cash management and commitment pacing are complex. This allows big picture decisions to be sensitive to the needs of the private equity allocation.

■ The third step is to implement a cash management model that computes future contributions, distributions, and valuations. There are many models out there for the choosing. You can even build your own.

Probabilistic versus Nonprobabilistic Models

We categorize cash management models as either probabilistic or nonprobabilistic. Nonprobabilistic models are usually very easy to understand and require a handful of inputs. Inputs are subjective and may include the rate of contributions, rate of distribution, and the return on invested capital.

In contrast, probabilistic models base their forward-looking assumptions on an empirical analysis of historical data. The tricky part, of course, is locating a legitimate source of data. Some portfolio managers use their own portfolios as a source of historical data; others use homegrown databases of information collected during due diligence; still others may purchase a commercially available dataset.

NONPROBABILISTIC: THE YALE MODEL

In 2001, Dean Takahashi and Seth Alexander (2001) of the Yale University Investments Office published a paper titled "Illiquid Alternative Asset Fund Modeling." It details a nonprobabilistic model that has become known simply as the Yale model. In this section, we walk through a brief explanation of this cash flow model.

Bottoms Up

A cash flow model must be built from the bottom up. This is logical: in order to understand the cash flows of a portfolio, you must know those of each investment or related group of investments.

In its early years, a fund is a voracious consumer of capital. In the middle years, its value peaks and, if successful, produces even larger amounts of capital. At life's end, a private equity fund will usually have relatively little cash flow. The current valuation of a fund can be used as an indicator of the amount of the cash it might return. Add up the activity for each fund and you get the activity for the portfolio.

Here are the criteria set forth in the Yale model:

■ First, the model should be simple and sensible on a theoretical basis.
■ Second, the model should be able to incorporate and respond to actual capital commitment experience and current partnership asset values.

- Third, the model should be able to analyze the portfolio impact of varying return scenarios and changing rates of investment and distribution.
- Fourth, the model should be useful for a variety of asset types.

Takahashi and Alexander (2001, 3)

The Yale model meets these criteria. As well, it is useful to note that their investments office has a very large private equity portfolio, thus providing it a rich source of data. Although the model can be run frequently, the paper implies that Yale runs this analysis only once a year. We are in agreement that a cash management exercise should not be done too frequently as this can create a short-term focus. Our recommendation is to run it once a year, or twice at most.

EXPLANATION OF THE YALE MODEL

1. For each fund, for each year of the fund's remaining life, estimate remaining contributions.
2. For each fund, for each year of the fund's remaining life, estimate remaining distributions.
3. For each year, subtract contributions from distributions to get net cash flow.

The age of each fund is critical, and the model always uses the best available information for each step. For example: the estimated contributions are based on the then-current unfunded amount; the remaining distributions are based on the factors that include the current valuation.

Model Contributions for Each Year

Take the current unfunded commitment amount to the fund, and apply a factor that varies with the current age of the fund to arrive at the net contribution for the year.

$$\text{Period Capital Contribution} = \text{Unfunded Amount} * \text{Rate of Contribution}$$

You decide on the rates. The rates they use in their paper are in Table 15.1.

As a reminder, the amount contributed depends on the unfunded amount at the beginning of each year, which may be zero. If it is zero, there are obviously no contributions.

TABLE 15.1 Rates of Contribution for the Yale Model

Year	Rate of Contribution (%)
1	25
2	33
3	50
4	50
5	50
...	50

Theoretically, this rate schedule could be customized for each fund. More practically, this might better be assigned by sub-asset class or vintages. The authors of the paper note that this schedule implies that the commitment will never be fully funded, but that this is representative of reality: many funds never do call all capital pledged.

Model Distributions for Each Year

This is a bit trickier, but we expect you will find it fairly straightforward. According to their model, the year's predicted distributions depend on three factors, a rate of distribution, the valuation of the fund, and a growth factor for that valuation.

$$\text{Period Distributions} = \text{Rate of Distribution} * \text{Prior Period's Valuation} *$$
$$(1 + \text{Annual Growth Rate})$$

Because of their fourth goal, that this should be useful for a variety of assets, the Yale model adds a twist to the Rate of Distribution factor, making it a choice between the greater of two factors, a fixed yield or a rate proportional to the age of the fund. The second choice of the rate of distribution is more directly useful for private equity and uses what they call a "bow factor." The bow helps estimate when distributions may occur.

$$\text{Rate of Distribution} = (\text{Age/Term of the Fund in Years})^{\wedge} \text{Bow Factor}$$

The higher the bow factor, the longer it takes for the projected distributions to occur. Table 15.2 is a table of rates of distribution corresponding to various bow factors and ages. A bow factor of 1 assumes that 10 percent of the projected distributions will occur each year for a fund with a term of 10 years.

TABLE 15.2 Rates of Distribution Using Various Bow Factors and Ages

Age	Bow Factor			
	1	2	3	4
1	10.00	1.00	0.10	0.01
2	20.00	4.00	0.80	0.16
3	30.00	9.00	2.70	0.81
4	40.00	16.00	6.40	2.56
5	50.00	25.00	12.50	6.25
6	60.00	36.00	21.60	12.96
7	70.00	49.00	34.30	24.01
8	80.00	64.00	51.20	40.96
9	90.00	81.00	72.90	65.61
10	100.00	100.00	100.00	100.00

Figure 15.1 illustrates why this is called a bow factor. With a bow of 1, the relationship between age and distribution rate is a straight line. The higher bow factor flexes the distribution curve downward.

The choice of the rate of distribution is made by taking the greater of the yield or the rate proportional to the age of the fund:

Rate of Distribution = Maximum (Yield, (Age / Term of the Fund in Years) $^\wedge$ Bow Factor)

So for example, if the Bow Factor is 3 and it is the fourth year of the fund, which is assumed to have a 10-year life, then the rate proportional to the age of the fund is:

$$(4/10)^\wedge 3 = 6.40\%$$

Further, if we use a yield of 5 percent the Rate of Distribution is:

Rate of Distribution = Maximum (5%, 6.40%) = 6.40%

Of course, if you decide that the asset class doesn't need a Yield, simply set it to zero:

Rate of Distribution = Maximum (0%, 6.40%) = 6.40%

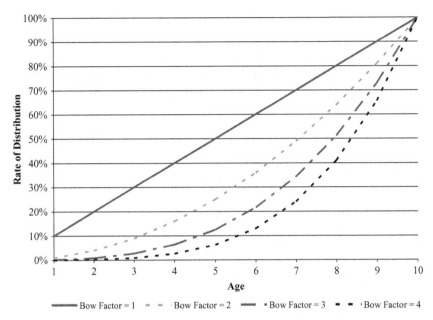

FIGURE 15.1 Different Bow Factors Change the Rate of Distribution

The Valuation

The Valuation in this model is a variation of the Adjusted Valuation, with a single difference, a fixed growth factor applied to the fund's *prior period* valuation:

Period Valuation = (Prior Valuation * Growth Factor)
+ Period Contributions − Period Distributions

With assumptions for the Rates of Contribution, Growth Factor, Yield, and Bow Factor, the portfolio cash flows are modeled year-by-year and fund-by-fund.

Each year is then summed to give you a modeled cash flow projection over the entire term of the current committed capital, usually 10 years. Of course, the further out you model, the less precision you have.

Benefits and Criticisms of the Yale Model

This model meets its goals. It is simple and can be readily implemented. There are relatively few inputs and the output is easy to understand. This makes the Yale Model a good place to start for this kind of work. Strengths, of course, can be weaknesses. If you choose poorly on the inputs, the output will suffer. By definition, a single run of this model creates one outcome, not the range of outcomes a probabilistic model would.

CASH MANAGEMENT: OUR EXPERIENCE

The map is not the territory.
—Hayakawa (1940, p. 27)

Do not confuse models with reality. Cash management is a day-to-day activity that should be planned year-by-year. No model is ever right, but we prefer cash management models that are probabilistic because they show a range of potential outcomes. A range can also show how your portfolio differs from what history might have predicted.

Before we lay out our approach to cash management, we have the usual disclaimers:

- This is *one approach* to a probabilistic model for cash management; there are many others.
- This section is only an outline, not a blueprint for implementation.
- Even with years of research and development on cash management modeling, we continue to tinker with various approaches as our thinking evolves.
- Chicken and egg: you need data to model data—the more the better. Our own modeling is based on a proprietary dataset (in our parlance, a sub-universe of funds).
- We use sophisticated statistical software to help with this analysis. In a departure from our text, we are not using simple out-of-the-box Excel functions.

This exercise is in two parts. The first builds a statistical model of how the data in your sample behaves on a year-by-year basis. The second part uses that statistical model with your actual portfolio investments to create a range of outcomes.

Categorizing Funds

Our experiences suggests that fund categories are statistically different. Our classifications currently are:

- Buyouts smaller than $1 billion
- Buyouts larger than $1 billion
- Early-stage venture capital
- Late-stage venture capital
- Mezzanine
- Distressed Debt

As a result, we use just these six asset classes when we model future cash flows and valuations. Funds of funds must be treated separately in light of the make-up of their portfolios. For example, a fund of funds position that is 50 percent late-stage venture capital and 50 percent buyouts smaller than $1 billion should be treated as two separate portfolios, with the year of life determined by reference to the underlying funds in each.

Aggregating by Year

Every year of a fund is different, but we make an assumption that for each year into the life of a fund within each category, funds behave similarly. Every dataset can be summarized in a simple chart like Figure 15.2.

We start to build our model by separately summing contributions and distributions for every fund in our sample database *for each year of its existence*. Similarly, we record the valuation at the end of the year for each fund. We then express each amount for each year as a percentage of the fund by dividing by the fund size. Table 15.3 shows how the data can be summarized.

With this data, you can answer questions like "What percent of a fund was drawn down in year 1? Year 2? As a percent of the fund size, what distributions can be expected in year 3?" The advantage of this approach is that you can easily compare funds of very different sizes. When this year-by-year summation is done for every fund, you usually have a great deal of data.

To complete the first part, we then apply statistical techniques to these results, including the fitting of probability distributions, to create a concise description of this behavior. We frequently observe beta, gamma, log-logistic, log-normal, and, infrequently, normal distributions. In determining the best-fitting probability distribution, we tend to use the Chi-square and Kolmogorov-Smirnov tests.

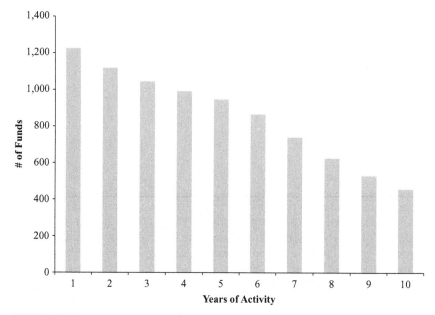

FIGURE 15.2 Data sets will always have less observations in later years when active funds are included.

TABLE 15.3 Summary Data for a Probabilistic Cash Management Model for a Fund

	As a Percent of the Fund Size		
Year	Contributions (%)	Distributions (%)	Valuation (%)
1	30	0	26
2	30	0	58
3	10	1	70
4	20	16	78
5	10	11	76
6	0	5	104
7	0	7	92
8	0	4	102
9	0	47	58
10	0	19	51
11	0	33	41
12	0	43	0

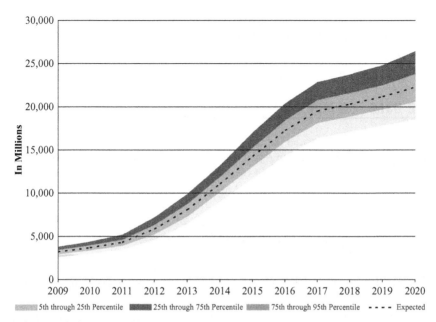

FIGURE 15.3 An Example of the Valuation Output from a Probabilistic Model

Finally, we then use the resulting underlying probability distributions in a Monte Carlo simulation to project contributions, distributions, net cash flow (distributions minus contributions), and valuation using the portfolio's current composition. We can also incorporate expectations for future commitments and so help with commitment pacing.

The results can be summarized in two stacked area charts, one for net cash flow, and the other for valuations on a year-by-year basis. See Figure 15.3 for an example of valuations.

SPECIAL NOTES

This cash management model assumes that contributions, distributions, and valuations are independent. Some may find this unacceptable, but we have found that adding the additional layer of complexity involved in time-series analysis has had mixed results because contributions are not necessarily related to distributions and valuations do not necessarily move in tandem with cash flow.

If you prefer to avoid the curve-fitting exercise, and if you have lots and lots of time, you can sample Monte Carlo outcomes directly from the source data.

OTHER USES FOR MODELS

If a cash management model is good, it can also provide you with a macro view of the portfolio, allowing you to quickly compare actual results to what history would suggest should or could have happened. Is my portfolio drawing down capital too quickly? Are my valuations on track? Has the industry changed?

For those of you already doing this type of work, there are probably many questions. Which model should I use? How can I improve my existing model? Or more simply, what makes a model successful?

Here we withhold judgment. We are encouraged when institutions acknowledge the need for cash management analysis and implement the necessary processes. But it is very difficult to prove one model superior to another. We expect the ideal model will be the subject of debates for years to come. Instead of offering specific answers we instead provide some guidance. Our requirements for a cash management model to be successful include the following.

- The model must reflect good judgment.
- The model must have adequate data.
- One size does not fit all. A model should have the capability to treat different asset classes differently. In fact, part of the process should be to test whether the asset classes behave differently.
- Ideally, the model should not just provide a single value, but a range of potential outcomes.

Strive to keep some details out of this analysis. Some groups want terms, conditions, and a raft of other variables incorporated into their model. In our experience, this is a leading cause of analysis paralysis in which no model is sufficient. Other groups prefer to color cash management models with opinion. "I think next year will behave like vintage 1993." We are not big fans of fortune telling. Models did not tell us how to act when venture capital came off the tracks in 1996. Subjectivity should be the exception, not the rule. Leave this thinking outside your model. Modeling is modeling—it is about the big picture, planning for the future, and staying disciplined.

YOUR MODELS

So where can you go from here?

The good news is that there has been a fair amount of research done in this area. For those groups without access to large historical datasets, start to learn about this process by using a nonprobabilistic model like the Yale Model. For those with access to comprehensive datasets, begin experimenting with some of the probabilistic models.

Although most investors only allocate a small portion of their portfolios to private equity, this asset class is usually thought of as a major driver of returns for the portfolio. Even a relatively small allocation to private equity can substantially impact an institution's overall return.

Effects of a Shortfall

If you fall short of your target allocation for private equity, you may have trouble making up the difference in returns from investments in other asset classes because the balance of the allocation is invested in inferior (purely on returns) asset classes. Shortfalls are all too common, but get buried in the portfolio's total performance. Moreover, returns are typically summarized by asset class, so the shortfall may be hidden because the capital awaiting investing in private equity was invested elsewhere in the interim.

Many of the most prudent investors are the most likely to be under-invested because of their reluctance to make sufficient commitments in the short time frame needed to achieve the desired allocation. We applaud their caution, but every quarter those prudent investors have to inform their boards that they have not yet achieved their desired allocation—and won't soon.

Cash Management and Risk Management

Knowing this, you could argue that these portfolio management processes should fall under the purview of risk management. Moreover, the risk of this asset class has not historically been in the returns. Any halfway decent portfolio manager can pick a few investments and beat the other institutional-grade asset classes on a return basis. Very real risks are hidden away from the naive observer because they exist before the capital is drawn down, after the capital is distributed and, of course, with allocation shortfalls. Preinvestment risk is related to the time you are waiting for the capital to be drawn down. Will you have enough cash on hand? Will it be an inopportune time to sell a different security? Reinvestment risk is associated with having to find a home for the cash distributed back to you after a realization takes place. Shortfall risk is related to the costs associated with not achieving the target allocation.

COMPENSATION

Many compensation plans include incentives based on the performance of the manager's investments. But what about the shortfall? Where does that come into place? Does it drag down the returns for that manager? It should. But it is not likely attributed to the manager's track record. This is a very serious topic that needs consideration. One could argue that incentives should be tied to the entire portfolio's performance, or perhaps the entire allocation of capital (including the shortfall) or some hybrid. The important thing to point out here is that the cost of the shortfall is naturally buried in the performance of the entire portfolio because that capital was invested elsewhere. As a result, it is easy to forget about it. The manager is not doing the job effectively if only half of the capital is deployed.

However, it is also important not to achieve the allocation by investing over some very short time frame, thus eliminating temporal diversification. The correct course of action is an optimization of a host of factors, including return, risk, and correlation, in addition to cash flow modeling.

COMMITMENT PACING

We said at the beginning of this chapter that cash flow management and commitment pacing are inextricably linked. It should be clear that by modeling cash flows throughout the life of the existing portfolio, you will have a better understanding of your current obligations and the patterns that they have created. If used as a regular part of your process, this type of modeling can help you make decisions about your current and future commitments.

How you pace them, of course, depends on your investment goals, including the growth of your overall portfolio and the role of private equity in it. In other words, if your asset allocation target is 15 percent, what is that 15 percent of? This is the stuff of detailed strategy discussions, with forward-looking changes at the institutional level. For example, a college endowment may want to fund a new building or a new campus five years out and so may have to plan for liquidity.

CONCLUSIONS

Portfolio managers have two principal operating responsibilities, manager selection and cash management. Good portfolio managers carefully balance these two responsibilities. They know that shortfalls are incredibly expensive and, as a result, are careful with how much time they spend chasing "exclusive" opportunities. Why? Because they know that the allocation they may get will be undersized and even if it was successful, it would have very little effect on their portfolio as a whole. Instead, they focus their efforts on deploying their capital effectively by locating suitable investment opportunities that permit them to make substantial commitments. The bottom line is that you cannot make money without having capital invested.

Cash management models ought to be used by investors with substantial exposure to private equity because they can be used to stay on track, stay disciplined, and generate realistic expectations. We prefer probabilistic models, but know that most will rely on nonprobabilistic techniques because comprehensive cash flow and valuation data are hard to find. Finally, it is important to remember that models cannot anticipate unforeseeable events.

PART Four

Conclusions

CHAPTER 16

The Private Equity Professional

We discuss our goals, the industry, and our hopes for the evolution of the private equity profession.

THE PROFESSION

Our goals for this book were to bring an awareness to the complexity of our profession, help advance its science, and perhaps elevate its art. Whether we were successful is for you to judge. Although this book is subtitled "The Professional Investor's Handbook" we are still not sure that such a thing can be written. In as complex a pursuit as private equity investing, there is too much unknown and there are few absolutes. There will be many who disagree with our techniques, recommendations, and conclusions. We agree we have much to learn.

The private equity industry is young and a bit naive, by which we mean that it is lacking in self-awareness. This stems partly from its nature: investing in private assets is done in isolation. Public assets can be bought and sold in the open markets at will, but a portfolio of private equity assets is a hard-to-assemble, hard-to-track, ever-changing bundle of positions in private enterprises. The bigger the portfolio, the more complicated they are. No two private equity portfolios are ever alike, and understanding one portfolio does not mean you can easily understand another—doing so takes considerable skill, time, and effort. The privacy that pervades the industry is both a strength and a principal weakness. Private transactions can create competitive advantages, and although private investors are rightly reluctant to share information, this may ultimately work against them, creating significant barriers to the evolution and growth of the asset class.

We have complained throughout this text about the lack of comprehensive industry-wide data. We complain in part because we believe that the myths and folklore of private equity should go away—they haunt the profession and stymie action and innovation. The macroeconomic effects of this private activity are in need of serious study. The published performance trends of the private equity sub-asset classes are lacking in foundation. In our opinion, the academic underpinnings of private equity are essentially nonexistent: most researchers and scholars desperately grab at insufficient data and as a result often draw unconvincing conclusions.

To be clear, we do not lobby for private transactions to be made public. Far from it. Data of this kind needs to be protected. What is needed is anonymized transactional data that can describe the kind of transaction that it was, and sufficient depth and uniformity of description to allow it to be analyzed, aggregated, and put into greater context.

Despite these handicaps, what we have argued here is that there is much you can do to take a disciplined approach to private equity investing, that this activity is, in fact, a bona fide profession. By now it should be obvious that the private equity professional is involved in a very different set of activities from the manager of public assets.

Ideally, a professional approach to investing is ethical, critical, objective, and dispassionate. In the end, you are reminded that business is just business, and in addition to fiduciary duty you have the responsibility of entering into and, at times, ending relationships. On occasion you may need to take legal action against these partners, and such actions require judgment and distance, and so lines between the professional and the personal must be drawn, fully understood, and respected. It is a bit ironic that the private equity professional works in an industry where personal relationships count, but cannot count too much.

The professional life rafts are associations and organizations that put you in a contact with like-minded colleagues. For example the Institutional Limited Partners Association, an international nonprofit organization, focuses exclusively on the needs and concerns of limited partners.

NEW SKILLS

There was a time, not long ago, when $20 million commitments were done across a table between LPs and GPs who barely knew each other. This is not hyperbole. One of the principal traits that made those deals possible, judgment, is still the most valuable skill that anyone brings to the investment process. But those simple days are no more. As the market has grown, this way of doing business has all but disappeared. Given the demands of transparency, the prominence of private equity, the complexity of the regulatory environment, and the mantle of fiduciary responsibility, today's professionals are required to research, document, and justify their investment decisions with increasing rigor.

There are dozens of roles in this complex business, but at times you must be a jack-of-all-trades. In some college endowments and family offices, two or three people run the entire investment process and may have hundreds of ongoing relationships. In these shops, private equity may be only a small part. In a large private equity fund of funds, the investment team alone may number in the dozens, with people and offices all over the globe. The skill sets required for these scales of operation are the same, but as teams become bigger, one job gets more complicated and becomes two or four. Specializations develop. Teams evolve, and some split.

Succeeding Long-Term

Private equity investing requires at least a passing familiarity or more likely, substantial expertise in a variety of complex legal, analytical, and investigatory processes. Although specialized consultants can assist, the investment process has to be guided by individuals or teams with a deep understanding of the needs and philosophies of the investing institution. A substantial long-term commitment to private equity requires a professional staff to support it. For institutions just starting to invest, a team can be assembled over time, with senior staff mentoring newly-minted graduates. In a different take on this, at least one institution we know well hires recent college graduates into an intensive two-year rotation of duties and then pushes these fledgling professionals out of the nest. The benefits to the institution are enormous, with fresh points of view and ideas infusing life and energy back into its team. The benefits to the industry may be even greater as these knowledge and skill sets are dispersed. The size of the team should grow with assets under management.

The work of private equity, even for the experienced professional, is rarely boring. Fresh challenges abound. The long lives of private assets can transcend the professional tenure of managers. People move on or retire. Organizations reorganize. We have encountered situations where massive private equity assets are split among several institutions; where whole investment teams walk out the door; where long-neglected assets are found in a corner, dusted off, and discovered to be worth substantial (or insubstantial) sums. We know of institutions that have relied on the advice of consultants for decades, only to discover that their current private equity portfolio was not only undiversified but also substantially underperforming the public markets. There are no shortcuts to reviving or unraveling these kinds of portfolios, but without the skills and experience of a professional team, these assets, and their institutions, will be underserved.

CEDING THE GLORY

Only a few actors star in a movie, but at its end, as the sound track plays on and screen after screen of names scroll by, you are briefly introduced to the people that made it all possible. As we have noted, much of the business press focuses on the public exploits of private equity funds and their stars—these are often business and human interest stories of a grand scale. In some rare cases, they are the stuff of legend. Let them have their glory. Much of academia is also enthralled by the cult of private equity, and many an endowment is grateful for the generous donations of its practitioners. Let them be grateful to their benefactors.

But endowments, pension funds, foundations, and others should be equally grateful to those entrusted to build on these assets. As we have shown, this is hard work, and unfortunately there are few maps and signposts to guide you or cheering throngs to rally you along the way. But most important, as we have tried to show, not only is this work important and interesting, it can make for stimulating and financially rewarding careers.

LOOKING AHEAD

In Chapter 8 we said: "Whether you have access to data or not, the world of private investing tends to be isolating. Not knowing how you are doing in comparison with others can increase your isolation."

We look forward to a time when a comprehensive database will be assembled and can start to be mined to provide reliable information on performance and portfolio modeling. We know of several initiatives underway and expect that one of these efforts will result in a durable, independent repository of data that is safeguarded with the controls needed to make it a success. We believe that a database of this kind will have substantial benefits for the industry at large, and will help provide a degree of legitimacy that the current data sources cannot. Many would like to see the survivorship bias in all data sources disappear. An industry-wide database may encourage the academic efforts needed to bolster the legitimate role of private equity in the world economy. Ultimately, this repository will remove one of the principal barriers to the continued growth of the private equity industry.

In time, we also expect the industry to have more transparency and a wider acceptance and application of standards. With a more open dialogue, and a broader foundation of research, we would expect to see more innovation. Today, most academic institutions that offer courses in private equity focus their study on the activity of the general partner or the entrepreneur.

In service to the industry, we would hope to see the academic and professional programs that introduce private equity broaden their curriculums to include other perspectives, most particularly of the limited partner, to open this world to new generations.

FINALLY

The private equity industry is here to stay and despite its current handicaps will continue to grow. New players, small and large, will be joining in. As the industry matures, more will be expected of it. Myth and folklore have played their part in its youth, but for the private equity industry to grow up, they may have to become stories about the good old days.

We hope that you have a role to play in telling the stories of the good old days to come, and we look forward to hearing from you.

CHAPTER 17

Summary

Here we briefly recap our approach and highlight what we have introduced.

INSIDE PRIVATE EQUITY

This is both an introductory and a somewhat advanced text on private equity, with a particular emphasis on what you can measure and how measuring things helps you manage them. We began with a bit of the history of private equity. We emphasized that private equity means different things to different people. We gradually introduced some industry jargon.

We outlined the private equity investment process and noted that it is best built on a continuous cycle. We highlighted terms and conditions of contracts that we have found to be especially important. After setting out a simple data framework and challenges of capturing data, we introduced the standard measures of private equity. Understanding multiples and the IRR helps you see how wealth is generated and the effect of time on private equity performance.

The good news is that everyone in the private equity industry cares about and ranks their performance against the performance of others. The bad news is that there are few good sources. We discussed universes, symbolically demoting them to sub-universes because of their lack of representation, and noted some of our other concerns about them. We show how universes have been made and created a small universe from publicly-available data.

Much of the published research on private equity uses analytical techniques designed for the public markets, often simply substituting the IRR for the TWRR. We discussed some of the fallacies of this as a general analytical approach.

We then took a side path and introduced the use of a visual tool, the radar chart, for quantitative screening of funds. We also highlighted the use of bubble and area charts in useful ways as a prelude to the presentation of additional analytical techniques later in the text.

We moved onto more complex portfolio-level questions, such as "What drives performance?" We introduced a proven and accepted benchmarking technique that compares performance to the public markets. The Index Comparison Method (ICM) strips the IRR of the portion of the return due to the market. The difference between the IRR and the IRR_{ICM} is the IRR spread, a means to compare the absolute performance of any fund or portfolio.

We illustrated how you remove another IRR bias by employing time-zero analysis, clearing latent effects of early winners or losers on, for example, a manager's track record. We then showed you how to strip additional biases out of portfolio decisions by introducing the concept of neutral-weighting to reveal the impact of commitment size, strategy, and the like. We discussed these measures in combination and their meaning, bringing out separate measures of weighting, timing, selection, breaking the world into skill and luck.

We next answered the question "What portion of a portfolio generated the bulk of your wealth?" using the Lorenz Curve to depict the concentration of wealth. This technique is especially well-suited for fund and vintage year analysis.

We talked about diversification and how larger portfolios have a higher likelihood of a lower performance threshold.

Cash management is a big topic, but we introduced it with an explanation of the nonprobabilistic model from Yale University. We outlined, a probabilistic cash-flow model. We favor this probabilistic approach, but few organizations have enough data to employ it.

If you have read this text from its beginning, you may have a sense of the private equity industry from the perspective of an LP with a portfolio of funds. You will have been subjected to our biases. We leave you with some industry aphorisms, collected opinions, and common beliefs. Are these truths? That's up to you to decide.

- "You can't eat IRR."

  Return is just a measure. Only cash is cash.
- "GPs do not care about reinvestment risk."

  It is not the business of the GP to understand or care about capital once it is distributed. It is up to the LP to have a home for the distributions as they are received. This is trickier than it sounds.

■ "Despite slippage and leakage, this asset class is damn good."

It costs money to make money. It is expensive to do business in this asset class. This "slippage" or "leakage" is from various fees, consultants, services, personnel, and general overhead. Many of these costs are absent or minimal when managing investments in other asset classes. Some of the costs involve specialized expertise that might be in short supply.

■ "With private equity, illiquidity is not a risk, it is a certainty."

Your private equity investments are deliberate investments in a long-term asset. Many mistake this illiquidity for riskiness. It has nothing to do with risk, as risk implies uncertainty.

■ "You can construct a portfolio to have the degree of liquidity that is needed by your institution."

This is a complex topic, but the implication is that the liquidity of a portfolio can be modeled, monitored, and modified. This is not true of individual funds or undiversified portfolios.

■ "The valuation of a fund, and so a portfolio, is independent of cash flows."

A distribution does not necessarily drop a valuation as contribution does not necessarily increase it. There will be frequent surprises that change the valuation seemingly without connection to cash flows.

■ "Liquidity is expensive. If you don't need it, don't buy it."

Investors with long-term horizons, like endowments, foundations, and pension funds, can benefit from investments in private equity and other alternative assets that have higher historical returns than that of the public markets.

■ "A fund manager will not be able to deliver every time, every cycle, every year."

Do not rely on the past performance of even the best of fund managers to adhere to a schedule or an outcome.

■ "Missing a good fund is not as important as avoiding a bad one."

An LP's job is to say no, and occasionally, after considerable study, to say yes.

■ "Investments do not happen in isolation—it is the portfolio that counts."

Having a great return on a single fund is nice, but LPs should care first about the portfolio as a whole.

■ "Try not to compete with yourself."

Choose managers wisely. Avoid investing in funds in the same market, for they will frequently be bidding on the same deals.

■ "Nobody should own you."

Do not be beholden to a fund manager for the sake of prestige, habit, or comfort. You don't *have to be* in any particular fund, period.

Proposed Venture Capital Portfolio Valuation Guidelines

June 7, 1990

GENERAL

Venture capital funds are required by generally accepted accounting principles to account for their investments in portfolio companies at value. There can be no single standard for determining value because value depends upon the circumstances of each investment. These valuation guidelines are intended to aid venture capital fund general partners in estimating the value of their investments.

PRIVATE COMPANIES

1. Investment cost is presumed to represent value except as indicated otherwise in these guidelines.

2. Valuation should be reduced if a company's performance and potential have significantly deteriorated. Such reduction should be disclosed in the notes to the financial statements.

3. Valuation should be adjusted to equate to a subsequent significant equity financing that includes a sophisticated, unrelated new investor. A subsequent significant equity financing that includes substantially the same group of sophisticated investors as the prior financing should generally not be the basis for an adjustment in valuation.

4. If substantially all of a significant equity financing is invested by an investor whose objectives are in large part strategic, it is presumed that no more than 50 percent of the increase in the investment price compared to

the prior significant equity financing is attributable to an increase in value of the company.

5. Valuation of a company acquired in a leveraged transaction should be adjusted if the company has been self-financing for at least two years and has been cash flow positive for at least one year. The adjustment should be based on P/E ratios, cash flow multiples, or other appropriate financial measures of similar companies, generally discounted by at least 30 percent for illiquidity. Such adjustment should occur no more frequently than annually, and should be disclosed in the notes to the financial statements.

6. Warrants should be valued at the excess of the value of the underlying security over the exercise price.

7. The carrying value of interest-bearing securities should not be adjusted for changes in interest rates.

PUBLIC COMPANIES

1. Public securities should be valued at the closing price or bid price except as indicated otherwise in these guidelines.

2. The valuation of public securities that are restricted should be discounted appropriately until the securities may be freely traded. Such discount should generally be at least 30 percent at the beginning of the holding period and should decline proportionally as the restrictive period lapses.

3. When the number of shares held is substantial in relation to the usual quarterly trading volume, the valuation should generally be discounted by at least 10 percent.

On-Site GP Audit Program Guide

Audit Procedures for Transaction Files

Based upon the cash flows and valuations submitted by the GP in support of its candidacy for investment, the audit will cover all investments made by the GP since inception.

Audit Objectives

1. Determine whether historical investments have been adequately documented and approved in accordance with the policies and procedures stated in the structured interview.
2. Determine whether cash and/or in-kind transfers have been properly booked, supported, and approved in accordance with written policies and procedures.
3. Determine whether valuation policies and procedures used are in accordance with current policies and procedures.

Objective 1 Determine whether historical investments have been adequately documented and approved in accordance with the policies and procedures stated in the structured interview.

a. Referring to a sequential listing of the investments submitted by the GP as evidence of an investment track record, assign sequential numbering and sample using random numbers.
b. Examine all related files for each of the investments randomly selected in order to determine whether each has been adequately documented and approved in accordance with the policies and procedures stated in the structured interview.

c. Using quantitative data from the files, project the entire track record using the complete sample and compare to the actual track record for the following: paid-in, distributions, valuations, TVPI, and RR.

Objective 2   Determine whether cash and/or in-kind transfers have been properly booked, supported, and approved in accordance with written policies and procedures:

a. Trace and agree all cash flows submitted in the track record for the sampled investments with the books and records of the GP, including all supporting documentation.
b. Note any discrepancies, interview appropriate GP personnel to determine source(s).

Objective 3   Determine whether valuation policies and procedures used are in accordance with current policies and procedures:

a. For each investment sampled, determine the valuation policy and/or procedure used for all interim valuations, compare to the current policies and procedures stated in the structured interview.
b. Note any discrepancies, interview appropriate GP personnel to determine source(s).

Audit Completion

a. Complete and index workpapers.
b. Draft a summary audit opinion, include in due diligence files.

Qualitative Due Diligence: Structured Interview

Fund:
Date:

1. Organization Chart
   1.1 Ownership of principals
   1.2 Distribution of carried interest
   1.3 Infrastructure (back office)
2. Background of Principals (fill out fully for each)
   2.1 High School
      2.1.1 High points/low points
      2.1.2 Academics
      2.1.3 Athletics/other
      2.1.4 Employment
   2.2 College
      2.2.1 High points/low points
      2.2.2 Academics
      2.2.3 Athletics/other
      2.2.4 Employment
   2.3 Graduate School
      2.3.1 Why this school/degree?
      2.3.2 High points/low points
   2.4 Volunteer organizations
3. Work History
   3.1 Employer
   3.2 Location
   3.3 Title
   3.4 Responsibilities

    3.5 Major challenges

    3.6 Major accomplishments

    3.7 Major mistakes/failures

    3.8 Reason for leaving

4. Deal Inflow and Review Process

    4.1 Systems

    4.2 How assigned

    4.3 Criteria for review

    4.4 Flowchart?

5. Investment Approval Process

    5.1 System/steps

    5.2 Due diligence

    5.3 Unanimous

    5.4 If rejected

    5.5 Written report (get copy, and of rejected)

6. Structuring and Transaction Execution Process

    6.1 Who and how

    6.2 Term sheet (get example)

    6.3 Final documents (get set)

7. Monitoring Process

    7.1 How assigned

    7.2 Systems

    7.3 Reporting (examples)

8. Realization Process

    8.1 Systems

    8.2 Benchmarks

    8.1 Execution

9. Prior Investments (review quantitative due diligence analysis to prepare)

    9.1 Winners, why

    9.2 Losers, why (worst deal)

    9.3 Internal review process

    9.4 Investment returns (updated)

10. Relationship Maintenance

    10.1 Systems

    10.2 Co-investors (provide list of all co-investors in every deal)

    10.3 LP Reporting (K1, quarterly, annual, monthly)

11. Overall Business

    11.1 Personnel and responsibilities

    11.2 Compensation (incentives) and firm building

    11.3 Insurance

Qualitative Due Diligence: Structured Reference Calls

Fund:
Date:

1. Principals/GP
    1.1 Trustworthy
    1.2 Hardworking and motivated
    1.3 Track record
    1.4 Continuity
    1.5 Contacts
    1.6 Operational/Financial expertise
    1.7 Industry knowledge
    1.8 Business of the business
    1.9 Infrastructure of the business
2. Strategy
    2.1 Portfolio exposure
    2.2 Viable and understandable
    2.3 Able to implement (macro/micro)
    2.4 Term (investment horizon)
    2.5 Downside protection
3. Relationship Potential
    3.1 Your institution's potential influence (size relative to other investors, seat on the advisory board)
    3.2 Co-investment opportunities
    3.3 Duration (will they be around a long time)
    3.4 Competition
    3.5 Others with stronger principles
    3.6 Stronger strategy
    3.7 Better relationship potential
    3.8 Timing for competition fundraising

Request for Information (RFI)

Fund:
Date:

I. Organization
  1. Provide a list of all GP offices—where they are located (address/telephone), how they are staffed, and when they were established. Please also list and describe any affiliates of the General Partner. Please provide details (and diagrams if available) of the legal structure of the General Partner.
  2. Describe any other investment management, advisory, or agency businesses that the GP is either currently involved in or expected to be involved in during the term of the proposed investment vehicle. Describe the manner in which the professionals of GP will be compensated for these activities.
  3. Please provide resumes for each of the key principals and professionals.
  4. Prepare a table (using the following format) that describes the following information, in terms of time spent, for the professionals of the GP:

Name	Generating Deal Flow	Reviewing Opportunities	Due Diligence	Negotiating/ Structuring	Monitoring	Admin./ Other	Outside Activities	Total

5. For all principals, please advise on board seats held and board responsibilities.

6. Describe how the carried interest is distributed within GP. Is the carried interest shared with a parent or any other entity? What is the vesting period for the carried interest? Provide specific carried interest allocations for your current fund, previous fund, and planned fund by individual.

7. Please verify whether an acceleration of the vesting period will occur pursuant to a change in ownership of the management company.

8. How much capital, on an invested basis, does GP have under management? How much capital, on a committed basis, does GP have under management?

9. How many investment professionals are employed by GP?

10. Please provide current salary/bonus for the Senior Partners, Associates, and Analysts at GP for the past two years.

11. Please provide a list of investments made by members of the GP into other private equity vehicles, and discuss the benefits of those investments for the Limited Partners.

12. What has been the turnover history of employees at GP? Are there any anticipated staffing changes, additions, or deletions for the next three years?

II. Investment Strategy

1. Please review your investment strategy and market niche, include data on the market opportunity and how your strategy is different from the strategy of peers or competitors.

2. What is your partnership's specific competitive advantage?

3. What are some specific challenges, at both the micro and macro levels, that you will face when investing the current fund?

4. Provide expected return information, both gross and net. Explain how the return will be earned. What do you expect will be the average holding period for investments? Is this different from prior funds?

III. Deal Flow

1. What are your firm's competitive advantages with respect to deal sourcing and deal flow?

2. How were prior investments sourced? Please list the specific investments, and briefly describe the circumstances, including the name of the company and specific contact.

3. Provide a copy of the firm's deal flow log for the last two years.

4. Please discuss recent developments at the macro-economic level, as it pertains to geography or a specific industry that will provide investment opportunities for GP.

IV. Investment Process/Due Diligence

1. Explain the due diligence process. Who is responsible for these activities? Are any of these functions ever outsourced?
2. Provide an example(s) of due diligence analysis, documentation, and investment recommendation.
3. Explain the decision-making process for portfolio investments. Is there an investment committee? Who is involved?
4. Discuss how the GP will monitor portfolio investments. Are there specific individuals dedicated to monitoring investments?
5. Have you ever offered co-investment opportunities to limited partners in the past? If so, what is the track record of these co-investment opportunities? Do you plan to offer the limited partners of your new fund co-investment opportunities?

V. Fund Performance, Financial Terms, and Calculations of Fees

1. What are the Fund's targeted/expected returns both as an investment multiple and an IRR? Please indicate time periods, and provide both gross and net of fee examples.
2. Please provide year-end audited financials for the past three years for all active funds.
3. Please provide details of your planned management fee structure and an example of the calculation. What is the estimated total of management fees during the life of the fund and the estimated annual average net management fee?
4. Please describe the uses of the GP's management fees. Please address how surplus funds are used. In addition, please comment on your view of using a fixed operating budget ($-based) and then using excess fees collected to offset future expenses of the fund, that is, management fees as a source for operations, not profit.
5. Do you collect transaction fees from your portfolio companies? Are they shared with your LPs?
6. Please provide a mathematical example of your distribution waterfall.
7. Provide a detailed operating budget for the past two years and future five-year periods. Please include all sources of income to the general partner (transaction, monitoring, fees, and so on).
8. How will you manage publicly traded securities? Will in-kind distributions be made? If so, what is your distribution and valuation policy?
9. Does GP contribute performance data to a third party such as Thomson Reuters? If so, how do GP's previous funds rank versus industry benchmarks? If not, please explain why you do not contribute performance data.

VI. Communication with Limited Partners
   1. Provide the name(s) of the audit firm(s) that will be used by GP.
   2. Provide the name(s) of the legal firm(s) that will be used by GP.
   3. Please provide a typical example of a capital call as well as a distribution. Do you provide an investment overview with the capital call?
   4. Provide a list of current Limited Partners. Please include name, institution, and phone number. Also indicate Advisory Committee members.
   5. Describe the Advisory Committee's formal and informal role.
   6. Provide name(s) and contact information of those members of the GP responsible for financial/accounting information and for members responsible for LP relations.
   7. What is the reporting frequency to LPs? What is the reporting currency?
VII. Fund Raising
   1. When was the first closing? What was the aggregate amount of capital commitments? Please provide an updated list of Limited Partners and amount committed to this fund.
   2. How much capital will the principals contribute to the proposed fund? How will this investment be structured?
VIII. Legal Considerations
   1. Is GP or any of its principals and/or affiliates subject to any current, pending, or potential litigation? Please explain the circumstances relating to any such litigation and/or any related settlements that have been reached.
IX. Other
   1. Please provide references for the principals. Please include contacts at all portfolio companies in the last two funds, and a list of co-investors.

Advanced Topics: Duration of Performance

Duration of Performance relates TVPI and IRR in a way to help you gauge what degree of change in one will cause a change in the other.

We are tinkerers. Like many others, we like building on ideas and creating tools that help us better understand what private equity is all about. In this discussion, keep in mind that we are looking for useful tools, not mathematical purity. This topic has also been explored by others, this is simply our take on it (Phalippou and Gottschalg 2005).

The IRR and TVPI are two peas in a pod—you rarely see one without the other. TVPI is a ratio that gives you an idea of the relative magnitude of the return but tells you nothing of the time that it took to achieve the results; the IRR is a performance measure with time embedded in it that tells you nothing about the relative magnitude of the return. In this discussion we explore two things:

1. Can a simple relationship be established between TVPI and the IRR?
2. If a relationship exists, what does it tell you?

Here we introduce a simple relationship between TVPI and IRR that can be determined without reference to the underlying cash flows of the investment or portfolio and in fact can be done with a calculator.

The first building block for this discussion is the "zero-coupon bond." This type of bond has no periodic payment (the *coupon is zero*), has a duration equal to its life, is usually long-term, and is sold at a discount to its face value. Invest an amount in the zero-coupon bond at a specified interest rate, and you receive a lump sum when it matures. If you translate this concept to a private equity investment, you would put all the contributions together at the outset of the fund (Paid-In), and gather all the distributions and valuation (Total Value) at any date within the fund's life. This is straightforward but leaves hanging the fact that contributions and distributions of a private equity fund never follow this simple pattern. The idiosyncratic blending of the weights and timings of contributions and distributions typical of a private equity fund do not at all resemble a zero coupon bond. Bear with us for a moment on this.

A well-known formula relates the future value of an investment to its interest rate and the total time that it is invested. This formula is

$$\text{Future Value} = \text{Present Value } (1 + \text{Return})^{\text{time}}$$

Let us substitute our private equity terms:

$$TV = PI\,(1 + R)^{\text{time}}$$

Here we introduce a twist that takes a leap of imagination. Instead of solving for the return, we solve for the time, or what we will call d, duration of performance, by using the IRR for the return.

$$TV = PI\,(1 + IRR)^{\text{duration}}$$

or

$$TV/PI = (1 + IRR)^{d}$$

which can be solved with a pocket calculator:

$$d = \ln(TVPI)/\ln(1 + IRR)$$

We call this result the Zero Coupon Equivalent Duration (ZCED) or more simply, the "duration of performance" of the private equity investment. The mathematical leap here is that the IRR is not the usual suspect when this equation is thought about or used. The IRR, as we have exhaustively discussed, is not a simple return—it is both time- and money-weighted. Think of duration of performance as the money-weighted, time-weighted

TABLE F.1 Duration of Performance for Four Funds

Year	Fund A	Fund B	Fund C	Fund D
0	−10	−50	−50	−50
1	12	10	0	0
2	−10	10	0	0
3	12	10	0	0
4	−10	10	0	0
5	12	10	0	0
6	−10	10	0	0
7	12	10	0	0
8	−10	10	0	0
9	12	60	258	85
IRR (%)	20.00	20.00	20.00	6.00
TVPI	1.20	2.80	5.16	1.70
Duration of Performance	1.0	5.7	9.0	9.0

average holding period for the investment, portfolio, or vintage to which you apply it. In Table F.1 we illustrate this concept.

Part of what the duration of performance answers is how long it took to get your money back. This is easy to see with Fund A, where you get your money back every year. A duration of performance of 1 is obvious when you add 1 to the IRR and this value is equal to the TVPI:

$$d = \ln(1.2)/\ln(1 + .20) = 1.0$$

With Fund B, it took longer for your capital to be repaid, and so the duration of performance is higher. Both Funds C and D are textbook examples of a true zero coupon bond, and so you would expect that their duration is equal to their term in years.

Perhaps the most useful aspect of duration of performance is that it describes a relationship between IRR and TVPI. These two measures move up and down in tandem. Duration of performance tells you how much movement in one is required to meaningfully influence the other. If the duration of performance is high, TVPI will have to increase significantly in order to change IRR; conversely, if the duration of performance is low, relatively small changes in TVPI will have relatively large effects on IRR.

PRACTICAL USES FOR THE DURATION OF PERFORMANCE

The calculation of the duration of performance is useful for two primary purposes: quality control and secondary interest sales or purchases.

For quality control, the duration of performance can tell you whether a particular fund or vintage is behaving normally. If a fund in your portfolio is four years old and has a duration of performance of one, for example, either the IRR is much higher than you might have expected, or the TVPI is much lower than you might have expected. In either case, you can be sure that the relationship between IRR and TVPI, as expressed in the duration of performance, is out of line, and the investment therefore probably needs your attention.

In the purchase or sale of a secondary interest in a fund, the duration of performance can tell you how attractive a particular investment is likely to be to the market. As you saw in Chapter 9, the point-to-point IRR can be extremely volatile at the end of a fund's life.

- To a seller of a position in a fund, a high duration of performance of a fund may indicate that it is unlikely that TVPI will increase enough to have a meaningful effect on the IRR. A fund with a high duration of performance may be more valuable to another investor, since its IRR to the current investor is essentially fixed.
- To a buyer, who will begin the duration of performance calculation with a TVPI determined using the purchase price as the base capital invested, a very small movement in TVPI can have a very large outcome in terms of IRR. In other words, the typically very short duration of performance of a secondary purchase in the hands of the buyer means that the IRR will likely be high if the investment's remaining assets are valuable. This phenomenon has been a primary driver behind the growth of the secondary market, with institutional investors supplying more and more capital to groups that specialize in secondary funds, such as Coller Capital, Lexington Partners, Landmark Partners and others, in the hope of attaining a high IRR.

Advanced Topics: Correlation and Opportunity Costs

CORRELATION

If you own two stocks, do their returns mirror each other, dipping and rising together? Or are they countercyclical, one rising when the other falls? Perhaps there is no relationship between the two at all. In financial terms, correlation mathematically measures how the returns of two investments move in relation to each other over time and is a key ingredient in advanced portfolio analysis and planning. In this discussion, we introduce the concept of correlation in the private markets. But first, a little background.

Buyer Beware

While the correlation indicates the strength of a linear relationship between two variables, the correlation alone may be insufficient to evaluate this relationship, especially in the case where the assumption of normality is incorrect. This topic goes outside the scope of this text.

Use in Public Markets

Two investments that are precisely correlated move in lockstep with one another. An uncorrelated pair do just the opposite, moving in opposition. Correlations range from -1 to 1 with a value of zero indicating that there is no linear relationship between the values. These three correlations $(-1, 0, +1)$ are rare in practice. The Excel CORREL function takes two arrays of values. The most common use of correlation is to compute the correlation between periodic returns for two different securities. As an example, Table G.1 is a comparison of the Vanguard Emerging Markets Stock Index (VEIEX) and the Vanguard Total Stock Market Index (VTSMX).

TABLE G.1 Quarterly Returns for the Vanguard Emerging Markets Stock Index and Total Stock Market Index

Quarter	VEIEX Return (%)	VTSMX Return (%)
1998Q3	−17.72	−12.07
1998Q4	18.94	21.51
1999Q1	10.87	3.71
1999Q2	19.38	7.88
1999Q3	−4.87	−6.42
1999Q4	28.32	18.27
2000Q1	−2.40	3.84
2000Q2	−6.89	−4.39
2000Q3	−9.69	0.27
2000Q4	−11.72	−10.17
2001Q1	−8.60	−12.27
2001Q2	8.55	7.47
2001Q3	−22.03	−15.93
2001Q4	25.55	12.32
2002Q1	10.39	0.97
2002Q2	−8.33	−12.69
2002Q3	−17.12	−16.84
2002Q4	10.37	7.82
2003Q1	−5.64	−3.14
2003Q2	22.50	16.46
2003Q3	14.74	3.60
2003Q4	18.86	12.40
2004Q1	7.85	2.58
2004Q2	−8.76	1.28
2004Q3	7.98	−1.82
2004Q4	18.71	10.31
2005Q1	1.43	−2.40
2005Q2	3.69	2.18
2005Q3	17.23	4.01
2005Q4	7.10	2.17
2006Q1	11.22	5.37
2006Q2	−4.57	−1.99
2006Q3	4.00	4.50
2006Q4	17.22	7.04
2007Q1	2.18	1.35
2007Q2	15.40	6.04
2007Q3	14.43	1.51
2007Q4	2.94	−3.31
2008Q1	−10.48	−9.50
2008Q2	−1.35	−1.56
	Correlation	0.891487

Source: Yahoo! Finance.

The correlation coefficient of 0.8915 indicates that there is a strong positive relationship between these two exchange-traded funds.

APPLICATION OF CORRELATION IN PRIVATE MARKETS

For all the reasons cited in Chapter 9, Flawed Research Methodologies, we should avoid any type of analysis that relies heavily on interim valuations. Computing quarterly returns for a private market investment that will then be used in a time series analysis is simply unacceptable. As a result, we put forth a new methodology that can be used to derive correlation and volatility without relying heavily on periodic returns.

We label our methodology an outcome-based approach. Outcome is meant to describe the since inception (as opposed to periodic) performance of an investment at a point in time. We then use many outcomes to compute the private market's relationship with the public market. Here are the steps:

1. Compute the IRR (or desired measure) for each investment.
2. Compute the IRR_{ICM} for each investment.
3. Compute the Correlation between (1) and (2).

The process can be summarized in a table similar to Table G.2.

This is a very different process from what has been conventionally used to compute correlations between private and public markets. At

TABLE G.2 Correlation Computed between Funds and the Public Market Using an Outcome–Based Approach

Fund	IRR (%)	IRR_{ICM} (%)
A	23.09	18.49
B	24.11	16.38
C	26.11	16.60
D	12.86	2.51
E	2.75	−2.41
F	−6.94	−3.70
G	−6.15	−0.01
	Correlation	0.928375

first glance, the methodology may seem objectionable, but consider the following:

- Short-term periodic IRRs (as illustrated in Figure 8.5) are not particularly useful or meaningful. We instead rely on the since inception performance (outcomes) to establish the relationship between the public and private market.
- The use of TWRRs in private market analysis is a mistake. See Figure 9.7 as a reminder of how far the TWRR and IRR can drift apart. Be skeptical of anyone providing you correlation coefficients that were produced using TWRRs for private equity investments.
- In order for the correlation coefficient to be meaningful, its inputs need to be comparable. The IRR of the investment and the IRR_{ICM} are absolutely comparable.

Wait a Minute!

You may be saying to yourself that Table G.1 and Table G.2 are not truly comparable because the former computes the correlation between two investments over time and the latter computes the correlation based on outcomes of many private investments to the public market. The good news is that you are absolutely correct. The remedy to this is to utilize the IRRs of the portfolio company investments and their related IRR_{ICM} to compute the correlation of a single fund to the public market.

OFF TO VOLATILITY, ON TO VARIABILITY

For those of you with statistics training, you know that correlation coefficients have their roots in linear regressions. Moreover, you know that this type of analysis will provide other meaningful measures like alpha and beta. In this section, we will take our outcomes-based style of analysis one step further to describe the variability of private markets.

First, to the task of fitting a line around a series of x-y points. The objective is a line that minimizes the squares of the errors between the points on the calculated line and the various data points that make up the graph. This is known as ordinary least squares linear regression.

The result of a linear regression is an equation in the form of $y = (\beta x + \alpha + \varepsilon)$ where β (beta) is the slope of the line and α (alpha) is its y-intercept. The goodness of fit of the line is usually expressed as R^2, the coefficient of determination, but may also be expressed as its square root, r or ρ (rho), the coefficient of correlation.

In Modern Portfolio Theory (public markets), the components of the linear regression represent the following:

- The beta parameter describes the relative riskiness of the investment, as defined by periodic volatility in the returns of the stock or portfolio relative to the overall market. This risk cannot be diversified away. It is a systematic risk. A negative beta indicates an inverse relation between the stock and the overall market.
- The alpha parameter expresses the stock or portfolio return associated with a market return of zero.
- The error term describes the idiosyncratic behavior of the stock or portfolio. It can be diversified away.

In order to visualize the process, we first plot the data from Table G.2 on a scatter plot (Figure G.1). Visually, it is pretty clear that there is a positive relationship between these data points. This, of course, is reflected in the correlation coefficient we computed earlier. The next step is to use statistical software to compute the linear regression equation (see Figure G.2). Excel has adequate facilities for this type of analysis. Simply add a linear trendline to the graph.

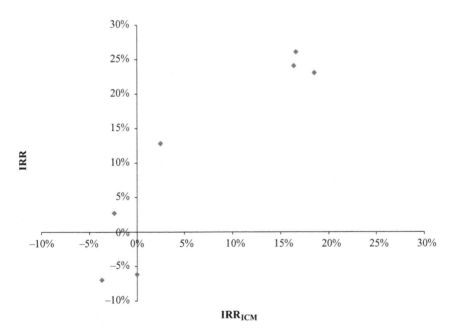

FIGURE G.1   Scatter Plot of the Data from Table G.2.

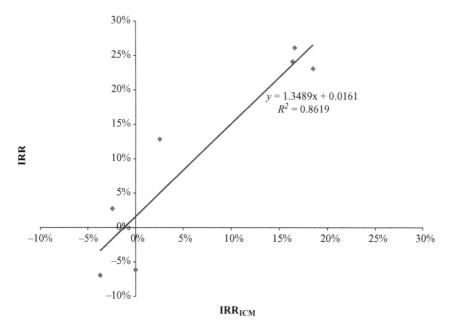

FIGURE G.2 Linear Regression Based on the Data from Table G.2.

You can interpret the beta of 1.3489 to mean that the IRR outcomes of the private equity investments are 34.89 percent more variable than the IRR outcomes of the same cash flows in the public markets. The alpha of 1.61 percent indicates that these private equity investments could be expected to return an IRR of 1.61 percent when the IRR_{ICM} is zero. The R^2 of 0.8619 tells you how well the regression line approximates the real data points. An R^2 of 1.0000 indicates that the regression line perfectly fits the data. In this case, it is certainly not perfect, but it does have a very high value.

In order to determine the relative risk of the private equity investments we have to calculate backwards from the known risk of the public markets expressed in TWRR terms. We must do some math before we can get there. We begin with the traditional definition of beta and then transform the equation to solve for the variability of the private market investment.

Beta is defined as the following:

$$\beta_S = \frac{\text{Cov}_{S,M}}{\sigma_M^2} \tag{G.1}$$

We use S to represent an individual stock and M for the market. Cov represents the covariance between the stock and the market. Correlation coefficient is defined as the following:

$$\rho_{S,M} = \frac{\text{Cov}_{S,M}}{\sigma_S \sigma_M} \tag{G.2}$$

Through some basic arithmetic we get to the following:

$$\beta_S = \frac{\text{Cov}_{S,M}}{\sigma_M^2} = \frac{\sigma_S \sigma_M \rho_{S,M}}{\sigma_M^2} \tag{G.3}$$

Now let us substitute the private equity (PE) for stock (S) and recognize that the market (M) we are referring to is the index used in the computation of the IRR_{ICM}.

$$\beta_{PE} = \frac{\sigma_{PE} \sigma_M \rho_{PE,M}}{\sigma_M^2} \tag{G.4}$$

We can then take this one step further and by solving for the variability of the private equity portfolio,

$$\sigma_{PE} = \frac{\beta_{PE} \sigma_M^2}{\rho_{PE,M} \sigma_M} \tag{G.5}$$

which simplifies to:

$$\sigma_{PE} = \frac{\beta_{PE} \sigma_M}{\rho_{PE,M}} \tag{G.6}$$

SO WHAT IS NEXT?

We already know two of the three components on the right side of the equation. The beta of 1.35 and correlation coefficient of 0.9284 were computed during the linear regression. This means that we need to compute the standard deviation of the market's returns over the related time period. Keep in mind that the market we are talking about is defined by the index used in the computation of the IRR_{ICM}.

Let us assume that the investments we have been discussing were active during the years between 1994 and 2003. We can compute the standard deviation by first computing the annual return for each year during that

TABLE G.3 Hypothetical Annual Returns for the Public Market

Year	Return (%)
1994	−5.40
1995	30.80
1996	15.90
1997	22.70
1998	21.20
1999	17.80
2000	−8.00
2001	−15.20
2002	−21.00
2003	32.90
Average	9.17
Standard Deviation	19.69

period. As you will see later, it is useful to compute the average return during the entire period.

So now we have all three of the components to the right side of the equation. Let's solve for the standard deviation of the private equity portfolio.

$$\sigma_{PE} = \frac{\beta_{PE}\sigma_M}{\rho_{PE,M}} = \frac{1.3489 * 0.1969}{0.9284} = 0.2861 \tag{G.7}$$

This approach shows that the private equity portfolio has a market-equivalent standard deviation of 28.61 percent.

Sharpe Ratio

The Sharpe Ratio, like most ratios, is easy to calculate and is used to compare different investments. Originally called the "reward-to-variability" ratio, it is the ratio of the expected return of the investment divided by the standard deviation of the investment's returns over time. The original formula includes the risk free rate of return, but we have omitted it for simplicity.

Simplified Sharpe Ratio = Expected Return/Standard Deviation

If we look back to Table G.3, we see the average return for the index is 9.17 percent, and the standard deviation is 19.69 percent. We can use the average return as the logical equivalent of the expected return and also fill in the value for the standard deviation.

$$\text{Simplified Sharpe Ratio} = 9.17\%/19.69\% = 0.4657$$

That was simple enough. Now let's do the same for the private equity portfolio. We already know that the standard deviation is 28.61 percent. We just need to determine the expected return. Recall that a linear regression equation takes on the form of $y = \beta x + \alpha$. We can solve for the private equity portfolio's expected returns by filling in the right side of the equation. We know that beta is 1.3489 and alpha is 1.61 percent. We also know that the average return of the index over the period is 9.17 percent so we can fill that in for x.

The rest is simple.

$$Y = (1.3489 * 9.17\%) + 1.61\% = 13.98\%$$

Thus, we have an expected return for the private equity portfolio over that period to be 13.98 percent. We can then compute its simplified Sharpe Ratio by dividing the expected return of 13.98 percent by the standard deviation of 28.61 percent. The result is 0.4886.

	Simplified Sharpe Ratio
Public Market	0.4657
Private Equity Portfolio	0.4886

Both of the ratios in this case are close. This suggests that the efficiency of the returns is similar.

INDIVIDUAL FUNDS VERSUS VINTAGES VERSUS PORTFOLIOS

All of the methodologies that we have introduced in the text can be applied at various scales. To determine the correlation, volatility, and/or Sharpe Ratios simply apply the methodology to the correct dataset. For an individual fund, you would use the underlying company activity. For vintages, you would create a composite for each vintage using their underlying fund activity. Portfolios would follow the same approach as vintages.

It is important to remember, however, that an entire vintage of private equity is composed of a large number of funds. Part of the investment efficiency calculated is therefore the result of the diversification inherent in the number of funds contained in the calculation.

Patent Summaries

Austin M. Long, III and Craig J. Nickels are the inventors of the following patents.

For more information, visit alignmentcapital.com.

METHOD FOR CALCULATING PORTFOLIO SCALED IRR—PATENT NO. US 7,058,583

The present disclosure thus includes a process for evaluating performance attribution in a private portfolio. Based at least in part on the discovery by the present inventors that an investment portfolio may be converted to a neutral-weight portfolio as described herein, the performance of a private investment portfolio can be analyzed to determine the contributions of investment selection, timing, and manager's contribution. The disclosed process and system are thus an important tool in evaluating the investment ability of portfolio managers and to improve their performance.

The process includes:

a. determining a return for the private portfolio by scaling the portfolio to a neutral weight portfolio with a common start date that is the earliest start date in the portfolio;

b. determining a return for the private portfolio with actual investment weights with a common start date that is the earliest start date in the portfolio;

c. determining a return for the private portfolio scaled to a neutral weight with actual start dates;

d. determining a return for the private portfolio with actual weights and actual start dates;

e. algebraically combining the returns of steps (a–c) to determine a manager's return; and

f. subtracting the manager's return from the portfolio index to determine performance attribution.

The disclosed system includes:

a. means for determining a return for the private portfolio by scaling the portfolio to a neutral weight portfolio with a common start date that is the earliest start date in the portfolio;

b. means for determining a return for the private portfolio with actual investment weights with a common start date that is the earliest start date in the portfolio;

c. means for determining a return for the private portfolio scaled to a neutral weight with actual start dates;

d. means for determining a return for the private portfolio with actual weights and actual start dates;

e. means for algebraically combining the returns of steps (a)–(c) to determine a manager's return; and

f. means for subtracting the manager's return from the portfolio index to determine performance attribution.

The system described herein includes a central processing unit or CPU (processor), which may be a main-frame computer connected to one or more work stations, or it may be a component of a personal computer that may be a "standalone" computer, or it may be networked to other computers through a common server. The system also includes an input device such as a keyboard in communication with the processor, at least one memory source, and software including instructions. The device may also include a display device such as a monitor in communication with the processor.

In the present disclosure, "algebraically combining" is understood to convey its ordinary meaning in the art, and as used in the examples herein, is the addition of numbers with positive and negative signs.

PROCESS AND SYSTEM FOR DETERMINING CORRELATION OF PUBLIC AND PRIVATE MARKETS AND RISK OF PRIVATE MARKETS—PATENT NO. US #7,421,407

The present disclosure may be described therefore as a system and process for evaluation of private market investments as a part of the investment procedure. The disclosed methods and systems include determining three values of the private investment, the excess return on the private investment over the public market, the risk associated with the return on the private investment relative to the public market, and the correlation of the private investment to the public market.

The disclosure may also be described as a process for determining the risk of a private investment portfolio relative to the public market, the correlation of a private investment portfolio to the public market, and the excess return of a private market portfolio over the public market by the steps of:

a. determining the internal rate of return of the private investment portfolio;

b. determining an index comparison return (ICM) for the private investment portfolio;

c. plotting the values of (a) and (b) as points in a scatter plot with (a) on the y-axis and (b) on the x-axis and applying least squares linear regression to the resulting plot to yield a linear equation in the form $y = \beta x + \alpha$, where β is the slope of the regression line and α is the point at which the regression line crosses the y-axis, and a value for R^2, the coefficient of determination;

d. determining the correlation of the private market portfolio with the public market index by taking the square root of the coefficient of determination determined in (c) to yield the coefficient of correlation r (also known in statistically literature as the Greek letter ρ);

e. determining the risk of the private investment of the portfolio by reference to the risk of the public market portfolio by solving the equation

$$\frac{\beta_{VC}\sigma_{S\&P}^2}{r_{VC,S\&P}\sigma_{S\&P}} \tag{H.1}$$

f. determining the excess return of the private investment portfolio over the public markets by reference to the a of the linear regression line.

The disclosed process may also be used to evaluate the return versus risk of a private investment portfolio by calculating the Sharpe Ratio and comparing the private investment Sharpe ratio to the Sharpe Ratio of an appropriate public market.

The disclosure further includes a system for evaluating private market investments including a central processing unit or CPU (processor), which may be a mainframe computer connected to one or more work stations, or it may be a component of a personal computer that may be a "standalone" computer or it may be networked to other computers through a common server. The system also includes an input device such as a keyboard in communication with the processor, at least one memory source, and software including instructions. The device may also include a display device such as a monitor in communication with the processor.

References

Accel Partners. 2008. Accel Partners and Erasmic Venture Fund team up, launch Accel India Venture Fund. www.accel.com (accessed September 12, 2008).

Ante, S. 2008. *Creative capital: Georges Doriot and the birth of venture capital*. Boston: Harvard Business Press.

Apple. n.d. Apple investor relations FAQ. http://phx.corporate-ir.net/phoenix .zhtml?c=107357&p=irol-faq#stock5 (accessed September 12, 2008).

Bailey, J. 1994. Are manager universes acceptable performance benchmarks? *Journal of Portfolio Management 18*: 9–13.

Bloomberg, M. 2001. *Bloomberg by Bloomberg*. New York: John Wiley & Sons.

Bodie, Z., A. Kane, and A. Marcus. 2004. *Investments*, 6th ed. New York: McGraw-Hill.

Brinson, G., L. Hood, and G. Beebower. 1986. Determinants of portfolio performance. *Financial Analysts Journal* 47:40-48.

Burgiss Group. 2008. Private equity trends: Report media & deliver times. The (i) Letter, July 2008, 4.

Bushner, E., C. Gigliotti, T. Judge, D. Park, R. Rose, S. Russell, D. Van Benschoten, and D. White. 1994. *Filling the vacuum: Alternative investments for pension plans, endowments and foundations*. Washington, Connecticut: Investors Press.

California Public Employees' Retirement System. n.d. AIM Program Performance Overview. www.calpers.ca.gov/index.jsp?bc=/investments/assets/ equities/aim/private-equity-review/overview.xml_ (accessed on April 13, 2008).

California State Teachers' Retirement System. n.d. Disclosure policy for CalSTRS alternative investment private equity partnerships. www.calstrs .com/INVESTMENTS/portfolio/disclosurepolicy.pdf (accessed August 25, 2008).

Cambridge Associates. 2008. Cambridge Associates LLC U.S. venture capital index as of March 31, 2008. https://www.cambridgeassociates.com/

indexes/docs/cambridge_VC_Index_with_Graph.pdf (accessed August 25, 2008).

Chaplinsky, S., and S. Perry. 2004. Calpers vs. Mercury News: Disclosure comes to private equity. http://papers.ssrn.com/sol3/papers.cfm?abstract_id=567525&rec=1&srcabs=909754 (accessed August 25, 2008).

Clark, A. 2008. Merrill Lynch sells its 20% Bloomberg stake for $4.5bn. www.guardian.co.uk/business/2008/jul/18/merrilllynch.jpmorgan (accessed September 11, 2008).

Clayton, Dublier & Rice. 2004. Clayton, Dublier & Rice completes sale of Kinko's to FedEx for $2.4 billion in cash. www.cdr-inc.com/news/articles/fedex_complete.shtml (accessed September 12, 2008).

Cohen, R. 2007. *The second bounce of the ball: Turning risk into opportunity.* London: Weidenfeld & Nicolson.

Conner, A. 2005. Persistence in venture capital returns. *Private Equity International*, March 2005, 65–67.

———. 2006. A method for quantifying concentration of returns in private equity portfolios. http://alignmentcapital.com/pdfs/research/acg_concentration_brief _2006.pdf (accessed August 25, 2008).

European Union. 1996. Council regulation (EC) no 1103/97 of 17 June 1997 on certain provisions relating to the introduction of the euro. Luxembourg. http://europa.eu.int/eur-lex/lex/LexUriServ/LexUriServ.do?uri=CELEX:31997R1103:EN:HTML (accessed August 25, 2008).

Financial Accounting Standards Board. n.d. Summary of Statement No. 157. www.fasb.org/st/summary/stsum157.shtml (accessed September 3, 2008).

Hayakawa, S. 1940. *Language in thought and action.* New York: Harcourt Brace Jovanovich.

Hsu, D., and M. Kenney. 2004. Organizing venture capital: The rise and demise of American Research & Development Corporation. http://papers.ssrn.com/sol3/papers.cfm?abstract_id=628661 (accessed September 13, 2008).

Intel Capital. 2007. Intel Capital fact sheet: Q3 2007. www.intel.com/capital/download/factsheet.pdf (accessed September 11, 2008).

J.H. Whitney. n.d. Firm/History. http://whitney.com/history.html (accessed September 13, 2008).

Judge, T. 1992. Annual meetings need to be made more productive. *Private Equity Analyst* 3: 1–2.

———. 1993. Financial reports from GPs need to be improved. *Private Equity Analyst*, 3:15–16.

Kaplan, D. 2000. *The silicon boys and their valley of dreams.* New York: Harper Perennial.

Kaplan, S., and A. Schoar. 2005. Private equity performance: Returns, persistence and capital flows. *Journal of Finance* 60:1791–1823.

Long, A. 2008. The common mathematical foundation of ACG's ICM and AICM and the K&S PME. http://alignmentcapital.com/pdfs/acg_icm_vs_pme_2008.pdf (accessed August 25, 2008).

Long, A., and C. Nickels. 1996. A private investment benchmark. Paper presented at the Association for Investment Management and Research's conference of Venture Capital, San Francisco.

———.2002. Method for calculating portfolio scaled IRR. US Patent 7,058,583, filed on Feb. 7, 2002, and issued on June 6, 2006.

Makridakis, S., and M. Hibon. 2000. The M3-Competition: Results, conclusions and implications. *International Journal of Forecasting* 16:451–476.

New York Times. 1996. Merrill Lynch reduces interest in Bloomberg to 20%. http://query.nytimes.com/gst/fullpage.html?res=9503E4D6113EF934A2 5751C1A960958260 (accessed September 10, 2008).

Phalippou, L., and O. Gottschalg. 2005. Performance of private equity funds. Paper presented at the annual meeting of the European Finance Association, Moscow. http://papers.ssrn.com/sol3/papers.cfm?abstract_id=473221 (accessed August 25, 2008).

Richards and Tierney. 1995. Opportunistic investing: Performance measurement, benchmarking, and evaluation.

Rouvinez, C. 2004. Beating the public market. *Private Equity International*, December 2003/January 2004, 26–28.

———, and T. Kubr. 2003. Enhancing private equity returns via diversification. *Private Equity International*, April 2003, 19–22.

State of Wisconsin Investment Board. 2007. 2006 annual report highlights. www.legis.state.wi.us/LaB/reports/07-10highlights.pdf (accessed April 14, 2008).

Swensen, D. 2000. *Pioneering portfolio management: An unconventional approach to institutional investment.* New York: Simon & Schuster.

Takahashi, D., and S. Alexander. 2001. Illiquid alternative asset fund modeling. Yale International Center for Finance. http://icf.som.yale.edu/pdf/AssetAllocationModel.pdf (accessed August 25, 2008).

Thomson Reuters. 2008. Despite economic slowdown venture capital returns remain positive in first quarter 2008. http://nvca.org/pdf/Performance Q108FINAL.pdf (accessed August 25, 2008).

Tufte, E. R. 2001. *The visual display of quantitative information*, 2nd ed. Cheshire, CT: Graphics Press.

Wang, C., and A. Conner. 2004. What's in a quartile? http://alignmentcapital .com/pdfs/acg_top_quartile_2004.pdf (accessed August 25, 2008).

Washington State Investment Board. 2008. Portfolio overview by strategy September 30, 2007. www.sib.wa.gov/financial/pdfs/quarterly/ir093007 .pdf (accessed May 24, 2008).

Index

CPSIA information can be obtained at www.ICGtesting.com
Printed in the USA
BVOW06*0030160715

408631BV00008BA/97/P